The Press and
the Carter Presidency

The Press and
the Carter Presidency

Mark J. Rozell

Westview Press
BOULDER & LONDON

Copyright © 1989 by Westview Press, Inc.

Published in 1989 in the United States of America by Westview Press, Inc., 5500 Central Avenue, Boulder, Colorado 80301, and in the United Kingdom by Westview Press, Inc., 13 Brunswick Centre, London WC1N 1AF, England

Library of Congress Cataloging-in-Publication data
Rozell, Mark J.
  The press and the Carter presidency.
  1. Press and politics—United States—History—
20th century. 2. Carter, Jimmy, 1924– —Relations
with journalists. 3. United States—Politics and
government—1977–1981. I. Title.
E872.R69 1989   973.926′092′4   88-20785
ISBN 0-8133-0765-7

Printed and bound in the United States of America

The paper used in this publication meets the requirements of the American National Standard for Permanence of Paper for Printed Library Materials Z39.48-1984.

10   9   8   7   6   5   4   3   2   1

For Lynda

Contents

Preface

This study is a revision of my doctoral dissertation written at the University of Virginia. As a student of the American presidency I became interested in how presidential leadership is defined, analyzed and assessed. Students of the presidency spend a great deal of time studying leadership theory and debating the merits of different measures of leadership "success." These students draw inspiration for their ideas from noted presidency scholars such as Edward S. Corwin, Clinton Rossiter, and Richard Neustadt.

Although the ideas of political scientists are crucial to our understanding of the presidency, these scholars are not the only "teachers" of the American presidency. Each day in the nation's newspapers, and each week in the news magazines, political journalists evaluate the performance of the incumbent president. For the vast majority of Americans political journalists are the most relied upon teachers of the presidency. Surprisingly, political scientists do not give much attention to how political journalists define, analyze and assess presidential leadership. While political journalists apply specific measures of leadership success, political scientists have yet to uncover and identify these measures.

This study is intended to open an inquiry into the role of political journalists as public teachers of the presidency. By examining national print reporting and commentary on one presidency I try to uncover some of the underlying notions of leadership held by political journalists. The categories of press evaluations adopted for this study can be used to analyze print reporting and commentary on subsequent presidencies so as to build a body of knowledge on contemporary presidential journalism.

I chose to examine the press assessments of Jimmy Carter's administration for two reasons: First, I wanted to study contemporary presidential journalism and concluded that an examination of the most recently completed administration was the most appropriate. Second, as an avid presidential observer I was fascinated, if not somewhat puzzled, by the highly negative portrait of Carter's presidency that prevailed in the national press. Despite evident presidential achievements, Jimmy Carter never overcame the generally negative press perception of his leadership. I wanted to learn what journalists meant when they characterized Carter's leadership as a "failure" and how they defined and measured presidential "success."

In researching, writing, and revising this study I benefited from the advice of four scholars at the University of Virginia: Charles O. Jones, James Sterling Young, James W. Ceaser, and Norman A. Graebner. Charles O. Jones, now at the University of Wisconsin at Madison, supervised the thesis and offered additional helpful suggestions when I revised the manuscript for publication. Norman A. Graebner also offered valuable suggestions for revising the manuscript. I wish to acknowledge the permission granted to me by the Carter Oral History Project's Director, James Sterling Young, to use the transcripts of the Carter Oral History for this study.

I have benefited from my association with four political science colleagues at Mary Washington College: Lewis P. Fickett, Jr., John M. Kramer, Richard J. Krickus, and Victor A. Fingerhut. I am grateful to my colleagues for providing an atmosphere most conducive to scholarly work.

The Mary Washington College Faculty Development Grant Committee supported my research while I revised this study for publication. A grant from the committee made possible the timely completion of this project.

Several individuals assisted with this book and deserve special recognition. Sally Furgeson, editor of this manuscript for Westview Press, proofread the text and offered many valuable suggestions for revision. Judy W. Singleton, a senior secretary at Mary Washington College, also proofread the text in its entirety, offering additional helpful suggestions. Michele McClain, a senior undergraduate at Mary Washington College, assisted with the proofreading of the manuscript. Donna Packard carefully and efficiently typed each draft of the text, from the early stages of the thesis through completion of the manuscript. My wife, Lynda Marie Rozell, now an attorney at Hunton and Williams in Washington, D.C., proofread and critiqued the manuscript at its various stages.

This book is dedicated to Lynda. She tirelessly and always graciously offered valuable ideas for improving the manuscript, even though she was most busy with her legal studies. My dedication of this book to her, though, is for all of the most important kinds of support that she gives to me each day.

Mark J. Rozell
Vienna, Virginia

1

Introduction

Jimmy Carter became president during a unique period in American political life. Widespread public distrust of national political leaders and institutions characterized this period which immediately followed the Vietnam and Watergate traumas. Public cynicism often focused upon the presidency. In the early 1970s it became fashionable for scholars and pundits to characterize the presidency as an "imperial" institution. Presidential usurpation of power and congressional acquiescence to executive initiatives allegedly resulted in a dangerous imbalance in the separation of powers. Public distrust of the nation's highest political office eventually became overwhelming.

Cleansing the presidency of its highly unfavorable reputation required much more than just a changing of the guard. Although President Gerald R. Ford sought to heal the nation of its anger and humiliation, public cynicism remained resilient. President Ford undermined whatever success he experienced at raising public esteem for national political leaders and institutions by pardoning Richard M. Nixon. Many observers concluded that only a new national leadership never associated with political Washington could rid the nation of its skepticism of public leaders and institutions.

For many Americans in 1976, Democratic presidential candidate Jimmy Carter embodied their highest aspirations for a "new beginning " in national politics. They hoped that this new era would be characterized by proper ethical and moral conduct in public offices. During the 1976 presidential campaign Jimmy Carter emphasized his desire to conduct an administration of the highest standards of decency and morality. His often repeated promise to "never lie" carried great appeal for many voters in the post-Watergate era.

The Nixon administration's excesses undoubtedly made possible a Carter presidency. The effects of Watergate, particularly public distrust of political leaders and institutions, and congressional reforms limiting presidential powers, made presidential leadership in the Carter years difficult. President Carter had to exercise presidential leadership in an environment of exacting scrutiny for any indication of improper behavior by public officials. Carter's rhetoric and campaign promises also focused attention on the issue of ethics in public service.

Political journalists led the scrutiny of the Carter presidency. During the early months of the presidential term journalists favorably evaluated Carter's leadership. Many believed that Carter's unpretentious, populist leadership style helped overcome public cynicism.

Carter's favorable press treatment did not last. When the administration's activities did not appear to fulfill the high standards that Carter adopted, press evaluations of the president's leadership turned increasingly negative. The Bert Lance controversy in 1977 particularly fueled negative press assessments of Carter's presidency. After the Lance controversy subsided the press-presidency climate remained very unfavorable to Carter. What is most striking about the press portrayals of Carter is their severely negative nature, despite considerable presidential achievements. Once journalists developed a negative perception of Carter's leadership, this perception framed their judgments of his activities over the course of the presidential term.

To a great extent, press negativity reflected the belief that the Carter administration did not always uphold the president's own high ethical standards. But Carter's negative press image cannot be attributed entirely to that belief. Carter also failed to meet journalists' basic leadership expectations. When evaluating contemporary presidents, journalists apply criteria that reflect their priorities and conceptions of presidential leadership. These priorities and conceptions of leadership are not always compatible with a president's own notion of leadership. During the Carter years, journalists frequently judged the president's leadership against idealized recollections of the leadership approaches of such previous Democratic presidents as Franklin D. Roosevelt and Lyndon B. Johnson.

This study identifies and assesses the national journalistic evaluations of the Carter presidency. In what follows I identify and discuss the major themes in national press reporting and commentary on Jimmy Carter and his administration from the latter stages of the 1976 campaign, through the conclusion of the 39th president's term in January 1981. One of my goals is to identify the underlying values and notions of leadership in presidential journalism during the Carter years. For example, during this period many journalists declared that the president was "failing" the leadership task. It is important to inquire into the basis of that judgment. What were journalists' criteria for success and how did they define "failure"?

Evaluating leadership is no simple task. It requires establishing criteria and judging whether those criteria are met. Scholars differ in how they define leadership and how they study it. Generally they have the time to ponder such matters. Journalists, on the other hand, work with short deadlines. Yet they too must develop a basic understanding of leadership in order to report it and make judgments about it. The day-to-day orientation of political reporting combined with time and print space limitations makes the journalist's task of evaluation significantly different from the scholar's task.

An important distinction between social scientists' and journalists' approaches to evaluation is that, unlike journalists, social scientists are expected to produce clear definitions and measures of leadership. Journalists are not expected to identify their evaluative criteria. Therefore, when journalists assess that the president is "failing" the leadership task, readers generally lack an understanding of the basis for that assessment.

Even though journalists do not explicitly identify their evaluative criteria, they operate with specific expectations of presidential leadership and performance. These expectations are not easily identified by daily consumers of political news and commentary, nor is there any motivation to do so.

Scholars should begin trying to understand the underlying notions of leadership in presidential journalism. Mass public and elite perceptions are strongly influenced by political reporting and commentary. It is therefore important to understand the values journalists bring to bear on their evaluations.

However, this study does not provide generalizations about presidential journalism for all administrations. The nature of presidential journalism has changed significantly over the years. Journalists during the Carter years, for example, approached presidential evaluation differently than journalists during the Franklin D. Roosevelt years. During Roosevelt's administration many journalists forged close relationships with the president as a means of enhancing their own professional stature. Many journalists were captured by their subject (if not captivated by him) and presented a sympathetic portrait of the president's activities. The post-Vietnam, post-Watergate environment in which President Carter served fostered an increasingly cautious press-presidency relationship. Journalists still wanted to form close relationships with the president, but were unlikely to become sympathetic observers of their subject.[1]

It is commonly believed that the events of Vietnam and Watergate in themselves brought about sudden changes in journalistic practices. But other influential developments preceded the tumultuous events of the 1960s and 1970s. Most important to this study, the nature of the printed media evolved as television emerged as a major news medium.

During the Franklin D. Roosevelt years the printed media were the major source of political news for most people. Many leading newspapers considered interpretive reporting unprofessional and reserved political commentary and analysis for editorial writers and syndicated columnists. The ethic of "objective" news reporting began to change with the rise of television in the 1960s. Newspapers and magazines could not match the immediacy of television reporting. Print journalism began to distinguish itself from television by providing news analysis articles by political reporters. Political interpretation in the print media was no longer restricted primarily to editorial writers and syndicated columnists.[2]

Contemporary journalistic reporting on the presidency therefore is an outgrowth of two important developments: (1) the growing acceptance of interpretive reporting, and (2) the post-Vietnam, post-Watergate skepticism of the presidency. Reporters today accept criticism of the presidency and of White House occupants as an integral journalistic function.

Journalists cultivate a number of sources of information and "inside dope" for their news analyses. These sources include White House press releases, press conferences, and informal meetings between White House officials and reporters. Yet journalists are often reluctant to rely heavily upon White House generated information. Journalists find that White House staff are frequently inaccessible, or choose to be available only on restrictive terms, or may purposefully slant and distort information to serve administration goals.

In their evaluative tasks journalists now tend to rely heavily upon Capitol Hill sources and low-level (often disgruntled) administration sources for information on the presidency. In his study of Washington's reporters Stephen Hess reveals that Capitol Hill sources are journalists' favorite news sources. In Hess's view, newspapers are "the medium of Congress."[3] Hess adds that there "is a well-known secret in the press corps: Washington news is funneled through Capitol Hill."[4] Hess explains that Washington news has a rhythm set by the major national news dailies (*Washington Post, New York Times, Wall Street Journal*). This news "travels a circuitous route back into the political government and out again to the rest of the country via the electronic media."[5] Print journalism thus becomes the focal point of national opinion development and journalists the molders of public perceptions of presidential leadership and performance.

Highly negative press commentary and reporting undoubtedly contributed to the unfavorable public perception of Carter's leadership and hampered the administration's ability to govern. This negative press commentary and reporting is not solely attributable to Watergate, Carter's own high standards, or to the fact that the Carter administration dealt with numerous complex problems—from energy shortages and inflation at home to Soviet adventurism and the taking of American diplomats abroad. While the inability to expeditiously resolve those complex problems opened Carter up to criticism, the evident incongruity between Carter's leadership and journalists' conceptions of leadership contributed importantly to the administration's negative press portrait. In their evaluations of President Carter journalists relied upon two general sets of expectations:

1. *General Expectations of Presidential Leadership.* These expectations included the proper "ingredients" for successful leadership and the leadership approaches presidents presumably should adopt. Ingredients for successful leadership often focused on the president's specific character attributes. This study reveals that journalists were enamored with presidents who exhibited energetic, forceful personalities. Popular images of Franklin D. Roosevelt and Lyndon B. Johnson were leadership models for many political journalists.

2. *Expectations of Jimmy Carter.* These expectations pertained to what journalists thought Jimmy Carter would and should do as president. For example, many journalists expected Carter to work carefully and closely with legislative leaders. According to Carter's press critics, the context of the post-Watergate era provided a unique opportunity for a Democratic president with large party majorities in Congress to initiate broad-scale legislative interventions.

Journalistic conceptions of leadership were not always consistent or stable. Journalists occasionally shifted their evaluative standards to explain apparent presidential successes and failures. Given the large number of journalists quoted here, divergences in journalistic assessments of Carter's presidency should not be surprising. What appears striking is the degree of congruence in journalistic interpretations across philosophical boundaries. For example, journalistic opinion of Carter's energy program varied widely. Many critics, such as the *Wall Street Journal*'s editors, characterized the program as an ill-advised response to the nation's energy problems. Other critics, such as the *Washington Post*'s editors, portrayed Carter's initiative as a bold and proper response to the "energy crisis." Despite these differences in opinion over the substance of the energy program, admirers and detractors agreed that the president failed the leadership task on this issue by not successfully "selling" the energy package to the public and Congress. This study shows that on a variety of policy initiatives journalists disagreed about the merits of specific administration proposals, yet they generally agreed that Carter's efforts to enact his proposals were deficient.

Method of Analysis

My analysis of the journalistic assessments of the Carter administration is derived from a comprehensive review of national print media sources from mid-1976 through January 1981. The selection of national print-media sources is adopted from Stephen Hess's definition of the news organization hierarchy in *The Washington Reporters* (Washington, D.C.: Brookings Institution, 1981).

In his study Hess describes what he calls "the solar system of Washington news gathering."[6] This system includes "the sun," or the "political government," and the various planets, the Washington news organizations. These news organizations, in Hess's scheme, form "an inner ring, a ring of middle distance, and an outermost ring."[7]

The inner ring constitutes the most influential news organizations. These organizations are also most important to the political government because "through them it learns what the country is learning about what it is doing."[8] Hess identifies the following news organizations as the inner ring: Associated Press, United Press International, American Broadcasting Company, National Broadcasting Company, Columbia Broadcasting System, *Newsweek, U.S. News and World Report, Time, New York Times, Washington Post, Washington Star,* and the *Wall Street Journal.*[9]

This study focuses on those inner ring sources that constitute the major focus of Washington journalism—the print media. As Hess notes, the television networks have "secondary impact" on the political government when compared to the information generated by print reporters and commentators. The wire services are excluded from this study because their purpose is not primarily news analysis. Print journalism today is the most influential medium of national opinion development.

Finally, I exclude one inner ring newspaper from my study, the now defunct *Washington Star*. In a *Wall Street Journal* survey cited by Hess, the three national newspapers cited most frequently by high-level federal officials as the news dailies they read regularly were the *Washington Post* (90%), the *Wall Street Journal* (62%), and the *New York Times* (45%). Moreover, a comprehensive reading of a seventh print media source would yield little, if any, substantive information beyond what I have found from the other six inner ring sources. Therefore, this study is based on the news analyses, commentaries and editorials on the Carter presidency contained in three national news dailies (*Washington Post, Wall Street Journal, New York Times*) and the three national news weeklies (*Newsweek, Time, U.S. News and World Report*).

In collecting data for this study I reviewed the above sources for reporting and commentary on the Carter administration. I surveyed these materials chronologically to gain insight into the development of the journalistic assessments of the Carter presidency. The material is organized to reflect the major themes in the press assessments of this presidency. From this material I selected numerous articles, editorials and commentaries that are representative of the general themes of these assessments. My decision to limit the use of quotations is based on (1) the necessity of making such a large data base manageable, and (2) excessive repetition of quotations reveals little more substantive information than is revealed by this study. For readers interested in examining my findings in greater detail, the footnote citations identify additional sources reflecting the major themes that are identified.[10]

Organization of the Analysis

The main body of this study is a chronological narrative of the journalistic assessments of the Carter presidency. This narrative begins with Chapter 2—"Early Evaluations"—which examines the press portrayals of Jimmy Carter from the latter stages of the 1976 campaign until inauguration day. Chapters 3 through 6 cover Jimmy Carter's four years in office with each chapter corresponding to a year in the term.

In these chapters I identify and discuss the major themes in the press portrayals of the Carter presidency. These themes are organized into five separate categories of activities: timing, symbolism and rhetoric, policy agenda, policy development, and staff.

1. Timing. This category of assessments has two aspects: first, the particular historic context in which the Carter presidency took place, and second, the different stages of Carter's term in office.

First, journalists assessed the Carter presidency at a particular historic period, and this context must be acknowledged in order to understand the journalistic evaluations of Carter. More specifically, the Carter presidency came in the aftermath of the national traumas of Vietnam and Watergate. In their assessments of Carter journalists revealed expectations of the presidency that were clearly influenced by the Vietnam and Watergate episodes.

Second, expectations of the president were also influenced by the stages of the term in which journalists viewed Carter. For example, journalists had ideas about how a president should begin his term and make use of the so-called "honeymoon period." In Chapter 3 we find journalists had expectations about the kind of first year agenda Carter should have adopted and the tactics needed to capitalize on Carter's initial popularity.

Timing is also a crucial factor in understanding the press portrayals of Carter in 1980—an election year. For approximately one year, beginning in late 1979 with the early party caucuses, journalists evaluated almost every action by Carter according to its political ramifications. The press portrait of Carter in 1980 was more negative than in any other year of the term. Journalists frequently judged the president's decisions (including those affecting the fate of the American hostages in Iran) to be politically motivated.

2. Symbolism and Rhetoric. A second category of journalistic assessments concerns the administration's symbolic efforts and political rhetoric. In their more general evaluations of presidential leadership journalists often focused on the president's role as public leader. They perceived the ability to project a leadership "aura" through the use of symbolism and rhetoric as an important element of the president's leadership task. More specifically, in an era of congressional resurgence and reform many journalists expected President Carter to use the "bully pulpit" to define a policy agenda congressional Democrats would follow. Leadership, in this view, is establishing the conditions which encourage followership. Journalists believed a "presidential" image to be an important part of establishing the leadership condition.

During the 1976 campaign journalists criticized Carter for failing to articulate a clear vision of where his presidency would lead the nation. They criticized Carter for seeking to appeal to all elements of a diverse electorate by being vague on policy issues in public speeches. A few journalists praised Carter's cultivating of the "outsider" image as a necessary response to public expectations for a divergence from the activities of the Nixon presidency. Yet some journalists expressed displeasure with what they perceived as the possible negative effects of a president leading the same establishment he had decried as a candidate.

In early 1977 the journalistic reviews of Carter's symbolic activities and political rhetoric were highly favorable. Journalists portrayed Carter as a "great communicator" seeking to establish his leadership by building public support through symbolic activities.

By the end of 1977 we see the beginning of the development of a negative assessment of Carter's symbolic and rhetorical abilities that became a base or touchstone returned to throughout the rest of the term. Journalists portrayed Carter as incapable of projecting the image of a "leader." They lamented what they perceived as a lack of "stature" or "presidentiality" in Carter. Journalists criticized the president most severely for allegedly failing to define for the nation a vision for the future.

During the term there were occasional divergences from this negative evaluation. For example, after the 1978 Camp David achievement and 1979 "Crisis of Confidence" speech there were reassessments in the press of

Carter's ability to inspire and to lead. In each case the president's "stature" was temporarily elevated only to sink again to the negative evaluation that formed the basic interpretation of his performance.

In 1980 journalists harshly criticized Carter's rhetoric, especially with regard to the presidential campaign. During this election year journalists characterized Carter's rhetorical attacks on other candidates as "mean spirited" and "vicious."

3. *Agenda.* The third category of journalistic assessments concerns the administration's policy agenda. Journalistic expectations of Carter's agenda must be considered within the context of the post-Nixon and Ford years. Through the use of impoundment and veto politics Republican administrations had frustrated the domestic policy agenda of congressional Democrats for eight years. Journalists therefore expected Carter's agenda to be highly compatible with the prevailing sentiments of congressional Democrats.

Journalistic criticism of Carter's early attention to human rights and arms control issues reflected this expectation. Several commentators complained that the nation elected Carter to focus his efforts on domestic economic dislocations. Presumably, congressional Democrats favored devoting their energies to problems of unemployment and inflation.

In the early stages of the term there was some confusion among journalists about the nature of Carter's domestic policy agenda. Early expectations were mixed, with some journalists predicting Carter would initiate large-scale social reforms and other journalists predicting the president would begin his term with a few carefully chosen agenda items. When Carter encountered difficulties working with Congress, though, journalists generally agreed that his ambitious agenda was a major source of the difficulties. So while many journalists found Carter's domestic policies individually to be meritorious, a press consensus that the domestic agenda was too ambitious and controversial developed early in the term. The general press assessment of Carter's agenda throughout the term was that it was too ambitious, ran counter to public and congressional sentiments, and appeared to lack identifiable priority items. For these reasons, journalists argued, Carter made Congress's job more difficult than necessary.

Again, there was some fluctuation in this base assessment. During the late-1978 post–Camp David euphoria many journalists observed that the administration had significant legislative victories in the 95th Congress. They even attributed these victories to Carter's allegedly new-found political skills. Journalists portrayed the Carter agenda for this brief period as more clearly focused on major priority items.

Generally, the press portrait of Carter's agenda as lacking a focus prevailed throughout the term. By late 1979, in light of the Iran and Afghanistan crises, journalists characterized President Carter's foreign policy agenda as hostage to external events. As these crises dragged on journalists increasingly held Carter responsible for not being able to alter the course of events that determined United States foreign policy.

4. *Policy Development.* The early press evaluations of Carter's efforts at policy development reveal a mixture of sentiments. Many journalists assumed

that a Democratic president with large party majorities in Congress aspires to be a legislative activist. They expected Carter to fulfill the role of a legislative-interventionist president taking advantage of one-party rule of the government. Many journalists anticipated early and frequent consultations between the president and members of Congress on major policy initiatives. These journalists focused on leadership opportunities provided by the political context.

Simultaneously, journalists who focused more on presidential character than on the leadership context found that Carter's personality was not conducive to highly cooperative relations with members of the legislative branch. Some journalists considered Carter a stubborn and uncompromising individual. These critics anticipated that Carter would not work closely with the Democratic-controlled Congress and would seek, instead, to pressure members of Congress to adopt administration initiatives without compromise.

Carter's foreign and domestic policy leadership quickly came under heavy journalistic fire. In foreign policy journalists lamented the apparent policy incoherence characterized by allegedly conflicting goals (e.g., arms control and human rights improvements) and the differing styles of administration policy spokesmen, particularly Secretary of State Cyrus Vance and National Security Adviser Zbigniew Brzezinski. In domestic policy journalists criticized Carter's efforts at developing public and congressional support for the following reasons: failure to consult adequately with members of Congress on policy initiatives; hasty preparation of major programs, with little attention given to their politically controversial nature; and unwillingness to compromise with legislators.

These themes persisted throughout the term, but were obscured temporarily on a few occasions (e.g., after the Middle East peace treaty signing and at the beginning of the hostage crisis). Journalists attributed a number of important incidents (including the 1980 United Nations vote mishap, foiled rescue mission attempt, and apparent policy reversal on the influx of Cuban refugees) to the administration's allegedly incoherent process of policy development and lack of clear and consistent policy objectives.

5. *Staff.* Journalists persistently assessed Carter's White House staff very negatively. The one exception was during the 1976–1977 transition period in which some journalists expressed delight that Carter's staff would be comprised of individuals from outside political Washington. In the immediate post-Watergate years a number of journalists believed that the federal government needed "new faces" and new perspectives.

This view did not represent a press consensus, however. Many journalists expressed concern about the White House potentially lacking the national political experience needed to lead political Washington.

A negative consensus view of Carter's staff more compatible with this latter perspective developed early in the term. During the first several months of the term journalists made a great deal of reports that Carter's staff members were not returning congressmen's phone calls and were failing to consult with members of Congress prior to the development of administration

policy initiatives. Journalists attributed these apparent slights to the inexperience of most staff members and even to a personal and professional
arrogance from having won the presidential race against major national
political figures. The press frequently complained of the apparent lack of
diversity in the Carter White House. This lack of diversity allegedly fostered
a kind of staff insularity reminiscent to some journalists of the Nixon White
House.

Journalistic assessments of events surrounding the Bert Lance controversy
in September 1977 best illustrate the negative press portrait of Carter's staff.
Journalists perceived the Carter staff as so insular as to be nearly blind to
the alleged financial improprieties of one of their own friends. A more
experienced and diverse staff, journalists reported, would have handled this
controversy competently.

This study shows that the negative press portrait of the White House
staff fluctuated little during the term. If anything, it grew steadily more
critical. The press generally credited major administration achievements to
the efforts of the president alone.

Following the chronological narrative of press reporting and commentary
on the Carter presidency I examine how selected Carter White House officials
perceived the journalistic assessments of their presidency. For Chapter 7, I
rely on two research sources: (1) the transcripts of the Carter oral history
project conducted at the University of Virginia's White Burkett Miller Center
of Public Affairs; and (2) the memoirs of Carter White House members. I
focus on the recollections of those officials in the Carter White House most
concerned with the rhetorical and symbolic duties of the presidency. This
group includes the speechwriters, members of the press secretary's office,
and selected individuals from the inner circle of White House advisers, as
well as the president himself.

The purpose of the chapter is to ascertain the convergences and divergences
between the way that public communications advisers in the White House
defined and evaluated President Carter's leadership and the way that political
journalists defined and evaluated his leadership. In their retrospective assessments Carter White House staff members also reveal how they sought
to deal with the Carter presidency's press image problem. The extent to
which these staff members recognized and accepted the bases of journalistic
evaluations is important corroborative evidence of the themes identified in
this study and of the similar values of leadership held by journalists and
these White House "insiders."

The concluding chapter reviews the major research findings of this study.
The concluding chapter draws together the major themes in the journalistic
assessments of Carter and identifies the elements of the press's implicit
theories of presidential leadership and performance. The chapter ends with
an analysis of the differing values and criteria journalists relied upon in
their assessments of Carter. The implications of my findings for the institution
of the presidency are also discussed.

The finding of central importance for this study is that journalists have
identifiable expectations of presidential leadership and performance. These

expectations need to be recognized by scholars who examine and wish to understand journalistic assessments of a presidency. Since journalists are influential public teachers of the American presidency it is important that we understand the values they bring to bear on their evaluations of presidential leadership and performance. In journalists' assessments of Jimmy Carter, we find a number of persisting themes revealing of journalistic expectations of presidential leadership and performance. The categories of themes identified here may be applied to studies of future presidencies. In this respect, a body of knowledge about contemporary presidential journalism can be developed.

Notes

1. James Sterling Young, *The Puzzle of the Presidency*, (Baton Rouge: Louisiana State University Press, forthcoming).

2. See Bernard Roschco, "The Evolution of News Content in the American Press," in Doris Graber, ed., *Media Power in Politics* (Washington, D.C.: Congressional Quarterly Press, 1984), pp. 7–22.

3. Stephen Hess, *The Washington Reporters* (Washington, D.C.: Brookings Institution, 1984), p. 98.

4. Ibid., p. 100.

5. Ibid., p. 96.

6. Ibid., p. 24.

7. Ibid.

8. Ibid.

9. Ibid., p. 24n.

10. See also Mark J. Rozell, "Journalistic Perceptions of the Carter Presidency" (Ph.D. thesis, University of Virginia, 1987). The doctoral thesis from which this book originated provides additional documentation of the journalistic assessments of Carter's presidency and further substantiates the existence of press themes identified here.

2

Early Evaluations

Jimmy Carter was very much a mystery to the press by the latter stages of the 1976 campaign. Journalists studied Jimmy Carter's past, as well as his campaign rhetoric, to develop clues about his character and philosophy. A number of themes dominated the journalistic assessments of Carter from the latter stages of the 1976 campaign until the January 20, 1977, inauguration. These themes are associated with my five categories of press assessments:

1. *Timing.* At this early stage there was considerable guesswork and speculation about Carter in the press. Many journalists believed Carter would begin his term proposing large-scale public policy interventions in the mold of Lyndon B. Johnson's "Great Society. " In their view, a Democratic president blessed with large Democratic majorities in both houses of Congress should begin his term with an aggressive legislative agenda.

Not every journalist shared this perception. A number of journalists expected Carter to begin his term cautiously and prudently. These observers believed that Carter's deliberate Cabinet selection process was a clue as to how the president would lead in the first year.

2. *Rhetoric/Symbolism.* For the most part journalists found candidate Carter's rhetoric unhelpful for defining his character and philosophy. Journalists portrayed Carter as a candidate and president-elect who tried to be all things to all people. They focused on Carter's apparently contradictory public statements. For some journalists this rhetorical approach was the hallmark of an astute politician trying to appeal to a diverse population. For others Carter's rhetoric reflected his eclectic, non-ideological political philosophy.

Journalists debated the efficacy of having a president who cultivated the image of an "outsider." The most optimistic journalists perceived the election of an outsider president as the beginning of a new era in American politics. They saw Carter's outsider image as symbolizing the end of a period in which access to the White House was vastly restricted. Many journalists, therefore, expected Carter the "outsider" to provide White House access to groups previously perceived as excluded from the decision making process. Other journalists were unenthused about the prospect of an outsider president. They believed that Carter risked putting himself outside the mainstream of political Washington by continually stressing his aversion to it.

3. *Agenda.* Journalists had conflicting expectations of Carter's policy agenda. Some expected Carter to initiate large-scale social and political reforms capitalizing on the large Democratic majorities in both houses of Congress. Others predicted the president-elect would propose a limited number of initiatives in the early stages of the term. Again, the perception of Carter's lack of clarity on the issues discouraged many journalists from attempting at this stage to evaluate specific agenda items (and, of course, no specific proposals had been announced yet).

4. *Policy Development.* Journalists varied in their opinions about Carter's ability to work constructively with Congress. A number of journalists expected Carter to be an "activist-achiever" in the mold of President Lyndon B. Johnson. According to these observers Carter's presidency would begin a new era of cooperative presidential-congressional relations after eight years of a Republican-controlled executive branch and Democratic-controlled Congress.

Other journalists predicted poor legislative-executive relations during the Carter years. They perceived Carter to be stubborn and uncompromising and viewed the president-elect's outsider image and national political inexperience as leadership liabilities. Some journalists also found the post-Vietnam, post-Watergate Congress unprepared to accept assertive presidential leadership.

5. *Staff.* A modest amount of press attention focused on Carter's White House staff. The two most common sentiments were: (a) that the group of "outsiders" Carter brought to Washington would offer a new, fresh perspective on American politics; and (b) that these "outsiders" lacked much-needed experience in national politics. Some journalists feared that this outsider status would encourage contempt for the Washington political establishment, making the president's job of persuading political elites precarious.

Most of the press's early evaluations reflected a good deal of confusion about the kind of president Jimmy Carter would be. Yet some elements of a negative base evaluation were developing. Several major themes in the early evaluations included: (1) the Carter "enigma"; (2) the Carter mandate; (3) Carter the "outsider"; (4) the energetic, activist Carter; and (5) the uncompromising, stubborn Carter.

The Carter "Enigma"

Many journalists acknowledged their inability to characterize Jimmy Carter in clear, unambiguous terms. Carter appeared to defy traditional political categorizations. He could please both political liberals and conservatives with his public statements and cause individuals of various persuasions to claim him as their own. Carter's pledges also invited strong criticism from traditionally Democratic groups. He aroused both widespread trust and skepticism across the political spectrum.

Two *Wall Street Journal* editorials published in July 1976 expressed this view. In an editorial entitled "Vagueness and All That," the *Journal* identified

Jimmy Carter's lack of clarity on the issues as the primary cause of public confusion about him. Finding a lack of any "coherent" ideology in the Democratic party candidate, the *Journal* noted its skepticism of the man who simultaneously espoused the virtues of free-enterprise and lambasted big business practices. While conceding the electoral benefits derived from such "vagueness," the *Journal*'s editors lamented that "there emerges no identifiable direction in which a President Carter would take the nation."[1]

In a follow-up editorial the *Wall Street Journal* asserted the common complaint that Carter tried to be "all things to all people" and that the Carter campaign was "studiously vague on the substance of government." In the view of the *Journal*'s editorial writers Carter failed to address difficult issues and focused instead on uncontroversial matters such as the need for honesty in government.[2]

The perception that Carter lacked a coherent or even identifiable public philosophy persisted throughout the 1976 campaign. An October 11, 1976, *Time* magazine news article observed: "There is some confusion between the relatively conservative Carter who speaks of love, healing and balanced budgets and the angry populist Carter who laces into fat cats and promises Government programs that sound expensive."[3]

A number of political columnists expressed similar views. For example, Stanley Cloud of *Time* assessed: "A line from a Kris Kristofferson song might well have been written about Carter's multifaceted personality: 'He's a walking contradiction/partly truth and partly fiction.'" Cloud added that Carter "developed a grab-bag political personality that offers something for almost everyone."[4] Cloud continued:

> . . . A candidate who tries to appeal to *Playboy* readers on the one hand and to evangelicals on the other, who promises tax reform but says he does not know enough yet to provide details, who talks both to God and Rock superstar Gregg Allman, violates all the unwritten political norms. By appealing to such differing constituencies, he has magnified the uncertainties about his character and positions.[5]

Peter Goldman and Eleanor Clift of *Newsweek* found similar contradictions in Carter's character. They believed that Carter, whose campaign for president faltered near election day, desperately tried to find campaign themes that would solidify public support:

> He has tried a bit of everything in his long autumn of on-the-job training in presidential politics. He has played the Gentle Jimmy preaching love and compassion and the Tough Jimmy attacking Gerald Ford as brainwashed; the Democratic Jimmy embracing the party tradition and the Independent Jimmy keeping his distance from it; the Zero-based Jimmy pledging a balanced budget by 1981 and the Bounteous Jimmy promising everything from full employment to a concert by the New York Philharmonic in Brooklyn. . . .
> He invoked the ghosts of Roosevelt, Truman, Kennedy and Johnson, then dropped the idea on evidence that it was spoiling his disestablishmentarian

appeal. He tried populism and frightened business away; he did issues speeches and found hardly anybody interested.[6]

Rowland Evans and Robert Novak attributed Carter's apparently inconsistent public positions to his lack of a philosophical "system" or "structure." Reacting to President-elect Carter's choice of personal friend Griffin Bell as Attorney General, a selection widely perceived as incompatible with Carter's promise to end political cronyism at the Justice Department, Evans and Novak exclaimed that this decision revealed that Carter's mind "is bound by no system or philosophy but is eclectic, pragmatic and instinctive."[7] In an earlier essay Evans and Novak found Carter's economic policy statements confused and contradictory, evidencing Carter's inability to adopt a coherent political philosophy.[8] Columnist Joseph Kraft agreed:

> Carter has a cast of mind that lacks what is called structure. He tends toward the marriage of opposites, toward the non-recognition of what most people consider either/or choices.
> Thus he favors stimulating the economy, but in the accents of fiscal conservatism. He wants new jobs in the private sector, but castigates fat-cat companies. He talks about being tough on the Russians, but he does not mention . . . the Soviet military buildup.[9]

In November 1976 Kraft wrote that a distinctive feature of Carter's campaign was to address every issue in this world and "some in the next." Kraft criticized Carter for failing to address "systematically" the crucial problem of inflation. He explained that Carter lacked a clear sense of direction on how to deal with inflation, then the nation's most pressing domestic problem.[10] Kraft also expressed disapproval with Carter's apparent lack of consistency on nuclear arms control issues.[11]

In its 1977 "Man of the Year" issue, *Time* magazine discussed the difficulty journalists and the general public had understanding Jimmy Carter: ". . . he is still an enigma to millions of Americans, including many who voted for him. He is complex and sometimes contradictory."[12] "He has been described with a catalogue of contradictions: liberal, moderate, conservative, compassionate, ruthless, soft, tough, a Charlatan, a true believer, a defender of the status quo, a populist Hamlet."[13]

Finally, the *Wall Street Journal*, in a January 20, 1977, editorial could muster up no more evidence of what a Carter presidency would entail than it had six months earlier. The *Journal* observed that Carter "remains something of a question-mark to the nation he will lead. We are still more than ordinarily unsure what he will do with his presidency, though his obvious native talent gives room for hope."[14]

The Carter Mandate

As with any presidential election journalists sought to define the extent of the public mandate for Jimmy Carter to pursue his preferred policies.

For the most part, journalists believed that Carter did not have a mandate to do much of anything. A number of journalists believed that Carter lacked a mandate for specific reforms because voters were uncertain of his intentions. For example, *Newsweek*'s Peter Goldman characterized the president-elect as "burdened by a kind of lingering public unease over who he really is and what he really stands for."[15]

In their post-election editorial, "A Change, But What Kind?" the *Wall Street Journal*'s editors expressed the same sentiment, but identified additional reasons for Carter's alleged lack of a specific mandate. First, and most obvious, was the closeness of Carter's electoral victory. Second, Jimmy Carter's appeal was predominantly regional rather than national. Yet unlike most journalistic assessments of this time, the *Journal*'s editors perceived this lack of a public mandate as a unique opportunity for the new president, which left him "remarkably free to choose what kind of president he will be. . . . In forming his administration and policies, President Carter will be free to address the needs of the nation as he sees them."[16]

Other editorialists and columnists agreed that President Carter lacked a public mandate for specific policies and provided conflicting interpretations of what that lack portended for the new administration. The *Washington Post* editorial on the national elections observed that,

> Mr. Carter's slim margin of victory takes nothing away from this achievement. But it does drastically diminish the unfettered "mandate" he openly sought. From all accounts he intended to assume the presidency blessedly and uniquely free of encumbering obligations to other members of his party and even to those groups and individuals who had gone out of their way to help him get elected. In fact, the election results place him deeply in debt—to organized labor, to big city bosses, to party workers, to certain elements of the traditional Democratic coalition.
>
> In particular, Mr. Carter now needs Congress more than Congress needs him.[17]

Peter Goldman perceived Carter's policy options as limited because of the "debt" the president-elect owed to party and labor leaders, "the men he had once run against." Goldman found Carter inhibited by the lack of a strong electoral mandate:

> He won finally as Democrats historically have won—mobilizing traditional Democratic voters by traditional Democratic means on traditional Democratic issues. The cost was the debt he incurred. "We won this election for him," said one big-city party leader. "The question is whether he'll show us any gratitude."[18]

Time magazine also found president-elect Carter encumbered by his lack of a strong electoral victory. *Time*'s news story noted that the closeness of the election showed Carter had "no commanding mandate for his campaign promises." The *Time* article pointed out that Democratic members of Congress would be unlikely to provide Carter with continued support given their own showings in the polls which were generally stronger than the president-elect's performance. The *Time* news story identified voter ambivalence about "taking a chance on Carter" as the cause of the closeness of the election and proclaimed that "Carter had won in a year in which nearly any respectable Democrat should have triumphed."[19]

Discussing the prospects for a Carter presidency, a November 7, 1976, *New York Times* editorial appeared restrained in its assessment of the opportunities provided Carter by his slim electoral victory. Rather than provide an early determination of the leeway, or lack of it, given to Carter by the voting public, the *Times* concluded that only the president could control his own political fortunes:

> Although Mr. Carter won with a popular plurality of nearly two million votes, he failed to achieve the desired mandate from every region of the country. Strong Presidents, however, create their own mandates. By their persuasiveness, political skill and sound judgment, they transform themselves from mere winners into leaders. . . . The voters have done their part. The responsibility for success or failure now rests with Mr. Carter.[20]

The Political Novice and "Outsider"

Although journalists characteristically called Carter an "outsider" both to his party and to the political establishment, they disagreed on the extent of Carter's standing as a national political novice. Journalists disagreed on whether the nation could be competently governed by an individual un-practiced in the art of national politics.

Two analyses in the post-1976 elections issue of *Time* magazine reflected the confusion about Carter's standing as a political "outsider." One article, "Marching North from Georgia," argued that Jimmy Carter won the pres-idency because his strategy of bringing together the old New Deal coalition "worked."[21] Another article, "The Route to the Top," offered a different assessment:

> Carter shunned the Democratic Party's horde of experienced organizers and brain-trusters. Apparently not fully trusting anyone but the Georgians who had helped him win the nomination, he stuck with them, even though they had little experience with national campaigns.[22]

Tom Nicholson of *Newsweek* agreed with the former assessment. Nicholson believed that Carter's election signified the revival of the Democratic party's traditional constituencies:

> Jimmy Carter's victory was not a personal triumph: he won because of the revival of the old coalition that first sent Franklin D. Roosevelt to the White House in 1932 and in some measure has been the main source of the Democratic party's strength in every successful Presidential election since.[23]

Most important, Carter's status as a political outsider was a source of both hope and anxiety for a number of commentators. An article in *Time* magazine's "Man of the Year" issue argued that Carter's "lack of ties to Washington and the party establishment" helped carry him to the White House. Yet this lack of a relationship with political Washington brought "potential dangers. . . . He does not know the Federal Government or the pressures it creates. He does not really know the politicians whom he will need to help him run the country."[24]

George F. Will disliked Carter's anti-elitism and political populism. In Will's view Carter's use of populist appeals violated the primary responsibility of a leader, which is to arbitrate between political elites. Will continued:

> Such populism is more than a bit murky on the subject of leadership. Carter frequently speaks about leadership . . . But for anyone whose populism is as pure as Carter's evidently is, there is not much for a leader to do, aside from drinking deep drafts of "the people's" wisdom.[25]

Meg Greenfield also expressed uncertainty about the need for a "populist" leader. Greenfield noted that Carter's populist image could be a positive development during a time of public skepticism with national leadership. Yet she warned that too much populism could undermine the pursuit of other desirable goods. President Ford, Greenfield argued, achieved closeness to the people by running an "open" presidency, yet he lost the election because of his handling of inflation and unemployment. Greenfield believed that populist appeals provided the potential for "self-delusion within the government itself" through rising expectations of what government could accomplish.[26]

In an October 11, 1976, editorial Greenfield presented a number of criticisms that eventually became part of Carter's press image. Greenfield noted that "Carter's self-professed and self-enforced role as the outsider" invited many problems for a Carter candidacy and presidency as well:

> I think if he is not careful he will put himself "outside" much more than the awful old venal, bloated Federal government he has identified as the enemy of American life. He is in danger of putting himself outside the mainstream of national politics and also outside the bounds of familiar, imperfect human experience. . . .
>
> Carter is overdoing a good and useful thing. That the aggregation of people, habits and ideas we think of as "Washington" is in need of both challenge and disruption strikes me as a truism beyond dispute. But there is something intolerant, unforgiving and even a mite ugly in the highly personalized and self-righteous way Carter has lately been pressing that claim. . . .
>
> What I suspect is that he is in the strong grip of a weak idea, namely, that this election is some kind of referendum on personal virtue, and that Americans want some kind of moral and political loner in the White House, one who is utterly and absolutely detached from the griefs and excesses of the past. But Carter, the "outsider" who is working this vein, is re-creating himself as an eccentric, a stranger to common experience, a man whose "we" becomes

increasingly unfamiliar and uncomfortable in its implications. I think people want him to come inside.[27]

Not every journalist shared Greenfield's reservations. *Time* magazine's presidency analyst Hugh Sidey assessed that Carter's "distance from the Oval Office has been his strength, and with luck and skill it could be his genius."[28] In another essay, "Not Laws But Inspiration," Sidey proclaimed that a Carter presidency may be noted "as much for what he is as for the legislation that he gets passed." Sidey added: "The simple act of trusting the American people, something that Richard Nixon could never do, can cement this society and can create a powerful force for the general good."[29]

Tom Wicker expressed the most pleasure in the prospect of an unpretentious presidency. Wicker feared that Carter might come "inside" to the political establishment and renew the practices of previous administrations. Rather than having a president who loved perquisites, Wicker proclaimed, "lots of us are rooting for more denim shirts, fewer neckties and maybe some softball on the old helicopter pad." Wicker offered a number of suggestions to help Carter maintain a people's presidency. Interestingly, among Wicker's suggestions ten weeks before Carter's inauguration were to cut down on playing "Hail to the Chief," replacing White House limousines with middle-American rental cars, having White House staff use commercial airlines, and having the president walk to his inaugural.[30]

Journalists therefore disagreed over the efficacy of having an "outsider" president. Perhaps the confusion over the prospects for a successful Carter presidency was best illustrated by *Time* magazine correspondent Stanley Cloud, who followed Jimmy Carter on the campaign trail for sixteen months in 1975 and 1976: "My own view is that he will either be one of the greatest Presidents of the modern era, or that he will be a complete failure."[31]

The Activist-Achiever

For a number of journalists the Carter presidency held out hope as the beginning of a new era in American public life. These analysts saw important evidence of this new beginning. First was the election of a man who for many observers evoked the image of other highly successful and energetic Democratic presidents, including Franklin D. Roosevelt and Lyndon B. Johnson. Some journalists expected Jimmy Carter to reproduce the significant legislative achievements of his Democratic predecessors. Second, the combination of a Democratic president and strongly Democratic-controlled Congress after eight years of a Republican-led executive branch created the expectation of harmonious White House–congressional relations. For example, Tom Wicker believed that Carter's election brought the prospect of great legislative achievements:

Despite the closeness of the Presidential election, Jimmy Carter may be coming into the White House in January with the best prospects for achieving a legislative program since the Johnson administration took over in 1965. With that one exception, in fact, Mr. Carter's legislative outlook probably is the best for any new President since 1948.[32]

Wicker identified a number of factors that created this favorable climate for sweeping legislative achievements. First, he noted that the Democratic party in January 1977 held nearly as many seats in the House of Representatives as the 89th Congress. The Democrats also held a 62 to 38 Senate majority. Second, Wicker perceived strong Democratic performances in the congressional races as evidence of the party's strength. Third, he proclaimed with Carter's election, the demise of the old Republican and Southern Democratic coalition in the House of Representatives. Finally, Wicker believed that reformed congressional rules made it "easier for legislation to be properly considered and brought to the floor for action." Wicker therefore advised the president-elect to move aggressively to carry out major legislative programs.[33]

Many journalists expected Jimmy Carter to accept this advice. Several *New York Times* contributors reflected this view of Carter as a committed political activist. Charles Mohr asserted that "to those who have studied him closely or know him well, there seems to be [great] likelihood that Mr. Carter will be relentless in trying to guide and, if necessary, force through his programs and changes."[34]

Times reporter Hedrick Smith also predicted that Carter would be an energetic leader: "As an activist who is committed to reforms, the President likes to place himself at the center of the action."[35] Smith found reason for cautious optimism based on Carter's commitment to political activism combined with, after eight years of divided leadership between a Democratic Congress and two Republican presidents, Carter's "new opportunity of working with overwhelming partisan majorities in both Houses."[36]

James Reston proclaimed Carter's election the beginning of a new era in American politics. In late December 1976 Reston observed that while all new administrations proclaim great changes and then disappoint, "as the Carterization of Washington proceeds, the idea is getting around that it may really be a New Year after all." Carter's broad, if not unprecedented inclusion of Vice-President elect Mondale in the Cabinet selection process convinced Reston of the president's commitment to change. Reston concluded that, "overall, there is a sense of change in the air, not only within the Cabinet and the White House staff but in their relations to one another, the President and the Congress."[37] Reston characterized Carter's staff as "intelligent and amiable young men" determined to avoid isolation and focus on the "mechanics" of running the government. "Above all they seem determined to keep in touch with the Congress and the public, and to use the authority of the White House to educate."[38]

A number of editorials reflected the notion that Carter's election constituted the beginning of a new era in American politics. On November 7, 1976, the *New York Times*'s editors offered an optimistic analysis:

The election of Jimmy Carter and Walter Mondale marks the start of a new political era. For the first time in eight years, the Presidency and the Congress are under the control of the same party, providing hope that legislative stalemate and government-by-veto may be finished.[39]

In its post-election editorial the *Washington Post* similarly viewed Carter's victory as the beginning of a new era:

People voted for Mr. Carter because they wanted a change. He has been elected with a very modest majority of the vote but with extraordinary advantages. One is the widespread feeling that the nation has reached the end of one era and is embarking on another. Mr. Carter is in a very strong position to become the embodiment of the nation's new hopes. Another is that he does enjoy the possibility at least of being helped by like-minded party colleagues in Congress and in local offices around the country. He also has available . . . the advice and services of Walter Mondale who begins with a large understanding of the workings of Congress and a great deal of good will and respect. So Mr. Carter has the potential for great success.[40]

Somewhat surprisingly, perhaps, the most optimistic expectations of Carter came from the conservative leaning news weekly, *U.S. News and World Report*. A number of articles in *U.S. News* predicted a new era of cooperation between the White House and Congress commencing with Carter's inauguration. Immediately following the 1976 elections *U.S. News* reported that the president "will find the new Congress readier than any in the last eight years to cooperate with the White House."[41]

While acknowledging that the White House–congressional relationship would not be completely "free of friction" because many of the new congressional leaders were independent and assertive politicians, a *U.S. News* story pointed out that one could not ignore the fact that the Democratic House majority was only two less than the 295 held by the 89th Congress:

Carter will confront this new Congress with one enormous asset: He is a Democrat. That asset shouldn't be underrated in assessing the prospects of restoring a harmonious working relationship between Congress and the White House. . . .

After being locked out of the White House for eight years, congressional Democrats will return to Washington in January eager to form a partnership with their new President.[42]

In late November 1976 *U.S. News* revealed the results of its interviews with many members of Congress on these members' expectations of Jimmy Carter. The news story reported that members of Congress expected Capitol Hill to be "much more receptive to President Carter's legislative program than it was to President Kennedy's." Also, a number of the interviewees asserted that they believed Carter should model his leadership approach after that of Lyndon B. Johnson. The report cited a number of factors as likely to enhance cooperation between the branches: (1) large Democratic majorities in both Houses; (2) the election of "new South" Democrats in the House who were less conservative than traditional Southern Democratic members; and (3) the erosion of power of committee chairmen in Congress.[43]

U.S. News and World Report's annual outlook issue of January 1977 predicted that the new year would "be one of change and—for the most part—change for the better." The news magazine's reporter predicted that "decisions are to be made in an atmosphere rid of much of the sourness that has lingered in the country since Watergate."[44] Another article in the outlook issue— "How Lawmakers Will Treat Ambitious White House Ideas"—offered a similar degree of optimism:

> For the first time since the mid-1960s, a large degree of harmony between Congress and the White House is in the cards for the new year.
> The heavy atmosphere of stalemate that has hung over Washington since 1969 is lifting, now that Democrats once again are to be in command at both ends of Pennsylvania Avenue.
> The shift will not mean that lawmakers and the new Democratic administration will see eye to eye on everything in 1977. But a new spirit of cooperation seems guaranteed.
> The immediate result will be to breathe new life into a variety of ideas previously doomed by the opposition of Republican Presidents.[45]

Journalists frequently compared Carter to his Democratic predecessors. In its 1977 presidential inaugural issue, *U.S. News and World Report* contained an article, "A New Era Begins," comparing Carter's ascendancy to the presidency to that of John F. Kennedy. The news story speculated that 1977 could be like 1961, the beginning of a new era of politics after eight years of Republican rule.[46] This article, though, was more restrained than the earlier *U.S. News* essays which "guaranteed" fruitful executive-congressional relations. *U.S. News*'s reporter cited the insights of unnamed political scientists who argued that Carter must still prove that he can work "effectively" with Congress. The report concluded that Democratic control of Congress provides "no guarantee of harmonious relationships between the two power centers. . . . "[47]

David Broder also exhibited optimism about Carter's ability to handle Congress and the bureaucracy. A week prior to the elections, Broder observed that, "More than most recent candidates [Carter] is a natural executive, with an instinct for command and a disciplined approach to decision-making." Yet Broder noted that a president with Carter's "ambitious designs" for government reorganization and policy reforms invites battles with Congress and the permanent government:

> He would plainly be an activist President and most of the voters appreciate the value of a take-charge executive, even knowing that such a President inevitably engenders tensions with Congress, the bureaucracy, the press and the private sector.[48]

The Uncompromising Carter
Heading Toward Problems Governing

Many journalists were not optimistic about Carter's prospects for accomplishing his policy objectives or getting along with the Democratic-controlled Congress. Looking at the same evidence provided by those individuals optimistic about Carter's ability to lead, these writers offered different conclusions. For a number of reasons several journalists predicted that Carter's tenure as president could be fraught with policy stalemate and unfriendly congressional relations.

First, some journalists alleged that Carter's experience as Governor of Georgia revealed a leadership approach not conducive to fruitful legislative-executive relations. Second, many writers perceived a stubborn streak in Carter's personality and a propensity to adopt policy positions not open to compromise. Third, Carter's policy agenda appeared to focus on highly divisive issues. Fourth, some journalists perceived Congress as unlikely to follow the lead of an energetic, ambitious Chief Executive in the aftermath of Vietnam and Watergate. Journalists also noted that since most Democratic members of Congress ran ahead of Carter in the 1976 elections, many congressional leaders felt little, if any, debt to Carter. Finally, some journalists believed that Carter's campaign for president as an "outsider" set a combative tone between the president and political Washington.

Stanley Cloud of *Time*, for example, reported a disturbing pattern of stubbornness in the former Governor of Georgia. One month prior to the 1976 elections Cloud noted that as Governor, Carter relied heavily on his own counsel and adopted "uncompromising stands that threatened to undermine the goals he wanted to accomplish." Cloud concluded:

He almost lost his battle to reorganize the Georgia government when his all-or-nothing stance irritated the state legislators. Only at virtually the last minute did he heed the advice of friends and agree to compromise on several relatively minor points. A troubling question is, if he is elected President, whether Carter would follow expert advice in making his decisions.[49]

In its annual "Man of the Year" issue in January 1977, *Time*'s lead story portrayed Carter's experience as Governor as a bad omen for the Carter presidency:

The obvious danger of (his) self-confidence is that President Carter may be unwilling to listen to advice or compromise when thwarted, as he will inevitably be. As Governor, Carter condemned his state's legislature as "the worst in the history of the state" when it refused to pass a consumer-protection bill that he favored. Although there have been charges to the contrary he was a good Governor. . . . But his steady scrapping with the legislature hindered him from accomplishing even more.[50]

A *Time* magazine article in the pre-1976 elections issue predicted what Jimmy Carter would do as president if victorious. The article portrayed Carter as an activist who needed on the job training in national politics:

> From his first day in office, Jimmy Carter wants to be an activist, innovative President in the boat-rocking mold of Franklin Roosevelt. Carter will require a lot of on-the-job training; he should need at least six months to a year to locate the power levers and learn how to pull them.[51]

According to this news article Carter's combination of political activism and inexperience was hardly the ideal formula for effective leadership. The *Time* article also noted that Congress no longer accepted a secondary role in defining the national political agenda:

> Many people see an advantage in having a President of the same party as the congressional majority. But Carter's dealings with Congress may be difficult. . . . He strongly criticizes "dormant" Presidents like Dwight Eisenhower and Gerald Ford for giving—by default—too large a policy role to Congress. Nonetheless, Congress is not likely to stop trying to influence strongly foreign policy or to change the Administration's proposed budgets. To get some of his programs through Congress, particularly those that will offend special interest groups, Carter may have to compromise. He often finds that hard.[52]

Finally, in its post-1976 elections analysis *Time* reported cautiously about Carter's ability to lead Congress. The *Time* article argued that the strong showing of Democratic members at the polls, combined with Carter's narrow victory, would shorten the traditional "honeymoon" period:

> Now, with both the White House and the Congress in control of the same party, there will be a new opportunity for the two branches of Government to work together. But since so few Senators or Congressmen rode on Carter's coattails—indeed, in some cases it was the other way around—the new President's traditional honeymoon may be fairly brief and subdued.[53]

David Broder argued that Carter's greatest difficulty governing "effectively" would be "to exert a leadership role against the claims of a Congress with a large and assertive Democratic majority whose members owe Carter next to nothing." According to Broder, Carter had to strengthen his support in the country in order to "exert a leadership role" over Congress. Broder concluded that this would be an especially difficult task for Carter since White House occupants have traditionally expanded their political bases through the skillful use of "political and public relations techniques."[54]

Albert Hunt of the *Wall Street Journal* found many members of Congress discouraged by Carter's gubernatorial tenure. Hunt pointed out that while Capitol Hill held out high expectations of a Democratic Chief Executive there was considerable apprehension about Jimmy Carter. Many members of Congress, Hunt reported, anticipated Carter's staff would show as much "disdain" for the Hill as his staff exhibited for the Georgia legislature.[55]

In January 1977 *U.S. News* predicted that the new president "will move fast early in 1977 to demonstrate that he will be an innovative, take-charge President."[56] Yet the magazine's reporter noted that according to some assessments, "down the road" the president may have difficulty leading Congress:

> Observers note that the President-elect showed a stubborn streak in pushing his programs through the Georgia legislature, and he is not expected to back off easily when he enters the White House. At the same time, lawmakers have lost some of their awe of Presidents in recent years and will insist on putting their stamp on major programs.[57]

Times columnist Anthony Lewis perceived a disturbing stubborn streak in Carter. Lewis argued that unlike "most successful politicians" Carter was intensely committed to a number of policy objectives. While implying that such devotion to principle was rare and admirable, Lewis concluded that Carter would meet resistance to his objectives, "But I doubt that he will give them up."[58]

Finally, the *New York Times* in a January 3, 1977, editorial, "Enter Majority Rule," speculated about Carter's congressional relations. The *Times* noted that Democratic control of both political branches provided the potential for overcoming the "policy stalemate" of the previous eight years. The editorial writers hoped Carter would take the lead in offering an atmosphere conducive to favorable executive-congressional relations:

> Will the change mean harmonious relations between the White House and Congress? Much will depend upon President-elect Carter's skills in working with Congress. Prior consultation, a willingness to compromise egos are inescapable requirements for a President dealing with the 535 politicians who make up Congress.[59]

Cabinet Selections

During the presidential transition journalists gave considerable attention to Carter's Cabinet selection process. The Cabinet selection process is the most visible activity of a president-elect during the transition period. It is the principal activity providing insight to the new administration's priorities and decision-making process. Carter's selection process sustained intense scrutiny and criticism because of Carter's many campaign pronouncements concerning the need for "new faces" to run the federal government. Carter's selections invited a combination of disappointment and praise.

Concerning Carter's Cabinet appointments, the following themes dominated the national print media assessments. First, a number of journalists expressed disappointment with the choices. For the most part, these critics found the majority of the selections too tied to the Washington establishment. These critics accused Carter of breaking the promise to bring new faces into his administration. Second, some critics assessed that Carter made extremely wise Cabinet choices. Having opposed the idea of appointing political outsiders to the Cabinet, many journalists expressed their relief with Carter's choices of individuals experienced in government service.

A third theme focused on the process of selection itself rather than on Carter's choices. While some critics found Carter's selection process excessively slow, many other analysts praised the president-elect for not making important decisions in haste. A number of journalists believed that Carter's deliberative selection process revealed a prudent, cautious style of presidential leadership.

To begin, Anthony Lewis criticized Carter for turning to the Washington establishment for major Cabinet choices. Lewis argued that Carter should have appointed new, young individuals to the Cabinet since, "after all, Jimmy Carter did run as an outsider." Lewis pointed out that while many observers were skeptical of the idea of appointing political outsiders, a greater number of people voted for Carter because of the promise of "risk and challenge." For that reason "it would be wrong for Mr. Carter to seek safety now in old ways and old faces."[60]

To emphasize the point that Carter's choices were generally too tied to the political establishment, Lewis remarked that Carter's Cabinet "could have been picked by Gerald Ford—or Dwight Eisenhower." Lewis criticized the "unoriginal character of Mr. Carter's choices." He concluded that Carter's Cabinet "is too conformist, too old, too tied to established interests."[61]

Carter's choices for the Cabinet and White House staff also bothered *Times* reporter James T. Wooten. Despite campaign rhetoric to the contrary, Wooten complained, Carter eventually chose establishment individuals. Wooten perceived the Carter choices as evidence that the president was not genuinely committed to bringing in new faces and new ideas to the national government.[62]

The *Wall Street Journal's* editors also did not approve of Carter's Cabinet selections. The *Journal* lamented the lack of "diversity" among the Cabinet members and referred to Carter's choices as "a Cabinet of homogenized problem solvers." Carter's lack of national political experience was, for the *Journal*, one cause of concern about having a Cabinet of like-minded individuals.[63]

A number of journalists agreed with Carter's selection of "insiders." Joseph Kraft rebutted his colleagues' criticisms of Carter's selections. Kraft viewed Carter's choices favorably because during the presidential campaign Carter and his aides "demonstrated that they knew next to nothing about running the federal government." Kraft expressed delight that in an area presumably unknown to Carter—national security policy—Carter appointed a number of distinguished foreign policy experts.[64] Kraft also praised Carter's decision to allow Cabinet officers "to run their own shows."[65]

James Reston also agreed with Carter's Cabinet selections. Reston wrote that the Carter people were "absolutely right in their determination to come to Washington with a fresh team and not with a collection of distinguished has-beens."[66] In light of the criticisms of Carter's Cabinet selections Reston dissented from the view that these individuals constituted "a collection of competent retreads." Reston blasted Carter's critics for failing to name any brilliant new-comers who should have been chosen by the president-elect. He concluded that "the Carter team . . . deserves a better press than it has received, and at least a chance to prove its worth."[67]

Perhaps the strongest defense of the Carter selections came from a *New York Times* editorial, "Ideals and Realities." While acknowledging that nine of Carter's seventeen Cabinet choices served in other administrations and another three were members of Congress, the *Times* dismissed the criticisms of Carter for picking too many "insiders." In Carter, the *Times* found a president-elect who wanted first and foremost to run an efficient and responsive government. Carter needed the "old hands" for that purpose. Also, given Carter's lack of foreign policy experience, the *Times* argued that it was wise to bring into the administration people like Cyrus Vance, Harold Brown, and Zbigniew Brzezinski. The editorial concluded that Carter "has assembled a strong Cabinet."[68]

A number of journalists assessed that Carter's Cabinet selection process exhibited his thoughtful, prudent decision making instinct. During the transition, James Reston, for example, noted that Carter's slow beginning in choosing the Cabinet assured political opponents that the president was thoughtful and listened to outside advice.[69]

Significantly, most of the journalists who praised Carter for his deliberation in Cabinet selection held less lofty expectations of the president-elect than those critical of his appointments. Peter Goldman asserted that Carter's selection process displayed an understanding of political "realities" that force decision making delays and compromises. Goldman asserted that, "the first thing not to expect quite clearly was the transubstantiation of Plains into Camelot."[70] A *New York Times* editorial echoed this view and praised Carter's "deliberative approach to government" as evidenced by the Cabinet selection process and early legislative proposals:

> This willingness to go slow and to develop new programs incrementally is all to the good. Mr. Carter was not elected as a miracle maker. He was elected because a majority of the voters shared his belief that a compassionate Government could also be a competent, hard-headed, thrifty Government. The new Administration can validate that belief only by the careful planning and strong management that the Carter approach envisages.[71]

Peter Goldman offered a similar view of the Carter Cabinet choices. While disappointing to those who expected a radical change in the kinds of people running the federal government, Carter's Cabinet choices built confidence in those critics uncomfortable with his campaign promises to bring new faces and decision making processes to Washington:

> Carter's show of deliberation [in Cabinet appointments] was only one of a series of signs intended to display him as a man of sober reserve—and thus to quiet the Capitol's enduring fear of the unknowns he represents.[72]

And he signaled, by his [Cabinet] choices and his manner of making them, the kind of government he proposes to lead northward from Georgia to Washington next January 20—a safe-and-sane technocracy with button downs under its denims and moderation on its mind.[73]

Conclusion

A number of themes dominated early press assessments of Jimmy Carter. Significantly, there was broad disagreement within the media on most of the questions discussed above. This disagreement reflected a general confusion about Jimmy Carter, what he stood for, and what he would do as president.

General perceptions of what a president should do during the transition period were the bases of many of the media assessments of Carter. A number of journalists also based their expectations of Carter on the leadership approaches of previous Democratic presidents. Others developed expectations of Carter from his rhetoric and promises. While journalists emphasized many similar themes in their early assessments of Carter, their conclusions varied.

To review some of the major assessments, many journalists expected Carter to be an activist-interventionist president who could "bulldoze" proposals through Congress. These journalists assumed that a Democratic president with a large party majority in Congress had a philosophically compatible base of support in the legislative branch.

Some journalists were not optimistic about the prospects of fruitful presidential-congressional relations under Carter. Based on perceptions of Carter as a stubborn, uncompromising individual these analysts predicted a difficult partnership between the political branches in Carter's term.

On the efficacy of having an "outsider" president journalists differed. For optimists Carter's election constituted the beginning of a "new era" in American politics devoid of arrogance in the use of power. In contrast, a number of journalists perceived Carter as putting himself outside the mainstream of political Washington and creating a difficult leadership condition.

In the following chapter we find the development of the above journalistic themes. Throughout 1977 a negative press assessment of Carter's leadership begins to emerge. This negative assessment becomes compatible with the views of Carter as uncompromising and incapable of dealing competently with political Washington's "insiders."

Notes

1. "Vagueness and All That," *Wall Street Journal*, July 13, 1976, p. 18.
2. "A Soothing Southern Drawl," *Wall Street Journal*, July 15, 1976, p. 76.
3. "Carter Fights The Big League Slump," *Time*, October 11, 1976, p. 18.
4. Stanley Cloud, "Jimmy's Mixed Signals," *Time*, October 4, 1976, p. 28.
5. Ibid., p. 27.

6. Peter Goldman and Eleanor Clift, "Mr. Outside In Stride," *Newsweek*, November 1, 1976, pp. 23–24.

7. Rowland Evans and Robert Novak, "Carter's Choice for Justice," *Washington Post*, December 22, 1976, p. A19.

8. Rowland Evans and Robert Novak, "Carter's Twisting Economic Talk," *Washington Post*, December 16, 1976, p. A19.

9. Joseph Kraft, "The President Elect," *Washington Post*, November 4, 1976, p. A27.

10. Joseph Kraft, "The Challenge of Inflation," *Washington Post*, November 16, 1976, p. A15.

11. Joseph Kraft, "Carter's Blunder on Arms," *Washington Post*, February 1, 1977, p. A17.

12. "Man of the Year," *Time*, January 3, 1977, p. 11.

13. Ibid., p. 13.

14. "On the Uses of Diversity," *Wall Street Journal*, January 20, 1977, p. 14.

15. Peter Goldman, "The New Look," *Newsweek*, November 15, 1976, p. 24.

16. "A Change, But What Kind," *Wall Street Journal*, November 4, 1976, p. 20.

17. "The Election," *Washington Post*, November 4, 1976, p. A26.

18. Peter Goldman, "The New Look," *Newsweek*, November 15, 1976, p. 25.

19. "Carter!" *Time*, November 15, 1976, p. 14.

20. "The Carter Presidency," *New York Times*, November 7, 1976, p. E16.

21. "Marching North From Georgia," *Time*, November 15, 1976, p. 16.

22. "The Route to the Top," *Time*, November 15, 1976, p. 31.

23. Tom Nicholson, "The Old Coalition," *Newsweek*, November 15, 1976, p. 29.

24. "Man of the Year," *Time*, January 3, 1977, p. 22.

25. George F. Will, "Carter and 'The People,'" *Newsweek*, October 18, 1976, p. 118.

26. Meg Greenfield, "They, The People," *Newsweek*, January 17, 1977, p. 88.

27. Meg Greenfield, "Carter's Real Blunder," *Newsweek*, October 11, 1976, p. 120.

28. Hugh Sidey, "Closing Out the Interim Chapter," *Time*, November 15, 1976, p. 28.

29. Hugh Sidey, "Not Laws but Inspiration," *Time*, November 22, 1976, p. 15.

30. Tom Wicker, "Little 'd—A Little Humility," *New York Times*, November 9, 1976, p. A37.

31. Stanley Cloud quoted in "Man of the Year," *Time*, January 3, 1977, p. 22.

32. Tom Wicker, "Mr. Carter's Mandate," *New York Times*, November 7, 1976, p. E17.

33. Ibid.

34. Charles Mohr, "Carter, with a Long List of Campaign Promises, Now Faces Problem of Making Good on Them," *New York Times*, November 14, 1976, p. A1.

35. Hedrick Smith, "The Man From Plains and the Imperial Presidency," *New York Times*, January 23, 1977, p. E1.

36. Hedrick Smith, "A Call to the American Spirit," *New York Times*, January 21, 1977, p. A1.

37. James Reston, "Mondale as Chief of Staff," *New York Times*, December 29, 1976, p. A25.

38. James Reston, "Carter's Amiable Computers," *New York Times*, December 17, 1976, p. 27.

39. "The Carter Presidency," *New York Times*, November 7, 1976, p. E16.

40. "The Election," *Washington Post*, November 4, 1976, p. A26.

41. "Will Congress Seize Reins from a Democratic White House," *U.S. News and World Report,* November 15, 1976, p. 25.

42. Ibid., pp. 26–27.

43. "What to Expect When Congress 'Welcomes' Carter," *U.S. News and World Report,* November 29, 1976, pp. 17-18.

44. "Outlook 77—A Fresh Start," *U.S. News and World Report,* January 3, 1977, p. 12.

45. "Carter's Record as Governor—Clues to the Future," *U.S. News and World Report,* December 13, 1976, p. 28.

46. "A New Era Begins," *U.S. News and World Report,* January 14, 1977, p. 16.

47. Ibid., p. 17.

48. David Broder, "Indecision About Carter," *Washington Post,* October 27, 1976, p. A13.

49. Stanley Cloud, "Jimmy's Mixed Signals," *Time,* October 4, 1976, p. 30.

50. "Man of the Year," *Time,* January 3, 1977, p. 14.

51. "A Carter Administration," *Time,* November 8, 1976, p. 24.

52. Ibid., p. 26.

53. "Carter!" *Time,* November 15, 1976, p. 15.

54. David Broder, "Carter's Dilemma," *Washington Post,* November 28, 1976, p. B7.

55. Albert Hunt, "President Carter and Capitol Hill," *Wall Street Journal,* January 24, 1977, p. 16.

56. "Carter: A Strong Leader," *U.S. News and World Report,* January 3, 1977, p. 14.

57. Ibid., p. 15; see also, "Carter's Record as Governor—Clues to the Future," *U.S. News and World Report,* December 13, 1976, p. 28.

58. Anthony Lewis, "The Long and the Short," *New York Times,* March 3, 1977, p. A33.

59. "Enter Majority Rule," *New York Times,* January 3, 1977, p. 20.

60. Anthony Lewis, "Faces Old and New," *New York Times,* November 22, 1976, p. A25.

61. Anthony Lewis, "Why Not the Best?" *New York Times,* December 23, 1976, p. A23.

62. James T. Wooten, "Many Carter Aides Picked From Often-Tapped Source," *New York Times,* February 4, 1977, p. A10.

63. "On the Uses of Diversity," *Wall Street Journal,* January 20, 1977, p. 14.

64. Joseph Kraft, "They Remember the Future," *Washington Post,* December 28, 1976, p. A15; see also, "Carter Finding Few Outsiders," *New York Times,* December 16, 1976, p. A21; and "Mr. Outside Opts for Ins," *Time,* January 3, 1977, p. 40.

65. Joseph Kraft, "Government By Cross-Cutters," *Washington Post,* December 7, 1976, p. A15. On Kraft's view of Cabinet selections see also his "The Aftertaste of the Selection Process," *Washington Post,* December 26, 1976, p. C7.

66. James Reston, "The 78 Days," *New York Times,* November 5, 1976, p. A25.

67. James Reston, "Two Cheers for the Cabinet," *New York Times,* December 26, 1976, p. E9.

68. "Ideals and Realities," *New York Times,* December 21, 1976, p. A32.

69. James Reston, "Carter's Cautious Beginning," *New York Times,* December 12, 1976, p. E17.

70. Peter Goldman, "First, a Word of Caution," *Newsweek,* January 10, 1977, p. 14.

71. "Driving Slowly Up Capitol Hill," *New York Times,* January 16, 1977, p. E18.

72. Peter Goldman, "Mr. Carter Goes to Washington," *Newsweek*, December 6, 1976, p. 21.

73. Peter Goldman, "Picking the New Team," *Newsweek*, December 13, 1976, p. 20. Of all the Carter Cabinet appointments none was subjected to as intense criticism as Griffin Bell (Attorney General). The selection of Bell was initially perceived as a poor choice because of Bell's close friendship with Jimmy Carter and previous membership in an all-white private club. James Reston proclaimed the Bell selection "insensitive, willful, stubborn and even selfish." In Reston's view the appointment defied "the principles Mr. Carter had supported all during the election campaign" and was reminiscent of other presidents who put friends in charge of the Justice Department (see "Carter's First Mistake," *New York Times*, December 22, 1976, p. A29). An even less restrained assessment was offered by Anthony Lewis who proclaimed Bell not qualified "by character, breadth of mind or judgment." Lewis called Bell "a man of limited vision and sensitivity," (see "Why Not the Best?" *New York Times*, December 23, 1976, p. 23). The press criticisms of Bell are too extensive to discuss further. Significantly, Bell's performance as Attorney General brought nearly universal praise of him by the end of Carter's term.

3

Carter's First Year: 1977

The previous chapter reveals journalists' early expectations of the Carter administration. Journalists based their assessments of Carter on the following: what Carter revealed about himself in the 1976 campaign; what journalists understood about his performance as Governor of Georgia; the people Carter surrounded himself with and their own experiences and backgrounds; and what the Cabinet selection process revealed about the Carter administration's decision making process. The early evaluations of Carter provided an incomplete and impressionistic portrait of the new president. A more fully developed portrait emerges from a review of Carter's actions as president.

Journalists' evaluative efforts focused on different bases for judging the administration once Carter became president. There is an obvious reason for this change: journalists had the first opportunity to judge Carter's actions as president. Using my five categories of journalistic evaluations, let's review some of this chapter's major findings.

1. *Timing.* The criteria applied when assessing a president's leadership (or potential for leadership) differed significantly from the transition period to the first year in office. For Carter the early 1977 evaluations appeared very much like those of the transition period. That is, the early evaluations were based on vague impressions of Carter and the expectations journalists had of how this president would and should behave in office. Journalists identified a number of their expectations of how Carter would initiate his presidency and the kind of agenda he would establish.

The evaluations of Carter during the first year moved in a direction established somewhat by the administration (in the timing of events, pronouncements, and policy proposals). In the first few months journalists gave considerable attention to Carter's symbolic activities: his rhetoric, discourse, and methods of appearing to the public. Once the administration identified its major first year initiative—the energy program—and other policy proposals, journalists gave increasing attention to the nature of the agenda and Carter's efforts to build public and congressional support. Journalists also focused on the timing of these initiatives. By the end of the year we find many journalists criticizing the timing of Carter's policy initiatives and explaining the kinds of proposals presidents should offer to ensure legislative success at this stage of an administration.

2. *Rhetoric/Symbolism.* In the early months of 1977 a great deal of Carter's efforts focused on political symbolism. Lacking major concrete policy proposals by which to judge the administration, journalists examined the president's rhetoric and symbolic actions. Journalists therefore assessed Carter's "success" as a political leader according to how well he conducted his "campaign" in office. The very favorable nature of these assessments is striking. Many journalists expected Carter to reestablish public trust in the presidency and were pleased with his self-styled "open presidency."

The press reacted to a number of Carter's symbolic actions including the January 20 "people's" inaugural, characterized by the First Family's walk down Pennsylvania Avenue to the White House. Other symbolic actions included Carter's efforts to "de-pomp" the presidency by cutting back on unnecessary frills in the White House such as staff use of limousines and supplying every office with a television set. The energy crisis inspired the turning down of White House thermostats and Carter's wearing of a beige wool cardigan sweater in a "fireside chat" on national television. A number of symbolic activities demonstrated Carter's intention to remain "close" to the people. These events included the March 5 national radio "Ask President Carter" show, and a March 16 "town meeting" in Clinton, Massachusetts.

A number of themes dominated the journalistic assessments of Carter's symbolism. Many journalists admired Carter's unpretentious, populist style. They perceived his symbolic actions as necessary for building public support for forthcoming administration proposals. A number of journalists wrote that Carter was creating the leadership condition by developing a public "mandate" not provided in the 1976 elections. Many journalists even portrayed Carter as a "great communicator" and praised his "moderate" and "subdued" tone.

Not all commentary on Carter's rhetoric and symbolism was favorable. Regarding the "great communicator" thesis, some journalists feared that in the television age a charismatic president like Jimmy Carter could use his gift of persuasion to create a dangerous imbalance of power between the president and Congress. Also, by the end of the year journalists criticized Carter's rhetoric and symbolism for raising the public's hopes to an unrealistic level.

3. *Agenda.* Carter's first year policy agenda was ambitious. In foreign affairs Carter made human rights the hallmark of United States policy. The administration held arms control talks in Moscow in March seeking Soviet approval of a major arms reduction plan. In domestic affairs the administration's initiatives included a comprehensive energy program; an economic stimulus package including a $50 tax rebate (a proposal later withdrawn); major electoral reforms; executive branch reorganization; hospital cost containment; a major public works program; creation of a Consumer Protection Agency; and a controversial proposal to eliminate 19 major water projects nationwide. Despite the outpouring of proposals Carter declared that his administration's first year could be judged a success or failure based on whether Congress enacted the energy program.

The major themes associated with the agenda were: (a) *Foreign Policy.* President Carter's attention to foreign affairs issues early in his term surprised many journalists. These journalists expected Carter to focus early in his term on domestic economic dislocations. Journalists derived this expectation from perceptions of Carter as inexperienced in the international realm and as having campaigned primarily on issues of economic justice and equality.

(b) *Domestic Policy.* For the most part journalists agreed with Carter's portrayal of the energy crisis and his determination to deal with the crisis. Many journalists asserted that Carter correctly identified the nation's major domestic problem and offered a fair, though far-reaching, energy plan. Journalists portrayed other domestic policy proposals such as executive branch reorganization, hospital cost containment, and the elimination of major water works projects as meritorious initiatives.

4. *Policy Development.* A wide gulf existed between journalists' assessments of the administration's agenda and efforts to enact that agenda. The human rights campaign is a good example. Carter relied on public diplomacy to bring international pressure to bear on governments violating human rights. The United States government also reduced foreign aid to countries violating human rights standards. Many journalists sympathetic to the human rights concept found the administration's application of the rights standard arbitrary. Journalists often portrayed the administration's policy as conspicuous in its failure to criticize and pressure friendly nations as vigilantly as foes behind the Iron Curtain.

In general, journalists found Carter's foreign policy incoherent. These critics believed that in the foreign policy realm an administration should adopt a "coherent" policy approach in the mold of one administration official (either the Secretary of State, National Security Adviser, U.N. Ambassador, or the president himself). Carter's administration allegedly spoke with too many voices and tried to achieve conflicting goals. Journalists made a great deal of reported differences between Secretary of State Cyrus Vance and National Security Advisor Zbigniew Brzezinski. Journalists also perceived Carter's efforts to achieve human rights improvements abroad and arms control with the Soviets as contradictory goals. They viewed the human rights campaign as causing Soviet positions to harden, making arms control negotiations impossible.

The press severely criticized Carter's efforts at building support for the energy program. Criticisms of the administration focused on: (a) the failure to properly consult members of Congress about administration proposals; (b) the program's quantity of hastily devised, controversial provisions; (c) the president's unwillingness to compromise on some of these controversial provisions.

The argument that Carter "failed" as a leader in working with Congress on the energy package reveals some important journalistic expectations of presidential leadership. Journalists expected the president to engage in early and frequent negotiations with members of Congress on this legislative initiative. According to many journalists, a president succeeds legislatively by stroking congressional egos, consulting legislative leaders at each stage of a proposal's development, and engaging in political compromises to gain widespread congressional support. Carter's approach did not approximate this model, leading many journalists to assess his legislative leadership negatively.

5. *Staff.* Journalists subjected the White House staff to intense scrutiny. Early in the administration journalists severely criticized the congressional liaison team headed by Frank Moore for failing to follow the norms of political Washington. Journalists emphasized rumors of staff not returning phone calls from members of Congress. Journalists accused members of the White House staff of showing contempt for the legislative branch by not properly consulting congressmen about crucial administration decisions. They portrayed the staff as lacking both national political experience and regional diversity (as evidenced by the numerous journalistic caricatures of the "White House Georgians").

Journalists assessed the "Lance affair" as the inevitable outcome of an inexperienced White House staffed by collegial and parochial individuals. They argued that an experienced staff with diverse backgrounds would have handled the Lance affair competently.

Finally, journalists assessed the Carter staff according to criteria the president identified. Carter's frequent assertions of the need for a high standard of ethical and moral conduct by public servants resulted in the press applying the highest standards of conduct to the Carter White House. This was most evident during the early stages of the Lance affair. Lacking evidence of Lance's guilt or innocence, journalists noted that Lance violated the president's own ethical standards.

In what follows the journalistic assessments of Carter are organized chronologically to provide an understanding of how particular themes developed over time. The chapter is organized as follows: (1) Carter's Symbolic Activities; (2) Carter's First Year Leadership; (3) The Lance Affair; and (4) The First Year Retrospectives.

Symbolic Activities

President Carter's inaugural speech helped establish the rhetorical tone of his administration. In this speech Carter sought to reassure citizens that, with Watergate in the past, they could have faith once again in government:

> The American dream endures. We must once again have faith in our country—and in one another. . . . Let our recent mistakes bring a resurgent commitment to the basic principles of our nation, for we know that if we despise our own government we have no future.[1]

Carter outlined for his administration a number of goals, including a concern for human rights abroad, nuclear arms reduction, environmental quality, and creating a democratic system worthy of emulation. Finally,

Carter discussed the importance of realizing that there were limits to what government could do:

> We have learned that "more" is not necessarily "better," that even our great nation has its recognized limits, and that we can neither answer all questions nor solve all problems . . . we simply do our best.[2]

In their assessments of the inaugural speech journalists frequently emphasized Carter's theme of "limits." Consistent with the commentary during the transition period many journalists concluded from this speech that Carter intended to proceed with a limited, cautious policy agenda. For example, a *Time* magazine news report noted the "subdued" tone of Carter's address— a speech that offered no great vision and no Kennedy-like proclamation to "bear any burden."[3]

The *New York Times* pointed out that Carter's speech contained "nothing memorable" on where he planned to lead the nation. The *Times* editorialists praised Carter's "melody" and added that they expected Carter to "make us proud again of the purposes and competence of government."[4]

The *Washington Post* praised Carter's address for "gentleness of tone and lack of zealotry." The *Post* editorial added that some of Carter's proclamations appeared contradictory because Carter lacked a rigidly ideological frame of mind.[5]

Newsweek reporter Susan Fraker predicted that Carter "will not try to reconstruct John Kennedy's tinseled Camelot or recreate Franklin Roosevelt's kinetic Hundred Days." Rather, "the Carter Presidency will almost certainly proceed with far more deliberation than speed." Quoting a Patrick Cadell transition memo that warned against attempting early "sweeping changes," Fraker noted that Carter agreed that it would be imprudent to try to achieve too much, too fast.[6]

A "Symbol-Minded" President

At the beginning of this presidency, journalists showed the most interest in the Carter "style." Journalists discussed Carter's numerous symbolic gestures and attempted to develop from their observations some understanding of Carter's leadership approach. Some journalists favored Carter's unpretentious style while others complained of an administration that appeared to stress style over substance. Others feared that the administration's emphasis on political symbolism could become a form of public manipulation.

The most prevalent assessment during the first few months of Carter's tenure was that the emphasis on symbolism was exactly what Carter and the country needed. Carter presumably needed to focus on political symbolism to build the commanding political base not provided by his electoral victory in 1976. The country allegedly needed stylistic trappings to rebuild trust and confidence in our national political institutions.

The Carter administration began with many experiments in political symbolism. Carter's inauguration was proclaimed a "people's inaugural" and was highlighted by the First Family's walk down Pennsylvania Avenue. Carter's first speech to the nation as president, the so-called "fireside chat," was widely hailed as a masterful effort to convey an unpretentious presidential style. *Time* magazine quoted Franklin D. Roosevelt, Jr.'s assertion that "President Carter fits television like my father fitted radio." The news story added:

> Only two weeks into his presidency, Jimmy Carter has already proved himself a master of the symbolic act.
> During his fireside chat last week, Carter introduced what may prove to be the most memorable symbol of an Administration that promises to make steady use of symbolism—the beige wool Cardigan, a favorite of his.[7]

The *Washington Post* praised the fireside chat on energy policy for its unimposing, unimperial style: "Mr. Carter's informality accomplished its evident aim of confirming that the tone and manner of national leadership have changed." The *Post* argued that Carter's emphasis on shared sacrifice was a message suited to "the general public mood."[8]

While critical of the "fireside chat" on energy as plagued by "too many generalities," the *Post*'s Haynes Johnson noted that Carter's performance exhibited the president's command of television. Proclaiming Carter "a creature of the television age," Johnson observed: "In his first two weeks as President Jimmy Carter has shown he understands the symbolic nature of national leadership."[9]

The most favorable explanation of Carter's symbolism was that he was attempting to gain support for forthcoming policy initiatives by reestablishing trust in the presidency. *New York Times* reporter Hedrick Smith argued that Carter's "deliberate depomping of the Presidency" was not intended to diminish the powers of the White House. Instead, "what Mr. Carter is obviously seeking to do is to earn back the full power of the Presidency by regaining public respect and confidence."[10]

David Broder argued that Carter's image-building and symbolism not only "makes sense" but was "required" at such an early stage of the administration. Given a variety of conditions, including a stubbornly independent Congress, interest-group pressures, and the lack of a strong public mandate, Broder believed that image building was "a necessary preliminary for leadership." Broder found the turning down of the White House thermostat and a president working in his sweater useful symbols for conveying the enormity of the energy crisis.[11]

Newsweek reporters Peter Goldman and Richard Steele offered similar views. While calling Carter's first energy speech "More style than substance," Goldman interpreted the speech "as an attempt at once to reduce the office to human scale and to prove that he is large enough for it."[12] Steele added that while Carter's talk lacked substance there was a "method to his showmanship . . . setting a style of leadership now so that he will in fact be able to lead later on."[13]

Many journalists admired Carter's commitment to "depomping" the presidency. In his discussion of Carter's "symbol-minded Presidency," *New York Times* reporter James T. Wooten praised the administration's move away from the "tenseness and nervousness" of the Nixon years.[14] Tom Wicker agreed that Carter's use of symbols showed "how well he understands public discontent at the distance and insensitivity of government."[15] *U.S. News and World Report* observed that both Washingtonians and Middle America favored Carter's unpretentious style of White House entertainment. The news weekly added that the public was "pleased with the move away from what has been called an 'imperial presidency' toward a simpler life style."[16] Meg Greenfield offered the most positive assessment:

> . . . the objective of all the democratizing and sweater wearing and bus riding is to reassure a sour public that Washington is not a bastion of privilege, presided over by people who have lost touch with reality. . . .
> [Carter] is surely right in thinking that these symbols and gestures are required now as an antidote to the governmental excesses of the past. . . . I think the instinct is right that tells him how important it is to try to stay human in the White House.[17]

Carter's most creative effort to establish a direct relationship with the public was the March 5, 1977 "Ask President Carter" radio call-in program. Sponsored by the Columbia Broadcasting System (CBS) and mediated by television news anchorman Walter Cronkite, the program allowed citizens to call the president and voice their concerns about government and public policy. Peter Goldman, while acknowledging the lack of "substance" in Carter's responses, argued that "as theater, 'Ask President Carter' was a virtuoso turn indeed—the most innovative and best played performance yet in his ongoing mixed-media show of intimacy with the people."[18] *Time* magazine declared the call-in show "a public relations triumph in Carter's campaign to bring the presidency to the people."[19] The *Washington Post* declared the event "a great success in just about any terms you can think of. . . . The President was snappy, intimate, and impressively knowledgeable." The *Post* assessed that Carter's symbolism "may be instrumental in mobilizing for him the kind of public support that will be essential to getting hard jobs done."[20]

Finally, some commentators exclaimed that Carter's image-building campaign was an astounding success, capitalizing on the upbeat mood of the honeymoon period and providing the president with a substantial base of public support. David Broder asserted that "Carter the communicator" had "transformed himself from the very shaky winner of a bungled campaign into a very popular President, whose mastery of the mass media has given him real leverage with which to govern."[21] John Mashek of *U.S. News and World Report* proclaimed that Carter's "close-to-people style is paying off big." Mashek concluded:

In Washington and around the country Jimmy Carter is astounding people with a rare ability to win over both the public and the news media.

The President's flair for getting his message across in various forums is unrivaled in recent years. Some already are comparing Carter's success to the charms of Franklin D. Roosevelt in pre-television days and John F. Kennedy after TV made its impact on politics.[22]

In late March 1977, *New York Times* columnist James Reston asserted that President Carter "is turning into the greatest advertising salesman since J. Walter Thompson." For Reston, Carter's burst of symbolic activity was a clue to how the president would lead the nation for four years:

He is using the powers of the Presidency and the powers of modern com- munications to the full, and is clearly answering the question that has been on everybody's mind: He's going to be an activist, interventionist President.[23]

Some journalists criticized Carter's emphasis on style and symbolism. The negative assessments of Carter's political symbolism followed two separate paths. First, some critics lamented the disproportionate attention to style early in the Carter administration. Second, a few journalists feared that Carter's strategic use of political symbols could eventually upset the delicate balance of power between the political branches. George F. Will was representative of the former view:

Being didactic is part of governing. But government cannot live by gestures alone. Governments must be ready to inflict pain as well as to deliver exhortations. Fighting the energy crisis with the White House thermostat is, after a while, a bit like fighting inflation with WIN buttons.[24]

A *New York Times* editorial criticized Carter's emphasis on image-building. To the *Times*, "after six weeks in office, Mr. Carter continues to act like a campaigner." The editorial criticized the president for being "vague" on the substance of policy and for failing to explain clearly the details of the administration's energy policy.[25]

The *Wall Street Journal* also lamented the "widening gap between form and substance" in the new administration. The *Journal* expressed dismay with an administration that cut back on the use of White House limousines and televisions to display fiscal responsibility while proposing a $19 billion budget increase.[26]

Joseph Kraft questioned whether Carter's "folksy" style was sincere. Kraft believed that there was a touch of phoniness to the Carter style and that "the emphasis on the open style has tended to trivialize the intrinsic difficulties of government."[27]

The strongest criticism of Carter's emphasis on image-building came from journalists who believed the president's communications skills were so adept that he could use the media to manipulate public opinion and overwhelm Congress. These journalists perceived Carter as doing much more than simply enhancing his own power. For example, in an editorial on Carter's "masterful" energy speech the *New York Times* expressed its fear that the president's unconstrained access to the mass media could cause a troubling imbalance in our constitutional checks and balances system.[28] Anthony Lewis declared the program a "formidable performance" yet noted that he perceived "dangers" in any frequent use of this innovation since presidents already have an advantage over Congress in our constitutional system.[29] James Reston also feared Carter would use his media skills to distort the balance of powers between the political branches.[30]

The most serious warning about Carter's leadership tactics came from the *Wall Street Journal's* Alan Otten. Otten contended that Carter had "remarkable communications skill. He's shown himself a master of the art. . . . Mr. Carter's communications success is, in a way, a bit scary." Otten compared Carter's communications skills to those of Franklin D. Roosevelt and argued that such an ability in the television age gave Carter a "tremendous advantage" over Congress and any political opposition.[31]

The First Hundred Days Benchmark

Ever since the New Deal era all presidencies have been measured against the early, massive legislative output achieved by Franklin D. Roosevelt in the 73rd Congress, 1st Session (1933). Undoubtedly the conditions surrounding this legislative output were unique and difficult, if not impossible, to replicate. Yet in 1977, many journalists found enough similarities to expect a nearly similar feat from Jimmy Carter. For analysts relying on the Roosevelt standard, the Carter administration's first 100 days paled by comparison. Hedrick Smith concluded that Carter "has not only fallen well short of the legislative blitz achieved by Franklin D. Roosevelt during the first 100 days of the New Deal but he has also been unable to live up to his own campaign commitments to 'work in harmony for a change' and to eliminate the deadlock between Congress and the White House. . . . " Smith argued that Carter, while succeeding in establishing a rapport with the public, had largely "failed in his efforts to become a legislative leader."[32]

In its 100 days assessment of the Carter administration *U.S. News and World Report* provided a one-page chart comparing the policy achievements of Roosevelt's and Carter's respective first 100 days. Based on this comparison the news weekly concluded that "Carter's start has been a subdued one compared with Franklin D. Roosevelt's historic surge of 1933."[33] *Time* magazine assessed that "Jimmy Carter does not have much of a '100 days' mentality; he insists he is thinking more of long range accomplishments. But he has already gone far to prove that he could be the most activist President since FDR."[34] *Newsweek's* Peter Goldman added that "Carter has not attempted the 100-day wonders of a Franklin D. Roosevelt or a John F. Kennedy; he has used his time instead to reassure America, where FDR sought to innovate and JFK to excite." Goldman adopted political scientist James David Barber's characterization of Carter as an "active-positive" personality. Goldman concluded that Carter "regards the presidency as one big calculus problem—and honestly believes that he can will his way through it."[35]

Other journalists, such as Joseph Kraft and James Reston, offered similar positive appraisals of Carter's performance at this early stage.[36] Yet a number of journalists were not enthused. Most of the criticisms offered by commentators such as Vermont Royster and George F. Will focused on Carter's difficulties working with Congress.[37] These appraisals of Carter's performance at the 100-day mark will be integrated into the following section which discusses journalists' evaluations of the Carter administration's foreign and domestic policy leadership. In what follows, we witness the beginning of a press consensus on Carter's leadership style.

First Year Leadership

The generally favorable press assessments of the Carter administration did not last. As we move beyond the realm of rhetoric and symbolism to the more concrete areas of the policy agenda and policy development the assessments of Carter's presidency change significantly. We also find a great disparity between the press treatments of the agenda and of Carter's efforts to build political support for administration policies. In the areas of foreign policy and congressional relations there developed a widespread perception of the Carter administration as having no clear strategy for accomplishing its objectives.

Carter's Foreign Policy

The Carter administration offered an ambitious first year foreign policy agenda. In the inaugural address Carter revealed his intentions to commit the United States to a human rights policy, to reduce the dangers of nuclear proliferation, and to establish the United States as an example of democracy worthy of emulation abroad:

> Our commitment to human rights must be absolute. . . . the powerful must not persecute the weak, and human dignity must be enhanced. . . . We pledge perseverance and wisdom in our efforts to limit the world's armaments to those necessary for each nation's own domestic safety. We will move this year a step toward our ultimate goal—the elimination of all nuclear weapons from this earth.
>
> . . . our nation can be strong abroad only if it is strong at home, and we know that the best way to enhance freedom in other lands is to demonstrate here that our democratic system is worthy of emulation.[38]

In its first year the Carter administration made human rights the centerpiece of United States foreign policy. The president publicly chastised foreign governments whose domestic policies violated human rights. The president's public pronouncements were conspicuous for their emphasis on rights abuses occurring behind the Iron Curtain. Carter angered the Soviet government by publicly supporting dissenters within the Soviet Union. Carter reduced foreign aid to some Third World countries whose governments violated human rights.

Carter also sought to reduce the superpowers' nuclear arsenals. In March, Secretary of State Vance submitted to the Soviets a far-reaching proposal to reduce nuclear armaments. The Soviets immediately rejected the proposal as too one-sided.

Journalists generally assessed Carter's foreign policy negatively. They particularly criticized Carter's early activities in public diplomacy. Journalists characterized Carter's foreign policy as too ambitious, too "open," lacking a sense of direction, full of contradictions, and generally too moralistic.

The extent of Carter's early activity in the foreign policy realm surprised many political observers. Some observers expected Carter to focus his attention on the nation's economic dislocations. Believing Carter to be both inexperienced at and unknowledgeable of foreign affairs, many assumed that he would first attack unemployment and inflation while leaving foreign policy matters in the background.

Joseph Kraft argued that Carter should have focused on the domestic economy since that was "a far more critical matter" than foreign policy-making. Kraft believed that Carter had a unique opportunity to put foreign policy matters in the background and focus on the economy because, "when he came to office there was no overarching foreign policy crisis—no Berlin, no Korea, no Vietnam, not even a cold war."[39]

U.S. News and World Report, in a February 28, 1977, article, "Carter's World: Too Much Too Soon?" expressed reservations about the "unprecedented blitz in diplomacy by a new Administration." In discussing Carter's early human rights proclamations and intentions for a new arms control pact, *U.S. News* reported that, "Rarely has a new Administration moved with such speed to tackle so many problems in foreign affairs and to place its own stamp on new policies to solve them."[40] In September, the *Washington Post*'s Murray Marder proclaimed that "the Carter administration has launched more novel, controversial departures in foreign policy than many administrations did in their lifetimes."[41]

Stephen Rosenfeld initially supported Carter's early emphasis on international affairs. While having acknowledged that Carter moved "audaciously and with startling speed"[42] in foreign policy, in April 1977 Rosenfeld asserted:

> By moving so fast on SALT, human rights, and the Middle East, the President has gained at home a power of initiative, and at least a temporary freedom of maneuver, far surpassing his thin electoral mandate. He has taken maximum advantage of the widespread feelings that it was time for a new approach and that the new boy deserves the chance to show what he can do.[43]

Yet after observing Carter in office for one full year, Rosenfeld adopted a view much closer to that of Joseph Kraft's arguments of a year earlier than to his own April 1977 column. Rosenfeld argued that Carter had erred in focusing a great deal of the administration's efforts on international affairs: "His prodigious concentration on foreign affairs, far from filling in the gaps of his inexperience, has raised questions about his judgment." Rosenfeld concluded that "Carter was not elected to be a foreign-affairs president." In Rosenfeld's view the Nixon-Ford-Kissinger achievements in foreign policy made it safe for the nation to elect a "provincial man."[44]

A number of journalists believed that Carter's foreign policy lacked a coherent strategy or direction. Journalists portrayed Carter's foreign policy in 1977 as a series of *ad hoc* responses to international problems. *U.S. News* observed that Carter's hectic pace in foreign policymaking had "given rise to criticism that Carter is shooting from the hip and operating haphazardly without a considered strategy."[45] The *Washington Post* praised Carter's determination to deal early with arms control issues. Yet, only three weeks into Carter's presidency, the *Post* complained about conflicting policy statements by administration officials and the lack of a foreign policy consensus within the administration.[46]

Richard Steele of *Newsweek* also expressed frustration with his inability to identify Carter's foreign policy strategy and objectives. The source of much of this confusion was a series of foreign policy statements by Carter and his foreign affairs team. Steele asserted that, "it was not yet clear whether there was any underlying strategy—or even a sense of priorities—to Carter's far-flung efforts . . . With his Administration barely one month old, there is no distinctive 'Carter foreign policy' as yet." Steele concluded that the Carter administration needed to provide "some conceptual underpinning" to its foreign policy actions.[47]

Tom Mathews of *Newsweek* believed that the Carter administration's problems enunciating a coherent, identifiable foreign policy strategy were two-fold: first, Carter placed too much faith in open diplomacy and believed "that plain talk could become as common in diplomacy as it is on the farm—if diplomats would only give it a try." Second, Mathews noted that no one in the Carter administration "has yet emerged as a conceptualizer or strategic thinker in the Kissinger mold."[48]

Marvin Stone attributed the apparent confusion in the Carter administration's foreign policy to Carter's propensity to act like a political candidate. Stone charged Carter to stop behaving like a candidate and "to surrender the conduct of American foreign policy to President Carter." Stone characterized Carter's apparently conflicting foreign policy pronouncements as "aimed at wooing voters in America rather than improving relations abroad." Most importantly, Stone found foreign leaders "greatly disturbed" by what he saw as Carter's penchant for shooting from the hip on issues that vitally affected the interests of other nations.[49]

Other commentators offered similar assessments of Carter's foreign policy. *Time* magazine declared the administration's foreign policy approach "novel and often contradictory."[50] Hugh Sidey of *Time* complained that the administration's inconsistent foreign policy was a result of the inexperience of both President Carter and, strangely, Secretary of State Cyrus Vance.[51] And only three weeks into the term Stephen Rosenfeld portrayed Carter's foreign policy as fundamentally flawed due to its contradictory aspirations. In

Rosenfeld's view the desire to achieve both arms control agreements with the Soviets and human rights improvements abroad is like believing "we can have our cake and eat it, too."[52] In a July 1977 essay Rosenfeld contended that Carter's human rights campaign was leading the nation on a foreign policy "roller coaster."[53]

Joseph Kraft also argued that emphasizing human rights while pursuing arms control agreements added up to a confusing agenda. Like many journalists, Kraft criticized Carter's early foreign policy pronouncements as unwise and imprudent.[54] Kraft advised Carter to conduct diplomacy on an "impersonal basis" and to quit being such "a compulsive talker."[55]

While journalists often described the Carter administration as lacking a coherent approach to arms control, United States-Soviet relations, and North-South relations, no foreign policy issue invited as much criticism as the human rights campaign. Early in the term Carter had considerable support for raising the human rights issue. Much of this praise came from conservative opinion leaders. George F. Will, for example, liked Carter's criticisms of Soviet rights abuses. By "focusing attention on [the Soviets'] contemptuous disregard for international undertakings," Will contended, Carter distanced himself from the "preemptive appeasement" of the Kissinger years.[56]

Marvin Stone praised Carter's decision to cancel the sale of a sophisticated computer to the Soviet Union in response to kangaroo-court trials of Soviet dissidents. Stone believed that Carter's human rights campaign could convince the Soviet government "that humane leadership is the way to strength and respect in the civilized world."[57]

The *Wall Street Journal's* editors favorably assessed Carter's human rights campaign despite their belief that the campaign against rights abuses behind the Iron Curtain did not help the plight of Soviet dissidents. The main beneficiary, they argued, was "the American people":

> In raising the human rights issue, the administration is reminding the American public of our own basic values. America, we are saying, is not simply concerned with material comfort; we attach great meaning to personal freedom and the individual soul.[58]

> President Carter's condemnations of foreign governments that violate human rights has given U.S. foreign policy a principled tone and has put the Soviet Union, a prime offender, on the defensive.[59]

> [The nation's] international position is improved . . . in no small part because of Mr. Carter's skillful use of the human rights issue. His decision to put this concern near the center of foreign policy told the world, and most of all the American people, that this nation does stand for something. And it has put the Soviet Union on the ideological defensive.[60]

Most journalists expressed more skepticism than optimism for Carter's human rights campaign. Even those who praised Carter's policies had reservations. For example, the *Wall Street Journal* questioned the administration's practice of putting friends such as Brazil and Argentina in the same category as Albania, Uganda, and the Soviet Union and concluded that the

United States "should be careful to avoid unnecessarily affronting traditionally friendly nations."[61]

Like the *Journal*, *Time* magazine praised the president for giving "many Americans a renewed feeling that they are standing for something in the world." Yet *Time* was not confident that Carter's application of the human rights standard was necessarily in the nation's best interest: "At the same time, Carter has greatly alarmed both traditional friends and adversaries abroad and raised serious questions about his aims and methods in foreign policy."[62]

The *Washington Post* also assessed the rights campaign negatively. The *Post* feared a moralistic crusade in the international sphere that could damage United States prestige abroad and "produce a ruinous arrogance."[63] A *Post* editorial entitled "The Prophet Carter" characterized the human rights crusade as "morally satisfying . . . [and] politically useful," but questioned whether it was "sensible." The editorial argued that it is "idle to think that many other countries in the world appreciate our values either philosophically or politically." The *Post* concluded that it may be preferable to raise issues of human rights practices with other countries in private.[64]

The perception of Carter's human rights campaign as an attempt to compel foreign governments to accept practices rooted in United States society and culture formed the basis for many of the severest criticisms of the policy. For example, Stephen Rosenfeld perceived Carter's human rights policy as an attempt to "make the world uncomfortable for diversity." Rosenfield argued that Carter's human rights policy implied that the United States should reduce its involvement with nations that failed to measure up to our particular standards.[65]

U.S. News and World Report wondered whether Carter wanted the United States to be the "Moral Policeman of the World?" The magazine warned that if Carter's human rights standard became too stringent we could adopt a role in foreign policy similar to the one renounced in the immediate post-Vietnam years.[66]

David Broder accepted the reinvigoration of moral principles in U.S. foreign policy as "both necessary and proper" to overcome public cynicism in the post-Vietnam era. Yet Broder warned that, "a heavy dose of moralism can lead a President to either the ruin or the redemption of his realistic aspirations in the international arena." Broder advised Carter to reconsider whether the pursuit of absolute moral principles abroad enhanced our national interest.[67] He also suggested that the president intensified ideological conflict with the Soviets while professing to bury cold war antagonisms. He believed that Carter's human rights campaign made conditions for political prisoners behind the Iron Curtain worse rather than better. Broder linked Soviet crackdowns on internal dissidents to the Carter human rights campaign and argued that Carter's international "crusade" hardened the positions of our adversaries.[68]

Finally, a number of journalists characterized Carter and his foreign affairs team as generally too "weak" and irresolute on issues concerning the use of military force abroad. A number of foreign policy decisions during the first year led to accusations of weakness and vacillation in dealing with the Soviet threat. First was the appointment of Paul Warnke as chief arms control negotiator with the Soviets. Many conservative critics disliked Warnke because of his views on detente and military force. Marvin Stone proclaimed Warnke "an unfortunate choice . . . because his dovish record and inconsistency do not qualify him as the best man for the specific job."[69] The *Wall Street Journal* added that Warnke's appointment perhaps displayed Carter's approval "of unilateral restraint as a substitute for a solid arms agreement."[70] The *Journal* also perceived Carter's withdrawal of United States military troops from Korea as a display of the United States' unwillingness to protect strategically important positions.[71] The *Journal* later blasted Carter for offering concessions to the Soviets in the arms control process. The *Journal* lamented Carter's "lack of resolution" which allegedly invited the Soviets "to try pushing him around throughout the world."[72] Cancellation of the B1 Bomber also invited harsh criticism from defense-conscious critics, particularly the *Journal's* editors who called the cancellation potentially "disastrous."[73]

To conclude, the Carter administration received generally mixed reviews for its first year foreign policy agenda from political journalists. The human rights campaign was the most controversial aspect of Carter's foreign policy agenda and this controversy was reflected in the diversity of journalistic opinions of Carter's policies. Journalists disagreed as well in their interpretations of Carter's efforts at *policy execution*. Most journalists believed that the human rights standard was very difficult to implement in an even-handed, fair manner. A number of journalists found Carter's administration of the rights standard too arbitrary.

The Carter administration's early foreign policy activism surprised many journalists. For the most part, journalists expected Carter to focus on the domestic economy. This expectation appears to have influenced some of the negative reviews of Carter's first year foreign policy leadership. In these negative reviews, journalists most frequently criticized Carter's first year foreign policy for lacking a sense of direction.

Journalistic criticisms of Carter's foreign policy are similar to the criticisms of his congressional relations (e.g., the use of public pronouncements of policy rather than private negotiation, the efforts to achieve too many objectives too early, the lack of a coherent strategy of development). By analyzing the assessments of Carter's congressional relations we see the beginning of a journalistic consensus about the president's leadership.

Carter and Congress

No aspect of the Carter presidency received greater press scrutiny than the administration's relations with the Democratic-controlled Congress. Journalists generally expected Carter to work well with the large Democratic majorities in both Houses of Congress. Many journalists perceived a mood of reconciliation between the political branches after eight years of divided rule. But some journalists anticipated Carter's difficulties working with

Congress. Their assessments were influenced in part by Carter's relations with the Georgia legislature as that state's governor. Two early incidents in the Carter presidency, the nomination of Theodore Sorensen for CIA Director and Carter's proposed water projects cuts, also influenced journalistic perceptions of how Carter would work with the Democratic-controlled Congress.

Journalists generally portrayed the eventual withdrawal of Theodore Sorensen as the nominee for CIA Director as Carter's first significant setback. Many Senate conservatives opposed the Sorensen nomination for these reasons. First, Sorensen requested in 1948 draft classification as a non-combatant. Second, Sorensen filed affidavits in President Nixon's 1971 case against publication of the "Pentagon Papers," arguing that the federal government arbitrarily and excessively classified documents on national security grounds. And third, critics alleged that Sorensen, as President Kennedy's special assistant, used classified documents in giving background information to the press. After Sorensen withdrew himself from consideration, Senate Majority Leader Robert C. Byrd (D-W.Va.) complained that Carter could have avoided this controversy by consulting the Democratic leadership prior to announcing the nomination.

Many journalists criticized Carter for not properly consulting his party's members in Congress to develop support for the nomination. The *Washington Post* observed that the Sorensen withdrawal "amounts to the blooding of Jimmy Carter" and should remind him "that a President does not so much run the government as share control of it. This, you could say, is Political Lesson No. 1."[74] *Time* magazine also portrayed the withdrawal as a major rebuff of Carter's leadership of Congress and implied that the nomination would have succeeded had he consulted the party leadership.[75]

Some journalists believed that Carter erred by not fighting the Senate for Sorensen. *U.S. News*'s report asserted that Carter, by failing to fight for Sorensen, displayed a weakness that could encourage Congress to challenge the president's leadership.[76] Robert G. Kaiser of the *Washington Post* argued that the decision by Carter "not to fight harder for Sorensen may be a sign of strategic political tractability." Kaiser concluded that the Sorensen incident "does demonstrate [Carter's] vulnerability."[77]

The second incident that helped establish journalistic impressions of Carter as a legislative leader was the president's decision to cut funds for 19 water projects around the country. Carter believed that these projects constituted the ultimate wasteful, pork-barrel legislation. Yet in deciding to eliminate these projects from the FY 1978 budget Carter understood the congressional sentiments surrounding national water policy. In his memoirs Carter quoted his diary entry of March 10, 1977:

> Had a rough meeting with about 35 members of the Congress on water projects. They are raising Cain because we took those items out of their 1978 budget, but I am determined to push this item as much as possible. A lot of these [projects] would be ill advised if they didn't cost anything, but the total estimated cost of them at this point is more than $5 billion, and my guess is that the final cost would be more than twice that amount.[78]

For the most part journalists agreed with Carter's assessment that these water projects were wasteful and unnecessary. The *Washington Post* supported the Carter decision "on economic and environmental grounds."[79] From early on the *Post* generally favored Carter's proposed cutbacks:

> Mr. Carter is well within his rights in removing those 19 projects from next year's budget and reassessing plans which, in some cases, are more than a decade old. The Interior Department has already concluded that for 27 of 45 reclamation projects, future costs would be larger than future benefits. Such problems are worth thinking about before more millions and billions are spent.[80]

The *Wall Street Journal* praised Carter's instinct that "some capital projects are worthwhile and others are not." For the *Journal*, Carter's effort to eliminate these projects "demonstrates above all a refreshing willingness to oppose durable political sacred cows."[81]

Despite their agreement with the cutbacks, many journalists suspected that the action would invite trouble between the president and the Democratic-controlled Congress. Assessments of how Carter handled the policy decision differed significantly from the assessments of whether the proposed cutbacks were justified. The *Wall Street Journal* stated that "the administration still has a lot to learn about soothing congressional egos."[82] *Time* magazine predicted that Carter's relations with Congress would be combative if the president continued to neglect Congress's desire to be consulted on crucial policy decisions.[83]

The difference between journalistic interpretations of Carter's agenda and efforts at policy development was even more pronounced with regard to the energy program. President Carter proclaimed the comprehensive energy program the most important first year initiative of his administration. By any measure this program was a difficult proposal on which to stake an administration's reputation. It contained many controversial provisions and therefore had something for everyone to hate. Briefly, the package included an unpopular "gas-guzzler" tax on fuel inefficient automobiles; tax incentives for home insulation, gasohol production, car-pooling, and solar energy development; coal production; energy efficiency standards for home appliances; gradual decontrol of natural gas; and a gasoline tax intended to discourage consumption.

Most journalists regarded Carter's energy program to be meritorious. The major exception was the *Wall Street Journal*'s editorial writers who portrayed the energy program as a well-disguised tax increase. The *Journal* labeled Carter's energy bill "Mickey Mouse problem solving" and mockingly asserted that the president "should not conspire so willingly with Congress in implying that the problem somehow arose because householders prefer not to shiver in their own living rooms."[84]

A major basis for the *Journal*'s criticism of the Carter initiative was the belief that there would not be any future energy shortage. In the *Journal*'s view, Carter's "neo-Malthusian notion" of dwindling resources and the need to conserve "nurtures one of the most dangerous psychological impulses in society today."[85] In an editorial, "20 Million Years of Energy," the *Journal* refuted the contention that the world will run out of petroleum and natural gas "on a certain Tuesday near the turn of the century" and concluded that the solution to our energy consumption needs was "to deregulate the price and get the politicians out of the way."[86]

Rowland Evans and Robert Novak also lambasted Carter for not focusing on deregulation of natural gas and instead opting for "an ideological decision to solve the energy shortage through government regulation rather than market forces." They portrayed Carter's initiative as pandering to "passionate environmentalists."[87]

These negative assessments of the Carter program were generally the exception. The most prevalent view was that Carter was correct to be addressing future energy needs in a comprehensive fashion. Yet there were two major reservations with the energy package: (1) the controversial nature of many of the program's provisions made passage of the package unlikely; (2) the Carter administration's selling of the program was unimpressive.

In March 1977, the *Washington Post* praised Carter's energy initiative as an attempt to move beyond self-interested policy squabbles among and between bureaucrats, lobbyists, and congressional subcommittees:

> It is intolerable to leave public policy scattered in small fragments all over Washington, with each agency pursuing its own dinky purposes in disregard of all the others. It's not that this country has no energy policy; the real trouble is that we have too many. . . .[88]

One month later the *Post* displayed its excitement over Carter's proposed gasoline tax while admitting that such a controversial measure "will have no natural constituency."

> SPLENDID. President Carter's energy program is, evidently, going to include a stiff tax on gasoline. That's a pretty good test of presidential purpose. An energy program that reaches gasoline consumption is a serious one, deserving respect and cooperation. . . . But while the bite in the Carter plan is going to be real, it will also be delayed—the price, it seems of getting it through a reluctant Congress.

The *Post* editorial concluded that Carter's duty was to speak candidly of the national interest involved in this issue so as to rouse the populace to make the necessary, difficult sacrifices.[89]

Journalists identified the energy initiative as the major leadership test of Carter in his first year, not only because of the importance of the energy problem but also because Carter identified the energy program as *the* initiative by which his first year in office could be judged. Richard Steele of *Newsweek* asserted that, "his leadership in this crisis will likely be the greatest test of his powers of moral suasion."[90]

Time magazine in an April 1977 news report portrayed the energy proposal as a major test of Carter's ability to persuade Congress and public opinion.

Admitting the enormity of the task of convincing the public that the energy problem was serious, the news report noted that this was Carter's opportunity to cash in on his earlier efforts at courting public opinion. *Time*'s Congress specialist Neil MacNeil described the task ahead:

> It's going to be tough for a congressman to vote to punish his constituents when they can't see why. Historically, Americans don't mend the roof when the sun is shining, so there's reason for skepticism on whether Congress will go along with the President.[91]

Wall Street Journal columnist Norman C. Thomas's article, "Carter Not Playing by the Unwritten Rules of the Game," criticized Carter's tactical handling of the energy initiative. Thomas argued that Carter had a purely "personal approach" to leadership which neglected coalition building. He criticized Carter for putting forth too many energy proposals early in the term. Thomas argued that Carter erred by trying to go over the heads of members of Congress to the public when there was little support in the nation for such controversial proposals.[92]

By mid-July the *Washington Post* reported that after Carter's many efforts, "there is still no consensus in Congress, or the country, about energy." The *Post* regretted that Carter was "unable" to change the national predisposition toward energy consumption.[93]

Rowland Evans and Robert Novak presented one of the most severe indictments of Carter's attempt to sell the energy program. They observed that Carter's lambasting of special interest groups and his decision to appeal directly to the public to fight interest-group pressures signified a typical problem of the president's:

> The President is still inclined to moralize on issues that, far from being moral, are matters of practical politics and to appeal directly to the voters whenever he runs into trouble in Congress. . . .
>   Upgrading conventional political questions to the status of good v. evil is still an ingrained habit for Carter, but one that has not helped his energy program and could do him harm in the future.[94]

Invoking Carter's assertion that the first year of his administration could be judged a success or failure by whether or not his energy program was enacted, Robert G. Kaiser exclaimed: "By that standard, according to numerous congressional and administration sources, 1977 can now be judged a failure for Jimmy Carter." Kaiser believed that Carter's major failure was a lack of personal lobbying for the energy program. "Administration salesmanship was erratic," Kaiser proclaimed.

> The Carter plan was a technical device, an "engineering" solution to a series of problems that are highly political and sensitive to important power blocs in society. Moreover, it was based on a perception of "crisis" that the country never shared.[95]

From this review of the press discussions of the Sorensen nomination, water projects cuts and energy proposal we can develop some generalizations of the assessments of Carter's congressional relations. Journalists generally agreed with Carter's definition of the water projects as wasteful and with his definition of the energy crisis as the most important issue facing the nation. They agreed that, on the merits alone, the water projects deserved to be eliminated and the energy program given serious consideration. Yet they remained very critical of Carter's methods in developing support for administration policies.

First, journalists believed that Carter tried to do too much too fast at the beginning of the term. For the most part, journalists expected a less ambitious policy agenda. Instead, Carter began his term with a plethora of controversial legislative proposals, including the politically difficult energy package.

Second, journalists assessed that Carter lacked a clear strategy for garnering support for his initiatives. They perceived Carter as moving from one policy area to another with no apparent long-term strategy to achieve his many controversial objectives. As the *Wall Street Journal* stated nine months into the Carter presidency: "While of course we disagree with many of the policies resulting from this process, our greater impression is one of drift." The *Journal* blamed the administration for not gearing "itself up to decide what it really wants and how to get it."[96] David Broder made a similar point:

> What's missing is the sense of strategy—of choosing those problems that are important for the idealized goals and ignoring the rest; and of tackling the specific problems in a way that illuminates the principles, rather than contradicts them.[97]

Third, journalists attributed Carter's difficulties dealing with Congress to the lack of experience in the White House and congressional liaison staffs and a perception of poor political protocol. From both the Sorensen incident and the water projects cuts there developed an assessment of Carter as failing to extend simple courtesies such as informing congressional leaders of his decisions. By late April 1977 Hedrick Smith predicted that Carter would experience "enduring difficulties" with Congress because of the White House staff's inexperience and apparent foul-ups in personal protocol.[98]

Fourth, journalists contended that Carter failed to deal with the Democratic Congress in a manner that members of Congress expected from a president of the same party. Journalists criticized Carter for not fostering cooperative relations between the political branches after eight years of divided rule. They reported that Carter, much to the dismay of his party's leadership, (1) failed to consult adequately with members of Congress on major initiatives, and (2) refused to bargain or compromise with congressmen.

Gerald Parshall of the *Wall Street Journal* largely attributed the administration's difficulties with Congress to "President Carter's special brand of leadership":

Though Carter has been forced into some compromises, his style so far has been to shun compromise altogether or to delay it until the bitter end. In the little world of Capitol Hill, such idealism runs against the grain. Congress is not accustomed to settling issues on their merits. Instead, issues traditionally are settled through accommodation of competing interests.[99]

Dennis Farney observed that Carter was too preoccupied with the merits of policy proposals to pay attention to political considerations: "Like Jack Webb in the old 'Dragnet' series, Jimmy Carter is a 'just-the-facts-ma'am' kind of guy." Farney advised Carter to seek help from members of Congress and interest groups to develop support for administration policy initiatives.[100]

Five weeks into the Carter presidency, David Broder perceived forthcoming problems between the administration and Congress based on "muttering . . . among congressional Democrats about alleged incidents of neglect and abuse from the White House." In Broder's view, Carter "still believes what he said early in the 1976 primaries, that 'Congress is inherently incapable of leadership.' He sees Congress . . . as a body overly influenced by narrow parochial concerns, a playground for the special interests."[101]

In an important essay on Carter's congressional relations, "Jimmy the Engineer," Meg Greenfield argued that Carter's "radically different" approach to policymaking "accounts for much of the resistance he is meeting." Greenfield's April 1977 portrayal of Carter as a discrete problem-solver oblivious to political contingencies captured the prevailing explanation of Carter's unique leadership approach:

> . . . there is a curiously apolitical and genuinely radical aspect to this method of policymaking. It is back to the drawing board. All bets and assumptions are off. It is as if nothing had ever happened before. And policy—treasured policy—once arrived at is not to be toyed with; it is not to be compromised by dumb considerations such as that it might make the chairman of the relevant congressional committee wild. . . .

Greenfield continued that we can understand Carter's leadership approach if we examine it as the way of the engineer:

> There is first the conception of issues as problems for which there are—must be—technically feasible solutions. Carter has a very thin sense of the impossible. . . . You can tell him the program's design is flawed, but don't tell him that Russell Long won't let him have it. . . . His approach is clinical, orderly and— in Washington cultural terms—absolutely revolutionary.
>   Carter has no feeling for institutional political necessity and little visible appreciation of the human, folksy, disorderly relationships that are an important feature of political life on the Potomac. . . . [Carter] seems to be at a loss to understand the trimming and trading needed to get things done.[102]

Declaring "Jimmy's way is the way of the engineer," Russell Baker asserted that Carter's leadership approach "has practically nothing to do with politics. Aside from a mastery of the public relations skills needed to win the

Presidency in the age of media politics, Jimmy is as indifferent to conventional politics as a black jack dealer."[103]

Competing with this prevalent view of Carter as apolitical, uncompromising and unwilling to consult with members of Congress on administration policy initiatives was another view of Carter during the first year: that of a president who not only compromises freely, but also occasionally gives in too easily to congressional demands. The perception that Carter gave in too easily under pressure grew out of the Sorensen incident. Some journalists perceived Carter's apparent unwillingness to fight for this nomination as an indication that Congress could force the president's hand on important decisions. A number of journalists portrayed Carter as a president who backs down from his commitments under pressure. The *New York Times* reported:

> Taken individually, his retreats from the tax rebate, from defense cutbacks, from cancellation of costly water projects and from the human rights test in foreign affairs can be seen as prudent accommodations with the business community or powerful forces in Congress or simply reality. But cumulatively, the compromising suggests an excessive haste either in the embrace of policy or withdrawal from it.[104]

A *U.S. News and World Report* news story noted that Carter exhibited "an unexpected willingness to compromise with Congress by backing down on several major issues." The news weekly reported that to the surprise of many, Carter went "out of his way to meet with lawmakers and demonstrate that he wants friendly relations with Capitol Hill."[105] While this 100-day assessment of the Carter administration saw Carter working harder at cajoling legislators, *U.S. News's* six-month review noted that the president "is proving himself the pragmatist that his engineering background suggests." The review continued:

> Carter's disdain for the old politics of wheeling and dealing seems to have been subdued. He is trying to demonstrate a new resilience and adaptability.
> . . . more and more, the President is bending over backwards to foster a new spirit of give-and-take with Congress. He has veered away from the head-to-head confrontation with Capitol Hill that he almost seemed to be seeking a few months ago.[106]

David Broder also was not very alarmed by Carter's "retreats" from earlier positions. In Broder's view Carter altered "idealized" positions adopted as a candidate so as to come to terms with governing realities. By December 1977 Broder perceived Carter as "assimilated more to the practical wisdom of Washington's trade-off politics."[107] In an earlier essay Broder declared Carter, "The President Who Came In From The Outside," and pointed out that Carter had been transformed and was no longer a stranger to Washington ways.[108]

In November 1977 Evans and Novak went even further in declaring Carter "Washingtonized." As a result of Democratic party pressure, they wrote, "the highly personalized candidate has been slowly transformed into a regular Democratic President—Washingtonized."[109]

Most analysts did not perceive Carter as politically transformed or "Washingtonized" by late 1977. Journalists generally portrayed Carter's efforts to accommodate Congress as prudent efforts to salvage some of the administration's legislative proposals. Hedrick Smith wrote in August 1977 that Carter, after a difficult beginning, had developed good relations with Congress. Smith attributed this fruitful relationship to the fact that "Carter no longer shows the outsider's disdain for Capitol Hill but acts as though he is more sensitive to the prerogatives and feelings of powerful members."[110]

A *U.S. News and World Report* news story noted that Carter had learned to work hard "to cultivate key backing by playing host at breakfasts for members of Congress, staging 'down home' picnics, complete with square dancing on the White House lawn."[111] *Time* magazine noted that the president showed "that he can learn from mistakes and knows how to compromise."[112] In August 1977 *Time* observed that, "The President was getting along because he was going along."[113] Near the end of Carter's first year *Time* saw positive developments between the president and Congress:

> Carter is learning fast. . . . Last week Carter had a group of Republican legislators over for breakfast in one of the spiffier state dining rooms, and surprised them with effusive thanks for their help in overcoming Democratic opposition to a number of White House proposals.[114]

> Carter has already shown signs that his dealings with Congress in 1978 will be more deft. Having failed initially to lobby the Senate effectively for his energy proposals, he has been making the right moves as the showdown approaches. He has been inviting key Democratic leaders to the White House and telephoning others who can help.[115]

For the vast majority of journalists who did not see Carter as politically transformed or Washingtonized, there were a variety of explanations for Carter's troubles with Congress. The most prevalent explanations focused on the president's personal characteristics or alleged shortcomings (e.g., stubbornness, engineer's mind, political inexperience, moralistic views). Some journalists offered more charitable explanations of Carter's difficulties. These explanations included: (1) Carter tackled tough issues, such as energy, neglected by his predecessors; (2) post-Watergate anti-institutional sentiments still lingered; (3) the new Congress was more independent of the executive than previously; (4) Carter ran behind most Democratic congressmen in 1976 leaving few members feeling they owed their political fortunes to the president; (5) legislation limiting the president's powers, enacted in the 1970s, provided Congress with additional authority in foreign policy and the budget process; and (6) unlike his predecessors, Carter's agenda did not seek drastically to expand welfare-state benefits.

To begin, James Reston's explanation for Carter's difficulties was that Carter insisted on tackling politically difficult issues. In April 1977, Reston observed:

> He is asking us to do hard things with our minds: to think about shortages in a time of plenty, and to imagine the lives of our children, and even the entire human family, at the end of the century.[116]

By October Reston recognized that Carter was experiencing political setbacks. Yet the *Times* columnist continued to praise Carter for "facing up to what he regards as the central questions" despite growing opposition from all sides. While acknowledging the president may not prevail in many policy areas, "at least Mr. Carter is now dealing with the major issues of the next generation."[117] Reston added that Carter "is in trouble because he has had the audacity to face up to the most difficult . . . problems of our time."[118]

Evans and Novak who, recall, accused Carter of a lack of political savvy, recognized other factors contributing to Carter's difficulties dealing with Congress. In their view "the residual anti-White House attitude in Congress that has continued after Nixon's departure" could be blamed for Carter's inability to lead Congress: "Vietnam, Watergate and Richard Nixon generated a demand for congressional autonomy that makes relations with Capitol Hill much more difficult for Jimmy Carter."[119]

In an essay conspicuous for its almost loner status as an argument that Congress was to blame more than President Carter for executive-congressional squabbling, David Broder blasted Senate Democratic leaders for bickering over patronage matters. Many Democratic Senators, Broder added, "reacted like Tammany aldermen to Carter's threat to cut off some of their favorite dam projects." Broder's findings are worth quoting at length here because these sentiments appear almost nonexistent in the press otherwise when we consider the volume of columns devoted to Carter's alleged personal flaws:

> Much has been said, most of it critical, of President Carter's handling of Congress. Less has been said—and more is justified—about Congress's handling of the President.
> The end-of-the-session assessments proceed on the assumption that in the circus that is Washington, Congress is the lion act and the President's job, as lion tamer, is to turn those brawling "cats" into a disciplined troupe of performers. This year, that analogy is doubly in error.
> It is in error, first, because these "cats" in Congress have become increasingly immune to whip-cracking. If they need anyone, it is not the President (who trailed them at the polls on election day) but their own leaders. Second, the analogy is misleading because the tricks that had to be learned for the show to be a success were not things Carter could teach Congress, but things Congress could teach Carter.[120]

U.S. News attributed Carter's troubled congressional relations to organized pressure group activity and increased congressional demands to play a role in policy development. More importantly, Carter's agenda was not politically pleasing:

> One reason is the nature of Carter's proposals: They don't simply shovel federal money into the outstretched hands of various groups. Instead, they would put money in the pockets of some people and take it away from others. Hence, they hold political risks for the lawmakers.[121]

James P. Gannon of the *Wall Street Journal* conceded that "the Carter program is remarkable for its concentration of controversial issues over which the nation is deeply divided."[122]

A final assessment is provided by *Time* magazine presidency analyst Hugh Sidey. By late 1977 Sidey pondered a number of factors that made Carter's leadership task so precarious:

> Instead of giving to people as Roosevelt did, Carter often must take away. Instead of building industrial capacity, Carter must frequently change its emphasis and cleanup its mess. Instead of urging consumption, in some areas Carter must administer scarcity. These are negative choices.
>
> Arrayed against him at the same time is the most formidable army of doubters and special interest representatives ever to face a President. . . .
>
> The independence of Congress and its defiance of the President are established and growing phenomena. Perhaps Vietnam and Watergate injured the presidency even more than we thought. Reverence for the office is diminished.[123]

Thus, journalists generally portrayed Carter's first year relations with Congress negatively. In the chapter's conclusion we will also see how Carter's congressional relations largely framed the first year assessments of his presidency. First let's turn to the event of 1977 that resulted in the harshest assessments of President Carter—the Bert Lance controversy.

The "Lance Affair"

During the months of August and September journalists investigated the alleged financial improprieties committed by Budget Director Bert Lance in his role as a Georgia state banker. Most important to this analysis are those columns and editorials focusing not on whether Lance was guilty or innocent of charges against him, but rather, those evaluating the Carter administration's handling of the incident. In the numerous writings on the Lance affair that drew conclusions about the leadership of Carter and the White House staff three major themes prevailed: (1) that Lance, whether guilty or innocent, violated Carter's high ethical standards for public servants. Carter's willingness to fight for Lance therefore revealed a double standard—one for friends, another for everyone else; (2) that the isolation of the White House staff encouraged the defense of a friend despite political ramifications; and (3) that the inexperienced Carter team failed to handle the incident in a politically astute manner.

First, journalists characterized the Lance affair as especially damning to President Carter because of the high ethical standards he demanded of public officials. Dennis Farney and Richard J. Levine of the *Wall Street Journal* asserted: "Mr. Carter campaigned, of course, as an 'outsider' who was different from—and better than—the typical Washington politician. That's what makes the crisis especially threatening to him."[124]

Of the three newspapers only the *Wall Street Journal*'s editors showed sympathy for Lance. The *Journal* noted that Carter's high ethical standards, including demands that administration officials divest of all personal holdings in companies conducting business with government, could discourage many competent businessmen from serving the public sector. The *Journal* continued:

If Mr. Carter was serious about a Caesar's wife administration, then clearly Bert Lance must go. . . . The drama of the Lance episode is not so much about our affable budget director as about our fresh-faced President. We have already seen enough to know that Mr. Carter is no less hypocritical than our average politician. When we see how the Lance affair is closed, we will learn perhaps he is more so.[125]

The *New York Times*'s editorial chastised Carter's record in the Lance affair as "filled with dubious misjudgments and miscalculations." The editorial acknowledged that the affair was in part a "self-inflicted wound" largely related to Carter's standards of ethical conduct. The *Times* shared Carter's concern that a public official should not be removed by allegations alone yet argued:

What all this demonstrates to us is the danger of confusing due process in law with fairness in politics. The right not to be found guilty without proof is not the right to hold appointive office. . . . The most important issue is not Mr. Lance's probity as a banker but Mr. Carter's sagacity as a politician.[126]

And the *Washington Post* also reflected the consensus view that the Lance affair was largely the result of Carter's standards of ethical conduct:

The Lance case is much more than a routine charge of misconduct precisely because of the severe and rigid ethical standards that Mr. Carter has repeatedly laid down. If he wishes to keep Mr. Lance at the White House, he is either going to have to loosen the standards or to concede that there are exceptions for old friends.[127]

The news weeklies offered similar appraisals of Carter's handling of the Lance case. *U.S. News* assessed that the Lance affair created doubts about Carter's ability to handle a crisis.[128] *Time* called Bert Lance "an embarrassment to the Administration, a threat to its whole aura of stern moral probity."[129] *Time* reacted unfavorably to the president's September press conference defense of the Budget Director highlighted by Carter's comment "Bert, I'm proud of you":

> Carter's dramatic show of loyalty immediately injected into the affair questions about the President's own judgment and his moral standing with the public. Carter had pledged to avoid even the appearance of impropriety among his appointees. Now he has opened himself to the charge that he was willing to bend his rigid rules to save a close friend.[130]

> Certainly, Carter has been hurt by the Lance affair. His reputation as the champion of ethical purity has been permanently tarnished.[131]

Time's Rudolph Rauch observed that the Carter declaration of pride "managed to obliterate the one element that made him different—the innocence of the outsider, the incorruptibility of the unentrenched. That difference was his major hold on the American people."[132]

After the Lance resignation, a *Time* magazine news story asserted that the president's performance during his administration's first major crisis was somewhat disturbing in its implications for how Carter deals with adversity. The news weekly believed the crisis "raised troubling questions" about Carter's character and leadership:

> Repeatedly, Carter showed a sentimental streak and a moral blindness in assessing what his friend had done. The man who had campaigned against influential "big shots" and promised to appoint only top aides who met a Caesar's wife standard of honesty could not bring himself to criticize one who had obviously fallen short of that ideal.[133]

Newsweek's Richard Steele observed that Lance's problems were really "Carter's problems." That is, the crisis first and foremost damaged Carter's "carefully built reputation for honesty and integrity."[134] Carter's defense of Lance, Steele argued, was "raising questions about [Carter's] own ethical standards and the political judgment of his 'Georgia Mafia.'"[135]

Perhaps the most scathing indictments of Carter's handling of the Lance affair came from columnists David Broder and George F. Will. Broder compared the president's handling of the Lance case to that of the Sorensen nomination. In the case of Sorensen, Broder reported, Carter stepped back and allowed his nominee to withdraw once questions of whether Sorensen measured up to Carter's standards of behavior were raised. For Broder, Carter's handling of the Lance case was inconsistent:

> No one can doubt that Jimmy Carter is smart enough to know that the public record of Lance's financial transactions compromises the standard of disinterested behavior that Carter has proclaimed as the center of his own moral code. This is, after all, the same man who said he would fire the FBI director for accepting a window valence made in the FBI carpentry office![136]

Finally, George F. Will's criticisms reflected the consensus view that Lance came under intense scrutiny because Carter demanded unusually high standards of ethical conduct for public servants. In Will's view, "Lance's record would not arouse such interest were he not serving the President who invented ethics."[137] Will added:

> The Lance affair has reminded Americans that Carter is not a Moses, entrusted by God with new standards of goodness. It also has made Carter seem a bit like Gantry, not about to live by the rules he preaches.[138]

Journalists also believed that the isolation of Carter and his inner-circle of "White House Georgians" allowed the Lance affair to develop into a major issue. The Carter White House, in almost Nixonian fashion, critics alleged, was oblivious to those political sentiments that would have instructed the administration to handle the crisis differently. Hedrick Smith, conceding that White House improprieties in the Lance case were "more modest" than the Nixon White House's actions, still offered the devastating comparison:

> . . . they have exposed political frailties in the Carter camp that harps back to the Nixon era and before, and that have rubbed the lustre from the clean government image that Mr. Carter so carefully fashioned.

Smith argued that President Carter was ill-served by "loyalist" aides in much the same way that Richard Nixon was poorly advised on Supreme Court nominations. The result was skepticism about the sincerity of Carter's "new political morality."[139]

Allan Otten compared Carter's "isolation" in the Lance case to both President Nixon's withdrawal during Watergate and President Johnson's isolation during the Vietnam War. Otten asserted that the Lance case proved that Carter's inner-circle was "too small, too homogenized, too inexperienced, too self-confident." Otten concluded that Carter's key advisers were "all unable to appreciate that Congress and the public might not view good old Bert quite the same way as they did."[140]

Dennis Farney wrote a lengthy essay in the *Journal*, "Lance and the Small Town Boys." Farney argued that White House misjudgments over the Lance case could be attributed to the large number of small town Georgians advising the president. Farney drew on his own small town origins to derive some understanding of where the Carter people went wrong:

> A good part of the explanation lies in the small-town nature of the Carter White House—a White House dominated by small-town boys who think alike, react alike, stick together and resent the city slickers who second guess them or get in their way.
> The Lance case found Bert Lance of Gainesville, Ga., defended before the press by Jody Powell of Vienna, Ga., while Hamilton Jordan of Albany, Ga., monitored the overall operation from behind the scenes and advised Jimmy Carter of Plains, Ga., on what to do next. Their collective performance revealed some serious weaknesses in the Carter inner-circle.

In judging a man, small-town people tend to ignore the "technicalities" and rely upon the kind of person they "know" him to be. An impersonal city—particularly Washington in its cynical post-Watergate period—tends to concentrate on the "technicalities" and ignore everything else.[141]

Hugh Sidey also critically assessed Carter's inner-circle decision-making process. Sidey argued that the White House aides were "seriously hobbled by their own isolation."

They cannot see Bert Lance as having violated their code, if not the law. They cannot perceive that their insistence erodes trust, hurting the presidency and thus the nation. They have drawn the wagons in a circle and have so far placed Carter's pride and the feelings of their old friend Bert before the good of the country. It is a selfishness and arrogance of a sort.[142]

Related to the belief that Carter's staff were isolated was the claim that the White House staff members' political inexperience resulted in bungled decisions that might have been avoided by more savvy practitioners. Robert G. Kaiser posed a rhetorical question concerning the Carter staff's handling of the Lance case: "Did their emotional attachment to Bert Lance or their lack of experience make them ineffective political operators?"[143] Joseph Kraft's answer was an unambiguous "yes," declaring that the inexperienced White House staff led Carter astray and that Carter "needs to bring some new strength to his circle of intimates." The lesson of the Lance affair, Kraft observed, was that "the President turns out to be a lonely man surrounded by an inexperienced staff, who is not exempt from moral blindness and poor judgment."[144]

Undoubtedly the Lance affair was one of the most damaging incidents of the Carter presidency. The incident reveals the risks associated with a president setting the standards by which his administration should be judged. Carter admits in his memoirs that Bert Lance was a victim of "the very stringent standards I established for serving with me."[145] It is not surprising that journalists adopted standards Carter set for himself as the bases for evaluating his presidency.

The First Year in Retrospect

The end-of-the-year reviews are instructive in determining journalists' expectations of the president. Whereas the reviews during the transition and early stages of 1977 revealed journalistic expectations of Jimmy Carter specifically, the following reviews at the end of 1977 reveal more general expectations of presidential leadership and performance. The end of year retrospectives are particularly useful in determining journalistic expectations of the president since journalists are asking, implicitly, "What happened and why?"

To answer the first part of the question, "What happened?" journalists generally answered that Jimmy Carter "failed" as a political leader in his first year. For our purposes it is most important to identify and discuss journalists' answers to the "why" part of the question.

Significantly, almost none of the retrospective essays evaluating Carter's first year performance focused on the merits or shortcomings of the administration's public policy agenda. These assessments focused instead mostly on Carter's abilities as a political tactician. This emphasis on process over policy substance in drawing conclusions about Carter's leadership is revealing of the kinds of criteria journalists relied upon.

Four different themes dominated journalists' retrospective assessments. First, journalists believed that Carter overloaded the public agenda with too many controversial proposals. Second, many journalists perceived a lack of a coherent strategy for policy development in the administration. Third, many journalists criticized Carter for failing to engage in the traditional process of coalition building on Capitol Hill through negotiation, bargaining, and compromise. Finally, journalists characterized Carter's staff as inexperienced and unfamiliar with Washington's political norms.

Each of these views is discussed here beginning first with the assessment that Jimmy Carter overloaded the public agenda too early in his administration. Even Carter sympathizer James Reston conceded this criticism was "vaguely true." According to Reston, the major journalistic criticisms of Carter were that "[Carter] had tried to do too much too soon in his first year . . . with no sense of priorities or connecting rods between one program and another."[146]

Albert Hunt criticized Carter for offering too many policy proposals while failing to identify administration priorities. "The administration frequently floated up proposals like balloons and then often forgot them." Hunt believed that Carter's problems stemmed from trying to be an activist president in a "passive country."[147]

Time magazine offered a less than flattering picture of the president's leadership in his first year:

> In all, Carter's problem has been to assert his leadership when it counts. Having tried to do too much too fast, he has ended up accomplishing too little. He failed to concentrate on a few key issues such as energy and the Panama Canal treaty and thus dissipated much of his influence. He did not build the necessary crucial bridges to Capitol Hill; nor did he have the experienced staff to help.[148]

A *New York Times* editorial, "The Freshman," argued that Carter's propensity to deliver too many sweeping proposals was based on the belief "that all governmental problems could be solved only if they were worked at." The editorial continued:

> In domestic as in foreign affairs, policies proliferated. Energy? Give us a few weeks and we'll have a policy to solve the problem. Welfare reform? In another week or two? The President gave himself repeated hotfoots of hyperbole. In

the Spring, he described a bill to hold down rising hospital costs as "one of my most important priorities." By November, it lay dead at his feet.[149]

U.S. News also believed that Carter's first year accomplishments were limited because the president overloaded the agenda. "During the past eleven months, the President rushed to Congress a dizzying assortment of proposals, some of them controversial and complicated." Yet the magazine held out hope for the following year. *U.S. News* reported that Carter's "new game plan" for 1978 included an emphasis on a few limited policy priorities and other efforts to build public confidence.[150]

The second major explanation for Carter's alleged leadership failure was the administration's lack of a coherent strategy for policy development. Or, in Dennis Farney's words: "His problem is that he and his Georgian advisers share a seemingly innate tendency to 'wing it' on serious or complex matters."[151] And *Newsweek's* Tony Fuller wrote:

> As Jimmy Carter marked his first anniversary in office last week, there is in the land widespread confusion about who he is and where he is going, a sense of drift on which his personality remains evanescent and his leadership a matter of great doubt. . . .
>
> Carter is still seen as an outsider himself, a man not yet wise to the ways of Washington—and therefore weak and ineffective.[152]

A *Time* magazine news story reported that Carter perhaps did not know himself what he wanted to do as president:

> Perhaps the biggest challenge of all for Carter is how to manage the presidency and exercise power. For much of his first year in office, his Administration has remained strangely out of focus, suggesting that Carter may not be sure what he wants to do.[153]

The *Wall Street Journal's* January 23, 1978 editorial "Steady as She Drifts," reiterated a theme prevalent in the newspaper's assessments of Carter as early as 1976—that of a politician lacking any coherent or identifiable public philosophy. The *Journal* believed Carter's problems emanated from his relying on traditional Democratic party liberal dogma:

> While Mr. Carter campaigned as an outsider, he had no particular vision on what to do with power when he won it. So intellectually and philosophically his administration ends up falling back on the habits of his party, on the collective mentality of the Council on Foreign Relations, the Brookings Institution and Ralph Nader, Inc. But the reality is that there is no money to pay for that kind of liberalism, no great urge in the country for that kind of liberalism. . . .[154]

The third criticism of Carter's political leadership was that he was not attentive to the traditional Washington rituals of negotiating and bargaining with congressmen and interest groups. In Joseph Kraft's view Carter was an apolitical president who adopted policy positions because they were "right" rather than politically feasible. In response to the ironic question "Why Not The Best?" Kraft stated: "The answer is that 'the best is the enemy of the good.' The painful rediscovery of that ancient truth summarizes most of what had happened in the first year of the Carter administration." Kraft complained that Carter adopted either/or policy positions from which the administration was forced to back down after pressure from lobbies and Congress. The result, according to Kraft, was a year of backing away from large-scale promises and coming away nearly empty.[155]

Anthony Lewis argued that Carter simply had not learned to work with the Washington establishment and was therefore doomed to being at odds with it:

> The failures on energy and other legislation may be laid in part to faults in Mr. Carter's tactics. As everyone in Washington says, he took on too much too fast. He presented Congress with grand schemes on energy and welfare reform and the like, as if there were no room for give and take. He has not learned how to deal with the other potentates of Washington, notably Senator Russell Long.[156]

Three separate news reports from *Time* magazine portrayed Carter at the end of year one as an unskilled politician:

> The man from Plains is not the kind of bourbon-sipping, backslapping politician who gets along easily with the good ole boys in Congress.[157]

> He remains an enigmatic figure and one who has yet to learn the amorphous art of building constituencies to get things done.[158]

> He often seemed to bog down in detail and yet to slight the routine requirements of the job, such as sometimes twisting congressional arms. He has not demonstrated quite the same ardor in the presidency that he did in the campaign.[159]

Dennis Farney argued that Carter's major problem was that he attempted to govern in 1977 the way that he campaigned in 1976 (i.e., ignoring party leaders, showing distrust of the political establishment). Farney asserted that "the lesson of Mr. Carter's first year" is that political trouble results "from failing to cultivate interest groups." Farney concluded that Carter "is a President who prefers to make decisions by studying memos instead of thrashing things out with people."[160]

Journal columnist Vermont Royster generally agreed. Royster believed that Carter was an unpolitical figure occupying "essentially a *political* office." Royster observed that Franklin Roosevelt made the presidency powerful, but the office itself still has limited powers resting primarily on political influence. Royster observed that any president, "must understand the political groupings within the country and know how to marshall them, sometimes forming different coalitions for different purposes. That means he must be willing to push a little here, give a little there." Royster concluded that in running against the notion of an "imperial presidency" Jimmy Carter embraced

> . . . the idea of the unpolitical President. He sought to appeal to everybody in general and nobody in particular. He didn't even pay much attention to the Democratic Party. . . . It is no accident that the two strongest Presidents of the past 50 years, FDR and Harry Truman, were avowed political Presidents. Both understood that their power depended on influence and their influence on attention to the nitty-gritty of politics.[161]

Finally, journalists lamented the political inexperience and lack of political acumen of Carter's White House staff. *U.S. News and World Report* observed at the end of the congressional session "there are more minuses than pluses in the administration's record on Capitol Hill." The news story reported that in January of 1977 "a new era of unity between the executive and legislative branches seemed to be dawning, closing out eight years of fierce strife between Republican Chief Executives and Democratic Congresses." In seeking to explain why the "new era" never dawned the news report pointed to post-Watergate congressional attitudes, the weakening of national political parties, and the "inexperienced" Carter White House:

> Carter's status as a Washington outsider with almost no friends in Congress also has worked against him on Capitol Hill. So has the inexperience of his White House aides, who have shown so little savvy in their dealings with Congress that influential lawmakers have been nettled time and again.[162]

A news report from *Congressional Quarterly Weekly Report* asserted that the major journalistic assessments of Carter at the end of 1977 focused on inexperience and unfamiliarity in his administration with the "complexities" of national institutions:

> That image was all too true, agreed observers in Congress and the press. Mistakes made by the young administration were universally attributed to inexperience and unfamiliarity with the complexities of national issues and institutions, particularly Congress.
>   Carter gave these criticisms room to grow by surrounding himself with young loyalists from his Georgia gubernatorial staff and from his campaign days. The competency and experience of these young White House aides was widely questioned.[163]

Conclusion

High press expectations and eventual disappointment marked Jimmy Carter's first year as president. Journalists initially held high expectations for Jimmy Carter based on their perceptions of how Carter would and should lead the nation. These expectations, such as Carter needing to initiate a moderate, prudent agenda focusing on economic dislocations, were derived from an incomplete understanding of Carter based on his previous governing experiences and presidential campaign. Carter himself encouraged other expectations, such as the need to restore faith in government, establish a higher standard of morality in public service, and enact in the first year a comprehensive energy program.

Journalists did not make explicit early in Carter's term their more general expectations of presidential leadership and performance. Journalists, of course, did not explicitly define their major criteria for "success" at the beginning of this presidency. Rather, we begin to learn their implicit criteria for successful leadership in the ongoing assessments of Carter's difficulties. By the end of 1977 a clearer picture of these expectations develops. We learned in this review of Carter's first year a number of the ingredients for success identified by journalists. For example, a "successful" leader adopts an achievable public agenda and a clear strategy of development based on the traditional norms of political Washington of negotiating, bargaining and compromising. A successful leader will also bring with him a number of aides experienced in dealing with political Washington. A Democratic president with large Democratic majorities in the legislative branches is expected to achieve his major objectives if he follows the above rules of the game.

Journalists perceived Carter as having failed to meet their leadership expectations. In the views of most journalists Carter's first year performance was unimpressive. Following chapters show that many of the journalistic themes of 1977 became part of a dominant perception of Jimmy Carter: that of a politically inept, inexperienced president with no sense of policy priorities or clear strategy for policy development. As we shall see, this dominant perception forms the basis for later assessments of Carter's actions. Despite temporary upswings in journalists' assessments, the dominant perception of Carter as politically inept and inexperienced continually returns in the press portrayals of Carter's leadership abilities.

Notes

1. Jimmy Carter, *Keeping Faith* (New York: Bantam Books, 1982), p. 20.

2. Ibid., p. 21.

3. "Waltzing Into Office," *Time*, January 31, 1977, p. 9.

4. "From Micah to the New Beginning," *New York Times*, January 21, 1977, p. A22.

5. "The Spirit of '77," *Washington Post*, January 21, 1977, p. A22.

6. Susan Fraker, "Now It Begins," *Newsweek*, January 24, 1977, pp. 16–19; see also David Alpern, "The Big Problems," *Newsweek*, January 24, 1977, p. 30.

7. "Warm Words from Jimmy Cardigan," *Time*, February 14, 1977, p. 18; the news report also assessed that Carter's performance did not match Roosevelt's address in "rhetoric" or "sheer drama."

8. "The President's Message," *Washington Post*, February 4, 1977, p. A10.

9. Haynes Johnson, "The Quintessential Carter," *Washington Post*, February 3, 1977, p. A6.

10. Hedrick Smith, "The Energy Crisis and Carter," *New York Times*, February 3, 1977, p. A23.

11. David Broder, "The Carter Image," *Washington Post*, February 9, 1977, p. A21.

12. Peter Goldman, "Fireside Manner," *Newsweek*, February 14, 1977, p. 14.

13. Richard Steele, "Setting the Style," *Newsweek*, February 14, 1977, p. 14.

14. James T. Wooten, "So Far, It's a Presidency Trying to Do Without Pomp," *New York Times*, February 20, 1977, p. E3.

15. Tom Wicker, "Symbols and Reality," *New York Times*, February 4, 1977, p. A23.

16. "Now that the Carters Have Put Their Stamp on White House Social Life," *U.S. News and World Report*, April 4, 1977, p. 55.

17. Meg Greenfield, "Zero-Based Humility," *Newsweek*, February 28, 1977, p. 80; see also, "Just Call Him Mister," *Time*, February 21, 1977, p. 12.

18. Peter Goldman, "Dial-a-President," *Newsweek*, March 14, 1977, p. 12.

19. "America Gets on the Party Line," *Time*, March 14, 1977, p. 11.

20. "Dial-a-President," *Washington Post*, March 8, 1977, p. A14.

21. David Broder, "Mr. Carter When He's Out Front," *Washington Post*, March 23, 1977, p. A11.

22. John Mashek, "How Carter Spruces Up His Image," *U.S. News and World Report*, April 11, 1977, p. 43.

23. James Reston, "The Birth of a Salesman," *New York Times*, March 20, 1977, p. E15.

24. George F. Will, "Cold Comfort," *Newsweek*, February 7, 1977, p. 80.

25. "The Campaign Continued," *New York Times*, March 6, 1977, p. E16.

26. "Which Is For Real," *Wall Street Journal*, February 24, 1977, p. 22.

27. Joseph Kraft, "The Carter Style: Sincere or Phony," *Washington Post*, February 17, 1977, p. A19.

28. "The Chat By the Fire," *New York Times*, February 4, 1977, p. A22.

29. Anthony Lewis, "'Jimmy?' 'Hi Michelle,'" *New York Times*, March 20, 1977, p. E25.

30. James Reston, "The Birth of a Salesman," *New York Times*, March 20, 1977, p. E25.

31. Alan Otten, "Too Effective?" *Wall Street Journal*, March 31, 1977, p. 16.

32. Hedrick Smith, "Carter and the 100 Days," *New York Times*, April 29, 1977, p. A16.

33. "After 100 Days: The 'Real Carter' Emerges," *U.S. News and World Report*, May 2, 1977, p. 22.

34. "Ninety-Day Wondering," *Time*, April 25, 1977, p. 15.

35. Peter Goldman, "Carter Up Close," *Newsweek*, May 2, 1977, p. 32.

36. See Joseph Kraft, "The First 100 Days," *Washington Post*, May 1, 1977, p. C6; and James Reston, "Carter's First 80 Days," *New York Times*, April 10, 1977, p. E17.

37. See Vermont Royster, "The Hundred Days," *Wall Street Journal*, May 4, 1977, p. 22; and George F. Will, "The Good Ship Realism," *Washington Post*, April 24, 1977, p. C7.

38. Jimmy Carter, *Keeping Faith* (New York: Bantam Books, 1982), pp. 20–21.

39. Joseph Kraft, "Carter's Problems Are At Home," *Washington Post*, February 10, 1977, p. A15.

40. "Carter's World: Too Much Too Soon?" *U.S. News and World Report*, February 28, 1977, p. 15; see also, "Carter's New World Order," *U.S. News and World Report*, June 6, 1977, pp. 17–18.

41. Murray Marder, "Other Carter Negotiations May Hinge on Canal Pact," *Washington Post*, September 7, 1977, p. A12.

42. Stephen Rosenfeld, "The Risks of Human Rights Policy," *Washington Post*, February 11, 1977, p. A23.

43. Stephen Rosenfeld, "Carter's Fast Foreign Policy Start," *Washington Post*, April 1, 1977, p. A27.

44. Stephen Rosenfeld, "American Foreign Policy Still Undefined," *Washington Post*, January 10, 1978, p. A17.

45. "Carter's World: Too Much, Too Soon?" *U.S. News and World Report*, February 28, 1977, p. 15.

46. "When Is Talk Policy?" *Washington Post*, February 24, 1977, p. A20.

47. Richard Steele, "Carter's Global Blitz," *Newsweek*, March 28, 1977, p. 17–18.

48. Tom Mathews, "What Carter Is Up To," *Newsweek*, March 28, 1977, p. 32.

49. Marvin Stone, "Sir, the Election Is Over," *U.S. News and World Report*, May 9, 1977, p. 108.

50. "Cold War? Nyet. But It's Getting Chilly," *Time*, July 18, 1977, p. 11.

51. Hugh Sidey, "A Little Experience Is . . . Useful," *Time*, April 18, 1977, p. 13.

52. Stephen Rosenfeld, "The Risks of Human Rights Policy," *Washington Post*, February 11, 1977, p. A23.

53. Stephen Rosenfeld, "Carter's Foreign Policy Offensive," *Washington Post*, July 1, 1977, p. A27.

54. Joseph Kraft, "Crusader Carter and the Dissidents," *Washington Post*, February 24, 1977, p. A21.

55. Joseph Kraft, "Carter's Foreign Policy Method," *Washington Post*, March 15, 1977, p. A21. See also Kraft, "Foreign Policy Gospel," *Washington Post*, June 16, 1977, p. A23.

56. George F. Will, "Carter's 'Tougher' Soviet Standard," *Washington Post*, March 3, 1977, p. A23.

57. Marvin Stone, "Carter and the Kremlin," *U.S. News and World Report*, July 31, 1977, p. 71.

58. "Standing Firm Somewhere," *Wall Street Journal*, February 15, 1977, p. 22.

59. "Friends and Critics," *Wall Street Journal*, March 21, 1977, p. 18.

60. "The Carter Presidency," *Wall Street Journal*, June 30, 1977, p. 12.

61. "Friends and Critics," *Wall Street Journal*, March 21, 1977, p. 18.

62. "Carter Spins the World," *Time*, August 8, 1977, p. 8.

63. "The Right Track on Rights," *Washington Post*, February 27, 1977, p. C6.

64. "The Prophet Carter," *Washington Post*, March 20, 1977, p. C6.

65. Stephen Rosenfeld, "The 'Underside' of American Human Rights," *Washington Post*, March 25, 1977, p. A27.

66. "Moral Policeman of the World?" *U.S. News and World Report*, March 14, 1977, pp. 17–21; see also, "Tough Talk on Human Rights—Will It Scuttle Detente?" *U.S. News and World Report*, March 7, 1977, pp. 30, 35.

67. David Broder, "International Morality," *Washington Post*, May 29, 1977, p. B7.

68. David Broder, "Pushing Human Rights: To What Consequence?" *Washington Post*, June 15, 1977, p. A17; see also Joseph Kraft, "Time For An Informal Summit," *Washington Post*, June 28, 1977, p. A19; Joseph Kraft, "Soviet Dissidents on the Run," *Washington Post*, June 2, 1977, p. A19; Rowland Evans and Robert Novak, "A Mismanaged Human Rights Campaign?" *Washington Post*, June 20, 1977, p. A21; and "Carter's Morality Play," *Time*, March 7, 1977, p. 10.

69. Marvin Stone, "Why Not the Best?" *U.S. News and World Report*, March 21, 1977, p. 88.

70. "A Change in Accent," *Wall Street Journal*, February 10, 1977, p. 14.

71. "War in Korea?" *Wall Street Journal*, May 31, 1977, p. 16.

72. "Inviting a Crisis," *Wall Street Journal*, November 1, 1977, p. 2.

73. See "The B1 Decision," *Wall Street Journal,* July 1, 1977, p. 4; and "After the B1," *Wall Street Journal,* July 14, 1977, p. 18. Also, "Carter's B1 Shocker," *U.S. News and World Report,* July 11, 1977, pp. 13–14.

74. "Mr. Sorensen Withdraws," *Washington Post,* January 18, 1977, p. A14.

75. "Carter Takes His Lumps," *Time,* January 31, 1977, p. 21.

76. "Carter Takes Over," *U.S. News and World Report,* January 31, 1977, p. 11.

77. Robert G. Kaiser, "Sorensen Withdraws as Nominee for CIA," *Washington Post,* February 17, 1977, p. A1, 9.

78. Jimmy Carter, *Keeping Faith* (New York: Bantam Books, 1982), p. 78.

79. "The Water-Projects Vote," *Washington Post,* July 13, 1977, p. A22.

80. "Those Water Projects," *Washington Post,* March 16, 1977, p. A20.

81. "Water Projects and Sacred Cows," *Wall Street Journal,* March 8, 1977, p. 20.

82. Ibid.

83. "Water: A Billion Dollar Battleground," *Time,* April 4, 1977, pp. 16–20.

84. "Energy Mickey Mouse," *Wall Street Journal,* January 28, 1977, p. 12.

85. "Energy Psychology," *Wall Street Journal,* April 22, 1977, p. 16.

86. "20 Million Years of Energy," *Wall Street Journal,* September 14, 1977, p. 22; see also, "Some Fiscal Conservative," *Wall Street Journal,* May 11, 1977, p. 16. In this article Carter's energy program is characterized as "nothing but a massive tax increase." And in, "The Carter Tax Increase," *Wall Street Journal,* September 7, 1977, p. 20, the *Journal* calls the energy initiative "the most ill-conceived piece of economic legislation since the Smoot-Hawley Tariff of 1930."

87. Rowland Evans and Robert Novak, "The Washington-Can-Solve-It Approach," *Washington Post,* April 21, 1977, p. A23; and "Energy Politics," *Washington Post,* March 25, 1977, p. A27.

88. "The Energy Plan: First Bite," *Washington Post,* March 2, 1977, p. A18.

89. "The Emerging Strategy for Energy," *Washington Post,* April 13, 1977, p. A22.

90. Richard Steele, "Now the Gas Crisis," *Newsweek,* February 7, 1977, p. 19.

91. "Carter's First Big Test," *Time,* April 25, 1977, p. 14. House Democratic Whip John Brademas (Indiana) offered the same view: "It is tough enough with separation of powers and the absence of disciplined parties to enact legislation when there is some national consensus. It is really difficult when half the people don't even believe there is a problem." Quoted in "Congress: Showdown Ahead," *Time,* November 7, 1977, p. 18.

92. Norman C. Thomas, "Carter Not Playing By the Unwritten Rules of the Game," *Wall Street Journal,* April 22, 1977, p. 16.

93. "Damage Report on the Energy Bill," *Washington Post,* July 13, 1977, p. A22.

94. Rowland Evans and Robert Novak, "Carter's Energy Package: A Problem With Tactics," *Washington Post,* September 30, 1977, p. A27.

95. Robert G. Kaiser, "Energy Bill Status Judged a Failure for Carter," *Washington Post,* December 14, 1977, pp. A1, 4.

96. "Getting the Act Together," *Wall Street Journal,* September 27, 1977, p. 26.

97. David Broder, "A Lack of Strategy in the Carter Camp," *Washington Post,* June 8, 1977, p. A23.

98. Hedrick Smith, "Carter to Date," *New York Times,* April 24, 1977, p. E1.

99. Gerald Parshall, "Congress vs. the President: Behind the Growing Feud," *U.S. News and World Report,* May 23, 1977, p. 23.

100. Dennis Farney, "Building Coalitions Is Now the Key for Jimmy Carter," *Wall Street Journal,* May 16, 1977, p. 18.

101. David Broder, "Tensions Between Carter and Congress," *Washington Post,* June 11, 1977, p. A23.

102. Meg Greenfield, "Jimmy the Engineer," *Newsweek*, April 25, 1977, p. 104.

103. Russell Baker, "Something Different," *New York Times*, July 5, 1977, p. A29. A few other articles discussing the theme of Carter as unable to consult or compromise with members of Congress include: Albert Hunt, "Jimmy Carter vs. Congress?" *Wall Street Journal*, March 25, 1977, p. 26; David Alpern, "Tough Talk on Energy," *Newsweek*, April 25, 1977, pp. 21–22; David Alpern, "Give-and-Take Spirit," *Newsweek*, June 23, 1977, pp. 17–18; Peter Goldman, "A Party of One," *Newsweek*, July 4, 1977, pp. 13–14; "The New Washington," *Time*, February 7, 1977, pp. 17–26; "Now for the Substance," *Time*, February 28, 1977, pp. 12–15; "Sowing Seeds of Real Conflict," *Time*, April 18, 1977, pp. 12-13; and John Herbert, "The Carter-Congress Rift May Just Have Started," *New York Times*, March 27, 1977, p. E4.

104. "The First Quarter of Mr. Carter," *New York Times*, April 27, 1977, p. E22.

105. "After 100 Days: The Real Carter Emerges," *U.S. News and World Report*, May 2, 1977, p. 21.

106. "The First Six Months," *U.S. News and World Report*, July 25, 1977, p. 17.

107. David Broder, "Second Transition: New Faces, New Policy?" *Washington Post*, December 7, 1977, p. A27.

108. David Broder, "The President Who Came In From the Outside," *Washington Post*, July 31, 1977, p. B7.

109. Rowland Evans and Robert Novak, "Carter Has Been Washingtonized," *Washington Post*, November 1, 1977, p. A19.

110. Hedrick Smith, "Carter's Gain at the Capitol," *New York Times*, August 6, 1977, pp. 1, 30.

111. "Polishing the Carter Image," *U.S. News and World Report*, August 8, 1977, pp. 15–16.

112. "Ninety-Day Wondering," *Time*, April 25, 1977, p. 16.

113. "Working to Reform Welfare," *Time*, April 25, 1977, p. 6.

114. "Night of the Long Winds," *Time*, October 10, 1977, p. 14.

115. "Congress: Showdown Ahead," *Time*, November 7, 1977, p. 19.

116. James Reston, "Carter's Best Week," *New York Times*, April 24, 1977, p. E19.

117. James Reston, "Back to Basics," *New York Times*, October 7, 1977, p. A31.

118. James Reston, "Carter and the Lobbies," *New York Times*, October 9, 1977, p. A15.

119. Rowland Evans and Robert Novak, "Tip O'Neill: Keeping Carter at Arms Length," *Washington Post*, May 21, 1977, p. A11.

120. David Broder, "The Senate Has No Excuse," *Washington Post*, December 18, 1977, p. C7.

121. "A Defiant Congress," *U.S. News and World Report*, October 17, 1977, p. 25.

122. James P. Gannon, "For the President, the Senate is Hostile Ground," *Wall Street Journal*, October 7, 1977, p. 12.

123. Hugh Sidey, "What It Takes to Do the Job," *Time*, November 7, 1977, p. 21.

124. Dennis Farney and Richard J. Levine, "Budget Chief Becomes a Deficit for Carter Most Analysts Agree," *Wall Street Journal*, September 8, 1977, p. 1.

125. "Judging Mr. Lance," *Wall Street Journal*, September 19, 1977, p. 22.

126. "The Lance Hotfoot," *New York Times*, September 8, 1977, p. A26.

127. "The Domestic Test," *Washington Post*, September 7, 1977, p. A25.

128. See "Headaches Pile Up for Carter in Lance Affair," *U.S. News and World Report*, September 19, 1977, pp. 25–26; and "Lance Heads Home," *U.S. News and World Report*, October 3, 1977, pp. 17–18.

129. "The Sharpening Battle Over Bert Lance," *Time*, August 2, 1977, p. 6.

130. "Can Carter Afford Lance," *Time*, September 12, 1977, p. 15.

131. "Lance: Going, Going . . . ," *Time*, September 19, 1977, p. 15.

132. Ibid.

133. "Lance: Wounding Carter," *Time*, October 3, 1977, pp. 15–16.

134. Richard Steele, "What Damage to Carter?" *Newsweek*, September 19, 1977, p. 25.

135. Richard Steele, "Picking Up the Pieces," *Newsweek*, October 3, 1977, p. 22.

136. David Broder, "Lance and Carter: A Fateful Dependence," *Washington Post*, August 24, 1977, p. A15.

137. George F. Will, "A New (?) Standard of Scrutiny," *Washington Post*, September 1, 1977, p. A23.

138. George F. Will, "Lance, Carter, Babbitt and Gantry," *Newsweek*, September 19, 1977, p. 122.

139. Hedrick Smith, "In Lance Case, the 'New Morality' Echoes Some of the Old," *New York Times*, September 18, 1977, p. E1.

140. Allan Otten, "Little Learned," *Wall Street Journal*, September 29, 1977, p. 20.

141. Dennis Farney, "Lance and the Small-Town Boys," *Wall Street Journal*, September 23, 1977, p. 20.

142. Hugh Sidey, "The Persistent Perils of Inner-Circle Vision, " *Time*, September 26, 1977, p. 20.

143. Robert G. Kaiser, "Resignation Swings Spotlight Back to Carter's Programs," *Washington Post*, September 22, 1977, p. A16.

144. Joseph Kraft, "President Under Pressure," *Washington Post*, September 8, 1977, p. A27.

145. Jimmy Carter, *Keeping Faith* (New York: Bantam Books, 1978), p. 129.

146. James Reston, "What's Right with Carter?" *New York Times*, December 23, 1977, p. A29.

147. Albert Hunt, "Carter and the 1978 Elections," *Wall Street Journal*, December 27, 1977, p. 8.

148. "Now Back to Face the Music," *Time*, January 16, 1978, p. 9.

149. "The Freshman," *New York Times*, January 3, 1978, p. A28.

150. "Outlook '78: Carter—Will He Change Course?" *U.S. News and World Report*, December 26, 1977/January 2, 1978, pp. 18–29.

151. Dennis Farney, "Carter: Eroding Credibility at Home . . . ," *Wall Street Journal*, January 19, 1978, p. 12.

152. Tony Fuller, "Carter at the Grass Roots," *Newsweek*, January 30, 1978, p. 19.

153. "Now Back to Face the Music," *Time*, January 16, 1978, p. 8.

154. "Steady as She Drifts," *Wall Street Journal*, January 23, 1978, p. 8.

155. Joseph Kraft, "A Year of Almost Systematic Retreats," *Washington Post*, January 19, 1978, p. A25.

156. Anthony Lewis, "Pluses and Minuses," *New York Times*, January 2, 1978, p. A21.

157. "A Bold and Balky Congress," *Time*, January 23, 1978, p. 16.

158. "Sliding Down the Polls," *Time*, December 26, 1977, p. 12.

159. "Now Back to Face the Music," *Time*, January 16, 1978, p. 9.

160. Dennis Farney, "Carter's First Year," *Wall Street Journal*, December 23, 1977, p. 4.

161. Vermont Royster, "Presidential Power," *Wall Street Journal*, January 4, 1978, p. 14.

162. "Carter and Congress: Seeds of More Discord," *U.S. News and World Report*, November 21, 1977, p. 21.

163. "Carter's First Year: Setbacks and Successes," *Congressional Quarterly Weekly Report*, December 24, 1977, p. 2637.

4

Carter's Second Year: 1978

What makes the press assessments of Carter in 1978 so interesting is that this year, by any measure, was Carter's finest. In addition to journalistic assessments of the "failing" presidency there were highly favorable reviews of Carter's leadership. The persistence of the generally negative view of the administration and a few major foreign affairs achievements account for these relatively inconsistent appraisals.

For Carter, the highlights of 1978 were passage of the Panama Canal treaties, a civil service reform bill, a Middle East arms package, the lifting of the Turkish arms embargo, and the completion of an Israeli-Egyptian treaty at Camp David. In the aftermath of the Camp David treaties a number of journalists proclaimed the "great Carter revival," the "Carter miracle" and the beginning of the "new Jimmy." By the end of 1978 the tone of the journalistic assessments of the Carter presidency differed greatly from the analyses at the end of Carter's first year.

Despite the fluctuating views of Carter in 1978 there remained a generally consistent application by journalists of criteria identified above. Journalists relied on the explanations of failure identified above (inconsistency, inattention to conventional political norms, inexperience). They based their favorable assessments of Carter's leadership on two impressions: first, that Carter finally learned the arts of political negotiation and compromise; or, second, that journalists previously underestimated Carter's skills.

1. Timing. The journalistic view that a president should begin his administration with clearly defined and achievable priority items in order to establish a reputation for success persisted in 1978. Journalists portrayed the new year as the time for a "fresh start" for the administration. A number of journalists wrote that Carter's emphasis on such controversial issues as the Panama Canal treaties, airline deregulation, civil service reform, and the Middle East peace process was suited to a second presidential term. According to this view, a president succeeds by framing a limited, achievable agenda thereby establishing a reputation for success which later enables him to offer controversial proposals.

2. Rhetoric/Symbolism. In the 1978 State of the Union address the president spoke of the limits on government's ability to solve all public problems. Journalists criticized Carter's "conservative tone" and lack of any "bugle-call" to action. Some journalists reacted to Carter's speech as though the discussion of "limitations" introduced a new theme for the Carter presidency. This speech, in fact, reiterated many of the themes of the Carter inaugural.

During 1978 journalists discussed the "failed" presidency of Jimmy Carter. In assessing why the Carter administration failed to fulfill its promise many journalists found the president's rhetoric and projection of leadership lacking. Carter allegedly lacked "stature"—the kind of commanding presence that makes people respect a president.

Another explanation for the administration's troubles was Carter's inability to define and articulate a vision for the nation's future. According to this view, Carter spent so much time on the details of governing that he neglected the symbolic demands of the presidency. Many journalists believed that Carter should have paid a lot of attention to imagery as a means of communicating a sense of political purpose and direction.

In the aftermath of the Camp David summit in September journalists reassessed Carter's image. The unexpected achievement of an Israeli-Egyptian peace treaty led many commentators to admit they had "underestimated" the president. The treaty gave Carter a "new stature" at home and abroad. After Camp David, Carter allegedly exhibited that undefinable quality that Evans and Novak called "presidentiality."

The Camp David achievement influenced journalistic assessments of other Carter administration activities. At the close of the 95th Congress in October most journalists proclaimed the session a legislative "success" for Carter. Carter had a successful legislative session, in part, because he exhibited a commanding presence, had shaken that "crippling image of incompetence," and was a "presidential president at last." Unfortunately for the administration, the pre–Camp David portrayal of Carter as failing to symbolize strong leadership returned by the end of 1978.

3. *Agenda.* In the pre–Camp David months the journalistic assessments of the Carter agenda were similar to the 1977 assessments. In early 1978, the following themes prevailed: (a) Carter would attempt to gain the initiative and overcome problems working with Congress by offering a limited policy agenda; (b) Carter's emphasis on such controversial items as the Panama Canal treaties and arms control would generate further presidential-congressional friction; and (c) the State of the Union address reflected Carter's reluctance to rally the nation behind any grandiose policy objectives.

Many journalists expected Carter to offer a limited agenda seeking to achieve some early policy successes before proposing controversial items. When Carter's agenda ran into legislative roadblocks, journalists asserted that the president failed to offer a limited, achievable agenda. In the pre–Camp David months when a number of administration proposals moved unsteadily through Congress, journalists criticized Carter's ambitious and controversial agenda. Journalists criticized Carter for (a) overloading the policy agenda; (b) lacking identifiable policy priorities; and (c) offering legislation that ran counter to congressional and public sentiments. In the post–Camp David euphoria many journalists changed their opinions of the administration's agenda. At the end of the "successful" 95th Congress they praised Carter for pushing an ambitious agenda and viewed Carter's leadership favorably.

4. *Policy Development.* Carter's efforts at building congressional and public support for administration programs were persisting sources of journalistic criticism in the pre–Camp David months. In the pre–Camp David months of 1978 journalists emphasized Carter's insensitivity to conventional political norms; the president's tendency to seek comprehensive solutions and make appeals based on the merits of policies instead of political feasibility; the president's refusal to focus on a few achievable policy items; and the president's efforts to push the nation into conflicting foreign policy directions.

What is interesting about the persistence of these themes is that President Carter had major legislative victories in 1978. Carter achieved these legislative victories in very close votes, such as the lifting of the Turkish arms embargo (three votes) and the Panama Canal treaties (one vote). Significantly, journalists focused on the closeness of the votes, the political costs incurred in victory, and even the fact that Carter's initiatives almost lost.

The Camp David victory helped change, at least temporarily, the perception of political incompetence. Journalists attributed the victory to many of Carter's personal characteristics that they previously portrayed as destroying his efforts to build support for administration initiatives. For example, many journalists wrote that Carter succeeded at Camp David because of his idealism, stubbornness, tenacity, and mastery of detail.

At the end of the congressional session journalistic reviews of Carter's efforts at policy development were generally favorable. Journalists attributed Carter's legislative successes to the president's "new found ability" at engaging in the conventional norms of political Washington. Some journalists praised Carter for adding government veterans to the White House staff, making better use of the congressional liaison team, and seeking the advice of Washington insiders.

5. *Staff.* Carter's White House staff continued to receive severe journalistic criticism in 1978. A series of alleged incidents involving White House staff aide Hamilton Jordan resulted in numerous press commentaries about staff incompetence and boorish social behavior. Journalists even criticized the White House staff's handling of press accusations. They frequently blamed the "White House Georgians" for the alleged maladies of the administration. Carter's staff did not enjoy the benefits of the press's temporary, post–Camp David rehabilitation of Carter.

Initial Observations

At the beginning of Carter's second year we find a variety of predictions of how "successful" the president will be in 1978. The analyses reveal a continuous attention to the same themes pervading earlier assessments of Carter: Will he learn to compromise? Will his staff adopt a professional demeanor? Will he limit his agenda to a few priority items? Will the White House adopt a workable strategy for enacting priority items?

In Joseph Kraft's view, "the outlook is not for an improvement in the President's stock." Kraft's explanation for this prediction was twofold: *First*, to his great credit Carter attempted to deal with problems not recognized by the public. "How do you yell 'murder' when there is no corpse? That was Jimmy Carter's problem last year and the reason he did so poorly. It remains his problem this year." *Second*, Carter failed to play "inside politics." In Kraft's words, to be successful a president must

> . . . work with the congressional lobbies and the interest groups behind them. He has to practice a constant give and take. He has to trade effectively.
> If there is one thing the Carter administration has not been able to do, however, it is to trade effectively.[1]

U.S. News and World Report agreed that Carter's controversial agenda exacerbated congressional-executive tensions. *U.S. News* anticipated that issues on the 1978 agenda—SALT II and the Panama Canal treaties—would result in additional congressional resilience to Carter's agenda.[2]

Not all of the analyses at this time viewed Carter's prospects negatively. A number of essays noted that upon return from his nine day, four continent tour at the end of 1977 Carter expressed a desire to work with Congress, to compromise, and not to build public expectations too high again.[3] David Broder believed that Carter would adopt a limited agenda in 1978 in which legislative victories gradually occurring one at a time would precipitate future victories.[4]

Reactions to Carter's 1978 State of the Union address reflected different journalistic expectations for Carter's second year and the persistence of particular themes in evaluating the president. In the speech Carter emphasized a number of policy priorities for his second year, including arms control, the Panama Canal treaties, energy, tax policy, and creation of the Department of Education. Carter also reiterated a major theme of his inaugural address in asserting that "Government cannot . . . define our vision."

David Broder perceived Carter's emphasis on policy priorities as an attempt to regain the leadership condition by returning to the themes of the 1976 campaign.[5] In contrast, the *New York Times* saw the address as an attempt to establish Carter as a serious leader by abandoning the 1976 campaign themes. According to the *Times*, Carter was attempting to lead by adopting a conservative tone and a limited vision for the nation.

> Having tried, however ineptly, to rouse the nation only to be kicked for the effort, he invites us now to slumber on soundly but to let conscience stir our dreams. He is a soothing flatterer and a sensible President, but not yet a leader, or teacher, even for a quiet time.[6]

The "conservative tone" of Carter's speech and the discussion of "limitations" bothered many commentators. The president accused earlier of trying to do too much too fast, was lambasted for acknowledging government's inability to solve all public problems and for failing to set grandiose objectives comparable to the Great Society. According to Hedrick Smith, the "restrained rhetoric" of Carter's address "broke with the solemn historical tradition of earlier presidents who employed stately eloquence or seized upon a momentous occasion to summon the nation to arms directing it into a new era." Smith assessed that Carter instead "presented the nation with a balance sheet of its problems and a catalogue of his prescriptions for them."[7]

The *Washington Post* faulted Carter's speech for its lack of any sweeping legislative proposals. In the *Post*'s view, "Mr. Carter is determined not to be a bugle-call President. . . . Mr. Carter is now preaching the doctrine of limited government—and redefining the idea of the American presidency." Carter's assertion that "Government cannot . . . define our vision" produced a sermon from the *Post*'s editors:

> The federal government and, above all, the President contribute powerfully to the national vision. It is one thing to say that the United States can survive spells of bad government . . . but it's entirely another to suggest that it could get along indefinitely without a large sense of common purpose. Mr. Carter seems genuinely not to understand that truth—and it may well turn into the central defect of his presidency. He has not gotten his energy bill through Congress because he has not been able to give Americans a sufficiently clear idea or [sic] where it takes them.[8]

More "Scandal"?

In the early stages of Carter's second year the press assessments of the administration were influenced by the so-called David Marston affair and allegations of boorish social behavior by Hamilton Jordan. These incidents seem trivial since the allegations were never substantiated. Yet it is important to discuss these matters because the press treated them as major scandals, and each incident contributed to lasting impressions of the Carter administration.

The firing of Republican United States Attorney David Marston (Philadelphia, Pa.) developed into a major media investigation into an alleged cover-up of wrongdoing in the Carter administration. Marston had a reputation as a fiercely aggressive and partisan prosecutor. Allegedly at the request of former Rep. Joshua Eilberg (D-Pa.), Attorney General Griffin Bell, unaware that Marston was investigating Eilberg, suggested to the president that Marston be fired and replaced with a Democratic attorney. Marston's firing invited an avalanche of accusations. For the most part, the accusations against Carter were two-fold: *first*, that he lied by failing to acknowledge how much he knew about Marston's investigations into the activities of loyal Democratic politicians; *second*, that he broke a campaign promise to end patronage politics at the Justice Department.

William Safire accused Carter of obstructing justice and asked cleverly: "What did he know? When did he know it?" *Time* magazine proclaimed that, "In this case they were fair questions." *Time* recalled Carter's 1976 campaign pledge to "never lie" and alleged that Carter's handling of the

Marston case included a number of "lies." The news weekly added: "Jimmy Carter has some fresh tarnish on his escutcheon—with nobody but himself to blame for it."[9]

Hedrick Smith noted that the Marston firing made Carter appear to be not immune to "traditional patronage and protection politics." Despite proclamations of a "new moral leadership," the Carter administration "looked as inept and as partisan as its predecessors."[10] And Norman C. Miller of the *Wall Street Journal* asserted:

> . . . there is no way the President can square his campaign promise to depoliticize Justice Department appointments with the firing of a Republican prosecutor in the midst of an investigation of corruption involving Democratic politicians.[11]

Evans and Novak argued that Carter's actions were incompetent but did not obstruct justice. The real problem, they asserted, was that candidate Carter preached a new vision for the Justice Department. "Candidate Jimmy Carter's pious campaign promises to install a nonpartisan merit system at the Justice Department forms the base of this problem."[12]

The *Wall Street Journal* agreed that the most credible claim against Carter was that he failed to fulfill the promise of a merit only criterion for Justice Department appointments. The *Journal* claimed that the incident was sensationalized by the media, and defended the firing. The editors' main criticism was that Carter's handling of the incident exhibited poor political "instincts."[13]

Despite the numerous accusations and occasional defenses of Carter's actions, most journalists faulted the president's handling of public criticism. Many journalists portrayed the Marston case as another test of Carter's political acumen. Journalists perceived the failure to dissipate criticism as evidence of Carter's political ineptitude.

A number of journalists also considered the so-called "White House Georgians" as a source of problems in the Carter administration. Dennis Farney's discussion of the White House as overly influenced by small-town Georgians lacking any sense of propriety in the "big town" is revealing. A highly critical article by Hugh Sidey claimed that "the yahoo syndrome has been detected in the White House." Sidey proclaimed:

> As long as Presidents are successful, they are proud (indeed, some might say, even overbearing) about their geographical, cultural and intellectual identities. But when success begins to elude them, they detect in the world beyond the White House walls (particularly in New York and Washington) massive arrogance and contempt aimed at their humble origins and quaint folkways. They develop large chips on their shoulders, which weight them into self-pity.
>
> Some warning tremors of this sort are coming from the White House underlings who complain . . . that the Georgia boys are being called a bunch of yahoos.
>
> What makes a genuine yahoo, of course, is that he fears in his heart that he really is one and so spends a lot of time going around protesting how terrible it is that other folks think he is one.[14]

A photograph of Jody Powell holding a frog cleverly accompanied Sidey's article. The caption read: "Country Boy Powell and Friend."[15]

A series of alleged incidents involving Hamilton Jordan resulted in numerous columns condemning Carter for tolerating boorish social behavior. Meg Greenfield in January 1978 differed from Sidey's criticism of the White House staff. Greenfield argued that this notion that "the Georgians," those "bodice-tugging, necktie loosening, hard-drinking, free-cussing Georgians" are behind all of the problems in Carter's administration was overstated. Rather, "there are far too many Carter Administration Georgians in town who do not play the bumpkin game to lend credibility to the notion that the principal tension here is between a stuffy, decrepit Establishment and a bunch of bare-chested, peanut-feeding yahoos."[16] Yet only six months later Greenfield criticized White House aides for "embarrassing" Carter and the institution of the presidency. In an apparent turn-around from her earlier columns praising the openness in Carter's presidency Greenfield concluded:

> And there sits Jimmy Carter in the White House, Mr. Morality himself having to answer questions over the first nineteen months about his close associates' entanglements with the quest for dough, the use of drugs, boozing, whoop-de-doo and blabber mouthing. An open Administration, they called it. I think he had better close it down, if he can, at least in its chaotic, permissive aspects.[17]

This latter assessment more accurately reflected the press perceptions of the Carter White House staff by that time. The press accusations of White House staff inexperience, failure to cultivate party leaders, and failure to engage in Washington-based social events were serious enough. By late 1977 the stories concerning Hamilton Jordan's social adventures in particular became incredible. One month prior to Greenfield's more sympathetic column Jordan was accused of slighting the Egyptian Ambassador's wife at a dinner party by tugging her elasticized bodice and proclaiming his pleasure in viewing the "pyramids." The alleged incident was reported in the last three paragraphs of a 105-paragraph story concerning White House social behavior in the *Washington Post*'s "Style" section. No sources for the alleged incident were identified. The White House was not provided the opportunity prior to publication to confirm or deny the story. The wire services picked up the story and the media portrayed the event as accurately reported.

In February 1978, a *Post* gossip columnist reported in the Sunday paper's magazine that Jordan twice spat an amaretto and cream on the blouse of a young woman at a Washington, D.C., singles bar after the woman resisted Jordan's attempts to become acquainted. The source for the story was the allegedly offended woman, reported by other patrons as unruly and intoxicated. Again, no opportunity for a White House denial was offered prior to publication. Again, the story was widely distributed and reported. For example, *Newsweek* reported:

Hamilton Jordan has tried hard to keep a little south Georgia clay on his boots—and in his footprints around the White House. But in recent weeks Jimmy Carter's favorite good old bad boy has twisted Washington pomp only to run afoul of his own new circumstances. A de facto White House chief of staff, Jordan puts in a hard twelve-hour work day, but he also plays hard when the sun goes down.[18]

Journalists ridiculed the White House staff for responding to the accusations with a 33-page denial, including transcribed interviews with the bartender who served the alleged victim. Journalists paid little attention to which version of the story was correct. The press had more to say about the White House's efforts to control gossip column innuendo. The broad dissemination of these stories and replies contributed to the general press portrait of the Carter White House. For example, George F. Will's essay "Hamilton on the Town" referred to Jordan as "the man who symbolizes unbuttoned disdain for Establishment priorities." Will continued:

> it is arrogant for a powerful person to be scruffy and boorish in order to advertise his exemption from little conventions and courtesies. Besides, Jordan's comportment reinforces the growing belief that many of the most important people in the Administration, including the most important person, are out of their depth as well as their element.[19]

Time magazine carried a critical commentary on the characters of the Carter people by columnist Hugh Sidey. Without questioning the truth of the Jordan stories Sidey asserted that these incidents revealed the lack of "class" in the Carter White House. The Jordan barroom incident, Sidey believed, reflected on both Carter personally and on his presidency:

> One of the maladies of the Carter Administration these days seems to be a lack of class. Class is not always necessary for effective leadership; Lyndon Johnson demonstrated this. But if there is a dearth of achievement or other excitement, then a lack of class can be troublesome. The Carter Administration is drifting toward a description favored by the late Peter Lisagor of the Chicago *Daily News* who used to say of the buffoons who brought us Watergate, "class they ain't got."
>
> Jimmy Carter is the first modern president whose quotient of class seems to have gone dramatically down since his days as a candidate. . . . [Carter's] presidency is becoming tarnished by the antics of others and the fact that Carter tolerates them, indeed sometimes covers for them.
>
> Aide Hamilton Jordan's celebrated evening at Sarsfield's bar is only the latest episode in a continuing assault on traditional American sensitivities that probably began with Billy Carter.[20]

A *Time* magazine news story entitled "Tabulations of Harried Ham" acknowledged that little evidence existed for the two alleged incidents. The article focused on whether the White House exhibited oversensitivity to criticism by seeking to disprove the allegations. After acknowledging the lack of evidence in these incidents, the story concluded that Jordan's "effectiveness is becoming impaired, especially given Carter's almost Wilsonian public emphasis on personal morality and rectitude."[21]

Of the news weeklies only *U.S. News and World Report* discussed the Jordan incident with restraint. The generally cautious news weekly did not draw bold conclusions about the president and his staff's character or competence from gossip-column innuendo.[22] Such straightforward reporting was clearly the exception with regard to the Jordan stories.

Wall Street Journal commentator Norman C. Miller's analysis resembled that of *Time* magazine. While conceding the lack of evidence against Jordan, Miller noted that the White House reactions placed in doubt Carter's commitment to morality in public service. Proclaiming that the "overreaction" to the story "makes the White House a laughing stock," Miller concluded: "In political terms, jokes about boorish behavior by people close to the President in time can tarnish the image of high moral and ethical standards."[23]

David Broder also expressed concern for the Carter administration's image of high moral conduct. Broder acknowledged Jordan's political strengths, but he did not dispel the notion that journalists accurately reported Jordan's alleged behavior. Broder only advised Jordan to "live like a saint" to avoid negative publicity.[24]

Evans and Novak denied that the negative press for Carter's White House staff coincided with gossip page publicity. The columnists believed that the more important issue was that of "competence, not arrogance." They argued that

> . . . the unfavorable publicity coincided with the evolution of Jordan into a de facto chief of staff who will not and cannot fulfill the duties of the post. Because nobody else can perform those duties while Jordan holds the job, the trouble afflicting the White House in the first Carter year may be perpetuated.[25]

The numerous columns censuring Jordan's alleged actions contributed to a perception of the White House staff as unprofessional and to a negative view of Jordan that persisted throughout Carter's term. Columnists condemned the president for elevating Jordan's role in the White House long after these stories appeared. The lone press defense of the administration came over a month after the reporting of the alleged barroom incident. A *Wall Street Journal* editorial "Lay Off Jimmy Carter," asked columnists to provide Carter "a bit of a break" from this "misdirected" criticism. For the *Journal,* continual exposure of Jordan and later unsubstantiated accusations of Amy Carter's temper tantrums "may tell less about the character of this administration than they do about the childish crankiness of too many of this country's opinion leaders." Yet even this editorial accepted the gossip-column stories as truthful. In the same editorial the *Journal* argued that attacking Carter's "aides' competence misses the main point." The *Journal* complained that the presidential selection process elevated to the White House a group "of genuine outsiders. We shouldn't complain; we deserve it."[26]

The Panama Canal Treaties:
The "Jimmy Revival"?

It is reasonable to expect that following a major policy success journalistic assessments of Carter's leadership would turn favorable. Yet many journalists did not judge favorably Carter's leadership on the Panama Canal treaties. The themes dominating these assessments were (1) that Carter won because he worked hard at soothing congressional egos; (2) that Carter won despite his efforts at building support for the treaties. Many journalists emphasized the closeness of the victory margin (one vote more than the two-thirds majority needed in the Senate) and the political costs incurred by Carter in victory.

First, some commentators stressed in "I told you so" fashion that the only reason Carter achieved this legislative victory was that he finally decided to do what the press believed the president should have been doing all along: "Wheeling and dealing." Asking whether Carter's legislative victory constituted the president's "born again leadership," Hugh Sidey reported: "Carter shed some more of that evangelical sheen, orchestrating millions of dollars for a few votes, just like an old time pol. . . . [At] last he abandoned his 'I understand your problems' approach to a wavering legislator."[27]

U.S. News listed the alleged trade-offs Carter made to attain Senate votes. The news weekly reported: "The hairbreadth Senate win for the first canal agreement took a lot of doing, including wheeling and dealing never before seen in this administration. . . . Carter was backed into the unaccustomed position of personally pleading for senators' votes." U.S. News emphasized the costs incurred by the president in "pleading" for votes. The news story concluded that Carter forfeited a lot of political capital that he needed for future legislative battles such as the SALT II treaties.[28] After the Senate vote on the second canal agreement the magazine again stressed the costs of the victory and asserted that the closeness of the vote tarnished Carter's victory.[29]

Time magazine portrayed the Panama Canal votes as major victories at a crucial juncture for the Carter presidency. Time reported that: "A defeat of the Panama treaty over a heavily financed right-wing opposition campaign would have been a disaster for his presidency." Time's report also emphasized that these victories carried important political costs for Carter.[30]

Despite Carter's legislative victories Time characterized Carter's approach to selling the package as ineffectual. The news weekly responded to Carter aides who complained that the press faulted Carter for doing too much and then for doing too little. "Yet there is a measure of truth in both charges." Journalists accused Carter of overloading Congress with many complex issues (doing too much) and then on specific issues like the Canal treaties journalists portrayed him as too slow in building support (doing too little). "On this occasion as on others, Carter appeared to think that the announcement of a worthy project was enough to get it accepted."[31]

Newsweek also emphasized Carter's tactics of selling the treaties instead of the victories themselves. Richard Steele discussed Carter's lobbying efforts on behalf of the treaties and observed that, "He even went so far as to engage in the ritual that he most abhors"—wheeling and dealing with members of Congress.[32] Peter Goldman further stated that: "The victory had been too long in coming, too bumpy in execution, too little appreciated in the media—and too desperately necessary to a government in doldrums."[33]

A *Washington Post* editorial argued that Carter's approach to attaining the Canal treaties victory failed to demonstrate his foreign policy leadership. The *Post* judged that Carter achieved his goal "in a manner too precarious for much comfort. . . . [All] that can be safely concluded from the Panama cliffhanger, in our view, is that the president has survived."[34]

David Broder's retrospective on Carter's achievement noted that Carter's major leadership problem was that, "He has buried himself in administrative detail and failed in a president's first duty—to communicate his vision to the country." For Broder, apparently, the president could no longer be called "Carter the communicator," a phrase that Broder used earlier in the term. Broder added that Carter spent too much time "on the essentially secondary issue of the Panama Canal treaties."[35] In order to lead effectively, Broder concluded, it is incumbent on the president "to divide and politicize the country . . . on lines that reflect his priorities, not someone else's."[36]

Carter's April 1978 decision not to deploy the enhanced radiation (ER) weapon, or, as it became known, the "neutron bomb," resulted in additional press criticism of the administration's foreign policy making process. Opinion on deployment of the weapon was divided. Opponents expressed horror at the weapon's capacity to destroy human life while maintaining the integrity of buildings. Advocates argued that the weapon would reduce the chances of a Warsaw Pact tank attack on NATO.[37] The *Wall Street Journal* asserted that, "There are no serious arguments against deployment of this weapon." The *Journal* declared that Carter's "frightening" decision not to deploy resulted from his being persuaded by "the arguments of the flaky left."[38]

More importantly, many columns focused on the process surrounding the decision not to deploy the weapon. What was apparent to many journalists was that Carter initially supported development and deployment of the weapon, and then decided to cancel the project altogether. Carter linked his decision to the lack of commitment from NATO countries to deploy the weapon in Europe. Yet journalists portrayed the president's decision making in this case as "indecisive." Evans and Novak argued that "the agonized indecision that has marked the administration's handling of the neutron bomb is a signal example of superpower leadership succumbing to pedestrian politics."[39] *Time* claimed that the apparent reversal on whether to deploy the weapon set off a "transatlantic furor." *Time* characterized the decision as a "mishandled power play [which] produces international confusion."[40]

While Carter's Panama Canal treaties victories brought some press acclaim, journalists focused on Carter's tactics in seeking congressional support. Despite a major legislative achievement journalists emphasized the closeness of the vote, how Carter sought support, and what costs the administration incurred in victory. The "neutron bomb" decision brought additional criticism of Carter's decision making. In March 1978 journalists also criticized Carter for not promptly ending a major coal strike and for allowing ousted Budget Director Bert Lance to maintain a diplomatic passport. Despite all of this, a few observers declared that the administration made noticeable improvements. *U.S. News* reported that the coal strike incident was "forcing Jimmy Carter to overhaul the way his White House staff operates. . . . Now the Carter team seems determined to make mid-course corrections to avoid further problems." The news magazine declared that Carter was finally beginning to limit priorities, improve relations with Congress, make needed staff changes, and work with the Democratic leadership.[41]

In May 1978, only six weeks after he declared the Carter administration a clan with no class, Hugh Sidey observed that the White House staff and Carter finally learned to dress for success. According to Sidey, Carter "dresses a little more neatly and wears a few more white shirts and stiff collars. His principal aide, Hamilton Jordan appears more often in suit and tie and leaves his boots at home." Sidey proclaimed that the president was no longer hostile to conventional political norms. "[Carter] can knock back a couple of bourbons at night with a man he likes. . . . He is developing personal intuition about individual congressional leaders." Sidey concluded that Carter even began "relishing presidential perquisites . . . [and] sees more the need to act presidential."[42]

To what do we attribute Carter's transformation from an anti-political president to a leader who downs bourbon with congressional leaders and enjoys special privileges? Sidey doesn't say. Yet only three weeks later he changed course and declared Carter "wary of tradition, protocol and many of the rituals of advanced urban society."[43]

That same month *Newsweek*'s Peter Goldman declared the beginning of a "new Jimmy"—an "aggressive" leader "hardselling his own programs, plugging those deserving Democrats who support them, dispensing tens and hundreds of millions in federal bounty." Goldman noticed indications of Carter's political transformation:

> This new Jimmy seemed sensitized—or at least resigned—to the finicky requirements of Presidential politics as well. He and his people have learned a bit about the art of pampering members of Congress; the President himself spends more tête-à-tête time with them—twice as much as he used to, according to the latest of his relentless time motion studies—and the Georgians even drink with them after hours. Those who help Carter will be helped in return. . . .[44]

The Failing Presidency

Prior to the Camp David Accords the major theme in the journalistic assessments of the Carter administration in 1978 was the "failing" presidency of Jimmy Carter. From April through late August of 1978 a number of columns and editorials tried to explain the Carter presidency's alleged failures. In its May 1, 1978, edition a *U.S. News and World Report* news story observed that the Carter presidency "is popularly perceived as being on the verge of foundering. . . . Political experts agreed that unless the situation is turned around soon, White House leadership could be damaged beyond repair."[45]

This perception of the Carter presidency as deeply troubled was widespread. Explanations included, first, the inexperience of the president and his staff in national politics and their aversion to conventional political norms. Second, some interpretations focused on the administration's efforts at policy development—the emphasis on discrete problem solving over building coalitions in Congress and public support, the attempts to accomplish too many reforms too quickly. Finally, there was the president's lack of "stature."

We begin with the assessment that Carter lacked "stature." In James Reston's words, "Jimmy Carter is not a majestic personal figure like Roosevelt and he doesn't inspire fear like Johnson."[46] Evans and Novak asserted that Carter's problem was that nobody feared him. And, "to govern properly, a president must generate a respect bordering on fear." Evans and Novak concluded that Carter failed to show Washingtonians that opposition to him was "not risk free."[47]

The more prevalent press interpretation was that Carter failed to adopt a clear vision for the nation's future. Carter allegedly sought to deal with numerous problems never relating his proposals to some broad national goals. For James Reston this was a more serious indictment than the view that Carter lacked stature:

> . . . the main charge against him is not that he doesn't listen to anybody but that he listens to everybody, and cannot make up his mind—or maybe, that he makes it up too often. . . .
>
> [Carter] has not made clear to the American people the complexities and ambiguities that have to be resolved. His speeches are wooden and statistical, his priorities confused.[48]

Reston assessed that Carter failed to reduce the complexity of the policy environment "to identity so that the people can understand just how difficult it is to choose." Reston acknowledged that it is not solely a president's responsibility to resolve the complexity. "But he can give a clearer lead on how to attack these problems and in what order."[49]

William Safire also faulted Carter for failing to articulate a vision of the nation's future. According to Safire, Carter lacked a political philosophy that could bring structure to the confusing policy environment. In Safire's view, the president "should become predictable to the people around him."

> Unless some philosophy is articulated that gives an Administration its character and flavor—unless the trumpet is certain—the diffusion of power loses its purpose. All that is left is squabbling and backbiting and end runs.[50]

Vermont Royster acknowledged critics' frustrations in trying to identify Carter's priorities: "With the possible exception of the energy program, there is no Carter policy that is at the center of national debate. What his critics charge . . . is that they don't know what his policies are."[51] Allan Otten agreed that Carter's agenda lacked identifiable priorities:

> The President spends too much time on process and details, and not enough on developing broad philosophy and goals and providing strong, consistent leadership. He changes course erratically, moralizes too much, oversells bad decisions and undersells good ones.[52]

Joseph Kraft believed that Carter's leadership problem was an inability to be "sensitive to the conflicts between almost equally good things that are implicit in holding power." Kraft complained that Carter suffered from "a lack of structure." Kraft added that Carter "strives mightily for moral positions on every issue and then finds that his positions collide in ways that force him to retreat."[53]

According to George F. Will, Carter set forth moral postures that failed to elicit strong public support. Carter's problem, according to Will, could be attributed to: (1) the president's humble, anti-imperial leadership style, and (2) the decline of respect for the presidency.

> A President is disarmed unless he can seize the nation's moral imagination. Carter cannot seize it with his rhetoric: remarkably, 53 years with the King James Bible has not given him a flair for stirring cadences. So he needs all the help he can get from what remains of the nation's reverence for the Presidency. After an Administration of Prussian arrogance and Sicilian corruption it was fine for Gerald Ford to invite the networks to watch him toast muffins. But in other times, the Presidency should be clothed in majesty, not denim.[54]

The press image of Carter as a discrete problem solver incapable of providing a philosophical framework by which to lead was very pervasive in mid-1978. In late May 1978, Tom Wicker defined Carter's leadership problems as such:

> The inheritor of a profoundly political office, whose most successful occupants have all been experienced and skilled politicians, Mr. Carter seems more nearly to have an engineer's approach—concern with the details of program and policy rather than with the broad appeals and human exchanges of gaining acceptance for them.[55]

By late August 1978, David Broder offered one of the few favorable appraisals of Carter's standing at that stage of the term. In his column, "The President is Learning," Broder referred to Carter's Middle East negotiations and veto of a defense authorization bill as actions which "exemplify what presidents get paid to do, and what Carter did all too rarely in his first 18 months in office. They are decisive, well-timed and personal initiatives in matters of overriding importance." For the most part, Broder's column was a retrospective on the alleged sickness of the Carter presidency:

> The most important thing the president is learning is how to use his time, his resources and his energy to shape events. Until quite recently, he was listening to everybody in Congress, the administration and the world who wanted to see him. He was giving comfort to all of them, indicating sympathy, if not commitment to their points of view. But he was not defining the choices for them from a presidential perspective or enlisting their assistance for his objectives.[56]

Broder's portrayal of Carter as a revived leader came only one month after the columnist proclaimed Carter's presidency in shambles. Prior to the president's trip to the European economic summit in July 1978, Broder asserted:

> President Carter is going to Europe this week under the worst circumstances possible. Not since Richard Nixon made his pre-resignation visits to Moscow and the Middle East has an American chief executive conferred with his counterparts at a moment when there were more reasons for skepticism about his own capacity for leadership.[57]

The basis for such doubt about the president's leadership included, according to Broder: (1) Carter's inability "to hold his own idealism up to skeptical self-examination"; (2) the president's "confusing the expression of good intentions with the devising of a sensible strategy for achieving his goals"; and (3) Carter's "tendency to moralize rather than manage his way through the morass of conflicting interests and powers in the world."[58] This assessment is consistent with Broder's April 1978 judgment that Carter too frequently emphasized "style" over "substance."

> What defines a President—what draws or repels political support—is not his style but his substance. The goals a president espouses give the hard edge of meaning to his administration and politicize the country into meaningful blocs.
>   Carter has blunted that process by espousing a bewildering variety of contradictory causes in both foreign and domestic policy.[59]

Hugh Sidey's columns offer several criticisms of Carter's leadership. In April, Sidey attributed Carter's leadership problems to the president's scientific background: "Much of his trouble in the mystical arena of political leadership arises when he tries to apply these bloodless principles to human power and pride."[60] In May, Sidey opined that Carter's leadership problems stemmed from his populism, small-town heritage, and spiritual background:

> In his populist fevers [Carter] sometimes seems mistakenly to champion mediocrity rather than excellence. Some of his prejudice seems to arise more from his small-town background than from reason and experience in a diverse world.[61]

And, reacting to assertions by some members of the Carter administration that their low popularity was partially a result of Carter's insistence on handling "tough" issues, Sidey argued:

> Unwary politicians have been known to be seized by a malady normally found among spiritual leaders. In their relentless pursuit of evil, the lonely champions who bring enlightenment sometimes convince themselves that the more they suffer the better they are.
>
> In the pulpit . . . such an approach to leadership may be effective. But the recent record suggests that it can be an extremely hazardous way to run a republic that has brought the vast majority of its people undreamed of wealth, poise, and awareness.[62]

In June, *Time's* presidency watcher identified Carter's lack of political experience as a source of the president's leadership difficulties. "It is the riddle of leadership. Jimmy Carter's 17 months of training have taught him to appreciate the unnerving complexities of managing power. But his lack of experience still seriously fetters him."[63]

By July, Sidey returned to the theme that Carter's problem was that tendency toward "mastery of detail." Sidey reiterated his belief that Carter's propensity to govern like a spiritual leader was a foundation of the administration's maladies:

> . . . almost everyone attests to his mastery of detail. Carter moralizes when he should calculate and manage, he preaches when he should devise a strategy based on reality. Diplomats claim that Carter cannot see the relationships between events. Politicians claim he misses the psychological impact of his actions.[64]

Other journalists identified reasons for Carter's apparently faltering presidency. In July *Time* magazine declared that Carter's "presidency is in deep trouble. . . . There is a mounting mood in Washington that the Carter presidency may be fundamentally flawed and that the Chief Executive may, despite his widely respected intelligence and dedication, be unable to lead the nation effectively." The magazine offered the following evaluation of the Carter presidency:

> It is Carter's style of leading that may be at the heart of the problem. Although he is Chief of State of the world's most powerful nation, he seems more comfortable wearing his famed cardigan than the mantle of presidential leadership. Perhaps in an attempt to avoid the trappings and pitfalls of the imperial presidency, Carter has been too reluctant to assert himself, to lean on people, to operate, in a sense, with the ruffles and flourishes that this one job of all in the U.S. may demand. As admirable a trait as this may be in many callings, it clearly can be a serious liability for a President who sometimes has no weapon but sheer intimidation to reconcile conflicting interests or overcome congressional and bureaucratic opposition.[65]

The *Wall Street Journal* differed with the viewpoint that Carter's leadership difficulties arose from a peculiar "style" of governing. In an August 4 editorial the *Journal* asked opinion leaders to stop focusing on Carter's inability to build a favorable image:

> President Carter's malaise isn't just some kind of marketing problem. The reason every White House mishap settles so snuggly into the public mind is that the President can't manage to arouse any countervailing enthusiasm for the policies he's trying to promote. And that's because he and his advisers have seriously misread the direction the public mood is traveling.[66]

In a July 30 column Joseph Kraft blamed Carter's efforts early in the term for having created a perception of incompetence. In Kraft's view, Carter's water projects cuts and arms control policies created an unfavorable climate. "On both of those issues, as on a few others, the president was forced to retreat in highly visible ways. He is still retreating, which is why the impression has grown that he is indecisive and hesitant." Kraft added that Carter adopted unrealistic positions creating high expectations. Like the *Journal*, Kraft believed that Carter needed to prove his competence by deeds, not by attention to image making.[67]

Meg Greenfield assessed that "image is a vital, valid concern of anyone who hopes to govern. And image needs cultivation, attention, work." Greenfield attributed Carter's alleged leadership problems to an inability to create a favorable image:

> I think the problem is . . . Carter himself is resisting the creation or imposition of a clear and unambiguous image. By definition, an image is delimiting, partial, restrictive. It involves the prominence of some aspects of a personality or public role at the expense of others. . . . [Carter] resists definition, fights it, really refuses to concede almost any part of the personal or political spectrum of attributes that might be associated with a leader.[68]

Journalists debated the causes of Carter's alleged leadership difficulties. Anthony Lewis believed that not enough press attention was given to factors that created leadership problems in the post-Watergate era:

> Some of Mr. Carter's troubles are no doubt of his own making. He was naive in his expectations of quick reform. He evidently lacks a taste—a Rooseveltian savor—for political maneuver. And so on. The list is familiar.
> But his shortcomings by no means explain the scorn, the savagery of the attacks on him.
> . . . In many areas the problems are harder than they used to be, and the resistance of interest groups to any conceivable solution more intense.[69]

Meg Greenfield recognized many variables making presidential leadership uncertain in the post-Watergate era. She noted such factors as the reported decline of the national party organization, interest group pressures, lack of national spirit, and the lack of a war to unite the people. Greenfield believed that it was the president's duty to reverse the unfavorable trends afflicting America.

> . . . one must begin with the trends, and first among these is the much remarked upon popular loss of confidence in the nation's leaders and institutions.
> The Carter Administration has not exactly reversed the trend or covered itself with glory in this connection.
> . . . as Carter himself concedes . . . somehow the nation needs to recapture the sense of common purpose.
> I think Carter has accelerated the opposite process by an overwillingness to settle claims and demands group by group and to yield to various constituency pressures. And *although the troubles didn't start with him, he represents pretty much the only mechanism that can be used to deal with them now.*[70]

The press portrayal of Carter's presidency as on the verge of "failure" can be understood by examining two areas of continual criticism of the administration: congressional relations and foreign-policymaking. Let's examine press criticism of the Carter administration's efforts in each of these areas from January 1978 until the September Camp David Accords.

Congressional Relations

The administration's efforts to build congressional support for the president's agenda continued to be a source of press criticism. In January 1978, David Broder noted that Carter's first year congressional relations brought forth a now familiar list of criticisms: overloading the congressional agenda, too little consultation with party leaders, wasting the moral force of the presidency on the water projects cuts rather than on energy policy. The result was that "Carter saw much of his 1977 legislative program passed— but got little credit for it because of a few conspicuous failures. His reputation for accomplishment and competence were diminished, not enhanced." Broder expected Carter to adopt a limited, achievable policy agenda in 1978.[71]

At the beginning of 1978 many critics were uncertain whether Carter's congressional relations would improve. In late March 1978 *U.S. News* reported that the administration's "[p]roblems with Capitol Hill have been monumental." Neglecting to identify its measure of legislative success the story continued:

> Carter, in fact, scored only slightly better with Congress in his first year than did Richard Nixon, who was facing a hostile Democratic majority. The Georgian did significantly worse than Democrats Lyndon B. Johnson and John F. Kennedy did.[72]

The news weekly perceived change taking place within the administration. And, "of all the adjustments, none is more important than the need to improve relations with Congress." *U.S. News* described the "Carter team— [as] determined to make mid-course corrections to avoid further problems."

The report concluded that Carter would seek a conciliatory approach toward Congress.[73]

Time magazine also predicted improved White House–congressional relations in 1978. A January 1978 article conceded that renewed congressional assertiveness made presidential leadership of Congress difficult. The article acknowledged that political reform undermined "[t]he old cohesion within Congress" and the traditionally instrumental role of the party leadership in both legislative chambers. Yet the magazine did not view Carter as a victim of circumstances. Rather, Carter "hurt himself further by at first showing little patience with the legislators and by making no real effort to consult with them." Despite these assessments the news article closed somewhat optimistically:

> With Byrd's coaching, Carter and Congress seem headed toward mutual respect this session, though probably not affection. The man from Plains is not the kind of bourbon-sipping, back-slapping politician who gets along easily with the good old boys in Congress. But he intends to work harder at consulting and compromising with them.[74]

The *Wall Street Journal* had a different reason for optimism: the president's resolve to use the veto to control federal spending. The *Journal* perceived this commitment as a move by Carter away from his first year leadership approach in which, "He set out to exercise vigorous leadership of his party, the nation and Congress, rather than merely trying to hold Congress in check." The editorial contended: "The times demand a President who can control, not one whose administration scurries around trying to come up with innovations. . . . The veto is a control weapon. . . . When a President uses it judiciously it signals character and strength of purpose."[75]

Despite some initially optimistic assessments, most press analyses in 1978 reflected the earlier criticisms of Carter's handling of Congress. From the early stages of the new session in Congress up until Camp David, journalists criticized the Carter administration for (1) a lack of sensitivity to conventional political norms; and (2) a lack of political experience at the national level. Among those emphasizing the former view was John W. Mashek of *U.S. News*:

> Carter and his band of Georgians came in determined to change things. They are handicapped, however, by carrying chips on their shoulders about Washington. . . . [T]hey remain proud of their unorthodoxy, their lack of political ideology, their indifference to capital society.[76]

Responding to complaints of congressmen about phone calls not being returned by the White House, Evans and Novak noted other reasons for the "cooling" relations between Carter and Capitol Hill. One reason was Carter's "insensitivity" in forcing congressmen to deal with controversial issues such as the creation of a consumer protection agency. The failure to return phone calls "is barely the tip of the iceberg."[77]

Time magazine found Carter's relations with Congress by July only marginally "improved." In another comparison to 1977, *Time* found that difficulties between the branches persisted:

> During Carter's first year in office, the White House seemed chronically insensitive to congressional egos and needs. Leading congressmen were slighted socially, liaison was poor and the possibilities of horse-trading were ignored. This situation has improved: the liaison staff has been strengthened and Congressmen have been more skillfully courted.
>
> But serious problems between the two branches of government remain. According to Administration critics, the White House still fails to consult adequately with key Congressmen before measures are sent to Capitol Hill.
>
> . . . Indeed, only Jimmy Carter can make these repairs [in congressional relations]. In the American political system of checks and balances among competing interests, he must recognize that the Chief Executive can be effective only if he finds a way to lead vigorously. To do this, he must combine long-range vision with tough management and a willingness to engage in political give and take. In all these areas, despite great personal assets, Carter still has a way to go.[78]

Richard Boeth of *Newsweek* also believed that Carter was not living up to leadership expectations. Boeth found parallels between Carter's difficulties with Congress and earlier troubles with the Georgia legislature:

> In the course of his running war with the Georgia legislature, Governor Jimmy Carter used to rely on persuasion and sweet reason to a point, then take his case rancorously to the countryside. Last week, after seventeen frustrating months in the White House, Carter began playing his Presidency like "Georgia On My Mind."[79]

Six months after his prediction that Carter's relations with Congress would improve in 1978, David Broder proclaimed the president a liability to congressional Democrats. Lamenting the president's continued "neglect" of the party, Broder predicted that Carter would hurt congressional Democrats' reelection chances in 1978. Even if congressional Democrats fared well, Broder assessed, Carter would still be perceived as a liability. In Broder's view, impressive Democratic congressional victories could reaffirm Congress's independence of Carter.[80]

By August *U.S. News* observed that the administration's "domestic program is in shambles." The magazine found congressional Democrats "grinding up the proposals of their own administration one after another, and there's no let up in sight." The report emphasized that Carter was not living up to standards established by his Democratic predecessors. "Carter has seemed reluctant to use presidential muscle with Congress, a tactic that both Johnson and Kennedy were not shy about employing." The article listed other explanations for tenuous White House–congressional relations: Carter's lack of public popularity; controversial proposals being pushed by the president;

most Democratic congressmen ran ahead of Carter in the 1976 elections; and the demise of "the old system of autocratic leadership" in the House.[81]

The major press observation at this time concerned the alleged inexperience and incompetence of the White House staff. In its cover story of July 24, "Carter's 18 Months: What Went Wrong?" *U.S. News* observed that, "The high hopes of a new President have been cut down at home and abroad." After outlining the now familiar list of criticisms of the White House staff, the story concluded optimistically that Carter and his staff "are trying to operate in classic Washington style."[82]

Yet in the same issue of the magazine White House correspondent Jack McWethy offered a less optimistic view. McWethy saw the White House as isolated and dominated by a small band of native Georgians:

Despite charges that the President has a "Georgia wall" around himself, friends from home are strengthening their command at the White House.
[The inner circle's] power seems to be growing, fed by Jimmy Carter's fierce loyalty to the people who came up with him the hard way from the red-clay politics of Georgia.[83]

McWethy noted that the key members of Carter's inner circle were "all Georgians, all former Carter campaigners." He asserted that while Carter turned on occasion to the outside for advice, the "inner circle" was consulted for key decisions.[84] McWethy's major complaint was that these Georgian advisers would not give "lawmakers the deference they demand." For example:

. . . when it comes to thrashing out the roughest issues, it is Jordan, Powell and Rafshoon who are at the President's side, often joined by Eizenstadt, Moore and Kirbo as well. More than 18 months into the Carter Presidency, the so-called Georgia wall is standing firm.[85]

In May, Alan Otten proclaimed the Carter administration "spectacularly inept" and listed the familiar complaints against the Carter staff. Otten believed that staff inexperience hampered the administration's goals.[86] In August the *Journal* columnist assessed that the behavior of the president's aides "has too often been immature and self-indulgent—what Meg Greenfield in *Newsweek* terms 'Peter Pan Politics.'"[87]

Time magazine in May described Carter as still an "enigma" and added that "even those who sympathize with him are not sure what he is trying to do, and this gives them the uneasy feeling that he and his inexperienced staff may not know what they are doing either." The article continued:

. . . only a member of the Establishment knows how it [the political system] really works. The Carter White House has been lamentably short of skilled hands.
. . . the staff lacks heavyweights or even medium-weights to attend to the nation's business. Carter has reached a stage where he needs all the experience he can get. . . . While engaging and energetic, his present staff is not adequate

for the job of running the country nor is it properly supervised and directed from above.[88]

At the end of July *Time's* analysis of the White House staff continued in a similar manner:

> The White House staff reflects Carter's lack of success as a Government manager. . . . The tightly knit and provincial Georgia mafia, which dominates the staff and enjoys the best access to the President, has slowed Carter's integration into the Washington scene and has limited his effectiveness. . . . [The Carter] Administration's ignorance of Washington's ways (something Carter elevated into a virtue during his campaign) has made cooperation between the two branches even harder.[89]

The *Washington Post* identified the Carter administration's isolation as a source of the president's difficulty working with Congress. The deadlock on energy policy, the *Post* argued, called for Carter to "deal directly with and continuously with Congress. . . . The President is not particularly good at that kind of bargaining."[90] The *Post* criticized Carter's tendency to devise in private policy solutions "while the waiting multitude wondered what was going on." In the editor's view, such attempts at "comprehensive" solutions and "rational codification" rarely work in politics.[91]

Finally, the *Post's* Marquis Childs defended the press's harsh assessments of the administration's political acumen despite protests from Anthony Lewis and other Carter sympathizers:

> The pounding President Carter has been taking from many of us in the press centers on the lack of experience in high policy of the president himself and the Georgia followers he brought into the White House. The result has been delay, indecisiveness and an outflow of moral suasion as a substitute for policy.[92]

Foreign Policy

Journalists subjected the Carter administration's foreign policymaking to considerable criticism during the same time frame (early 1978 through August 1978). The administration claimed some foreign policy victories during this period, including the lifting of the Turkish arms embargo and a major Middle-East arms package. Carter even appeared to accept the *Wall Street Journal's* advice in vetoing a defense authorization bill as a means of exhibiting his seriousness about holding down federal spending. Despite these efforts, journalists chided the administration for failing to adopt a coherent, consistent foreign policy.

David Broder, for example, found foreign policymaking in the Carter White House "unsettling." Broder assessed that

> . . . unlike most of his predecessors back to Harry Truman, Carter has not clearly designated a single center for foreign policy decision-making outside

the Oval Office. There is no one with authority approaching that exercised in the past by a George Marshall, a Dean Acheson, a John Foster Dulles, or a Henry Kissinger.[93]

Joseph Kraft also noted that Carter's foreign policy approach deviated from the approaches of earlier administrations. Combined with the president's inexperience, Kraft argued, the failure to identify a single spokesman for the administration's foreign policy caused grave problems:

. . . the president himself is a tyro in foreign policy, not only unpracticed in diplomacy but also without even a good working knowledge of recent history. Indeed his personal inexperience is the main reason why the tilting back and forth between advisers has generated serious misgivings in a capital that normally takes rivalry at the top for granted.
    The intimate involvement in day-to-day foreign policy by a president with so little experience and grasp is dangerous. So the sensible thing for Carter would be to follow two previous presidents not versed in foreign policy— Truman and Eisenhower—who placed prime reliance on the secretary of state.[94]

Meg Greenfield argued that Carter's problems in foreign policymaking could be attributed to a failure to articulate a clear vision or set of priorities. Greenfield observed:

. . . I think Jimmy Carter needs sorely to articulate to the country and to the rest of the world what his Administration takes our vital interests and priorities in foreign affairs to be, and to formulate consistent, unambiguous steps to protect and advance them.[95]

A number of other critics viewed Carter's foreign policy as confused and without a clear direction. Karen Elliot House of the *Wall Street Journal* discussed the lack of consistency in Carter's human rights policies, a situation causing confusion abroad about the direction of U.S. foreign policy.[96] *U.S. News* reported prior to Carter's June 1978 economic summit in Europe that, "It's the President's inconsistency in handling critical issues . . . that troubles America's allies on the eve of a summit meeting."[97] Two weeks later the news weekly featured a cover story, "Tug of War Over Foreign Policy," which emphasized the internal struggles between Vance, Brzezinski and Brown for control of the administration's foreign policy.[98]

After Carter's June 7, 1978, speech at the U.S. Naval Academy in Annapolis, Maryland, outlining U.S.–Soviet foreign policy, some critics believed that the president had made the necessary changes. In its June 12 issue *Time* declared that the speech not only represented a major policy change (from conciliation to confrontation) but that Carter had elevated Brzezinski over Vance as the major force behind U.S. foreign policy.[99] Four weeks later *Time* declared once again that Carter's foreign policy had come together, only this time the magazine reported that Vance, not Brzezinski, emerged as Carter's principal foreign policy spokesman:

Shades of T.R.! After weeks of tough talk, apparent inconsistency, and the alarms about a revival of the cold war, the Administration last week seemed to have got its foreign policy act together. The policy, to put it in the simplest terms: speak a little more softly but carry a big stick.

The soft talk came chiefly from Secretary of State Cyrus Vance, who seemed to be making speeches and appearances everywhere as the Administration pointedly thrust him forward as President Carter's chief foreign policy spokesman. Lest there be any confusion, Zbigniew Brzezinski, the toughest talker of recent weeks, was keeping unusually quiet, turning down all requests for on-the-record interviews.

. . . The need for clarification had become palpable as observers in Washington and Moscow puzzled over which voice was articulating U.S. foreign policy.[100]

Three weeks later *Time* declared that "U.S.-Soviet relations have sunk to the lowest point in years." The news weekly attributed the reinvigoration of the cold war primarily to the administration's lack of consistency in foreign policy and to the president's inability to clearly articulate his foreign policy priorities.[101]

A number of journalists criticized Carter's Soviet policy. Evans and Novak found that the president's "vacillation" on the neutron bomb decision as well as the cancellation of the B-1 bomber undermined the United States' international leadership credibility.[102] In addition to accusations of indecisiveness, Evans and Novak blamed Carter for failing to respond to "the current Soviet worldwide offensive." The columnists, reacting to the president's "non-response" to warnings from the Afghan regime that a Soviet takeover was imminent, portrayed Carter as a leader unwilling to jeopardize SALT or a summit meeting with the Soviet leader.[103] George F. Will added that many Carter administration officials "think the United States is as much a threat to world peace as communist powers are."[104]

On the anniversary of Carter's foreign policy address at Notre Dame University (May 22), the *Wall Street Journal* lamented the "dangers" of the administration's continuing lack of resolution in dealing with the Soviet threat.[105] Two weeks later a *Journal* editorial praised the perceived change in the direction of United States foreign policy in favor of treating the Soviet offensive seriously. The editors noted that for "right now it seems that the President has been acting rather quickly to extricate himself from themes of the past year. . . ."[106] A June 12 *Journal* editorial returned to the former theme and lamented, once again, the administration's lack of resolution in dealing with the Soviets. The editorial writers believed Carter unwisely chose not to link acceptance of a SALT treaty to Soviet worldwide behavior.[107] Finally, by early July the *Journal*, in response to the Soviets' arrest of a United States businessman in Moscow, blasted Carter's failure to respond firmly to the action. The editorial concluded that there was only a "facade" of United States firmness under Carter's leadership.[108]

The *Journal* also criticized the president for vetoing a $37 billion defense procurement authorization because of the inclusion of an additional, and costly ($2 billion), nuclear aircraft carrier. The newspaper portrayed the decision as harmful to the national security and an indication that "the administration is striking an alliance with the anti-military faction in Congress."[109] Despite earlier praise of Carter for resolving to veto costly programs as a means of controlling public spending, the *Journal* found no substantial evidence to support the president's decision on the defense spending bill. The newspaper portrayed the decision in four separate editorials as a frivolous effort by the president to look "strong" by vetoing something. The *Journal* claimed that Gerald Rafshoon convinced Carter that such an action would make the president appear in command.[110] In the wake of Congress's failure to override the veto in September the *Journal* criticized the "administration's willingness to dissemble on defense issues in pursuit of image politics. . . ."[111]

The verdict on the veto was mixed. Evans and Novak echoed the *Journal's* sentiment that the veto was an attempt to project an image of toughness. "But in getting tough [Carter] has risked losing major defense items obtained as trade-offs for the carrier in the intricate congressional log-rolling process."[112] *Time* magazine found virtue in the veto which exhibited Carter's new "combativeness." According to the magazine's report, "Carter's combativeness—if it works—comes none too soon."[113]

As with the Panama Canal treaties victories, a few subsequent foreign policy achievements did not result in any reassessment of Carter's legislative or foreign affairs leadership. Congressional victories in May on the Middle East arms package proposal were, according to *Time*, victories which "never seem to come easy for Jimmy Carter."[114] The final vote in the Senate (54–44 in favor) was a "hard won and welcome victory for Jimmy Carter."[115] *U.S. News* saw the victories as indicative of the president having finally accepted "old-fashioned politics." Yet, the magazine concluded, "most people are withholding judgment on whether the 'new' President is an improvement over the one they have been seeing over the last 16 months."[116]

Carter's narrow legislative victory in August on the lifting of the Turkish arms embargo (208–205 in the House) earned the president, *Time* reported, "passing grades for leadership."[117] *Time* viewed the vote as "a major victory for President Carter's foreign policy."[118] The same weeks that these reports appeared in *Time* the other two national news weeklies covered major stories on Carter's continuing problems leading Congress.[119]

Apparently a more dramatic achievement by the administration was required to fundamentally alter press perceptions of Carter's leadership abilities. Such a turnaround in the assessments of Carter's leadership came after the conclusion of the Camp David Middle East treaties in September 1978.

The Camp David Treaties: Carter's "Born-Again" Leadership

The major press assessment of the Camp David achievement is that Carter's presidency was dramatically revived, or, in the words of many journalists, "born-again." The press anticipated that the president, as a result of Camp David, would be recognized as a formidable leader. While some critics warned that inflation could erode Carter's elevated stature, the immediate post–Camp David environment in the press was nearly euphoric.

About four weeks prior to the Camp David summit with Anwar Sadat and Menachem Begin, the *Wall Street Journal* praised the president's assertion that the world should not expect too much from the negotiations. The *Journal* found this comment a prudent accommodation to reality and concluded: "Our own guess is that the September summit's success will be measured mainly by the absence of negative consequences."[120] The *Journal* later acknowledged that Carter's achievement far exceeded this modest measure of success. A September 19 editorial noted that Carter's success exhibited his leadership and revived the chance for peace in a troubled land:

> President Carter has won a genuine achievement at the Camp David summit. . . . So at Camp David Mr. Carter was able to demonstrate not only a capability of taking command of events, but also personal flexibility and growing understanding. . . . Mr. Carter did revive hopes for peace in an atmosphere from which those hopes had all but disappeared, and that is no small cause for gratitude.[121]

The *Journal*'s front page "Washington Wire" column on September 8 hinted at a possible Carter comeback resulting from the Camp David talks. "The meeting shows Carter looking presidential, grappling with intractable issues." The column noted that this action could translate into future legislative successes on other matters such as Civil Service reform.[122]

In her September 18 report Karen Elliot House of the *Journal* exclaimed: "The agreement is clearly a major accomplishment for President Carter, who doggedly refused to allow the negotiators to give up without progress."[123] House wrote that the treaty enhanced Carter's stature:

> Besides enhancing his international prestige, the competence he has shown at making peace between the Mideast's longtime enemies promises to bolster his sunken domestic political standing; it helps refute the criticism that he isn't up to the job of President and promises to heal his rift with the American Jewish community.[124]

Norman C. Miller described Carter's role in the summit as an act of "true statesmanship" that greatly benefited the president's policy agenda. He applauded the president's "effective leadership" and "remarkable courage." Miller believed that the president improved prospects for future international negotiations (e.g., with the Soviets on arms control) and negotiations at home (e.g., with the Senate over SALT). As to the criticism of Carter's ability to lead, the *Journal* columnist stated, "Camp David changed all that."

> [Carter's] often-criticized habit of immersing himself in the details of problems was vindicated in this case.
> . . . it was the President's intimate participation in the vexing details of the negotiations that finally brought the parties together against great odds. Thus,

Mr. Carter has effectively answered the scornful charge that he is little more than an engineer tinkering with the mechanics of problems and lacking the savvy to fashion broadly acceptable policies.
. . . Mr. Carter has dispelled the doubts about his ability to handle great issues. . . . *No longer will there be a receptive audience for those debilitating stories about Mr. Carter's "ineptitude."* How can anyone deride as inept a President who has established the conditions for peaceful settlement of the most intractable crisis in the world?[125]

A *New York Times* editorial confessed that pundits and establishmentarians had underestimated the president. The editorial exclaimed that Camp David was not the only evidence of Carter's astute leadership. Carter also deserved credit for civil service reform, urban reform, and a "meaningful energy program."

Washington is a fickle mistress and anyone who doubts that is invited to recall what was being said about Jimmy Carter not so many days ago.
. . . What Jimmy Carter brought off in the twelve long days at Camp David demonstrates how skillful he has become at the substance of diplomacy—and how adept at political imagery to boot.
. . . Washington's faddish cynicism [shouldn't] obscure the fact Mr. Carter is entitled to recognition for winning several big ones, not just Camp David.
"I think you misread your President," Israeli Defense Minister Weizman said today. He may be right and it may be that Jimmy Carter's most important achievement at Camp David is that he has earned a new opportunity to be judged not by mood but by merit.[126]

Hedrick Smith found that in the aftermath of the Camp David summit the president projected confidence, "a boldness that sometimes seems bordering on cockiness." The president "was crisp, confident and commanding in dealing with the press." The *Times* reporter observed Carter's "increasingly self-assured tone toward Congress." Smith concluded that Carter was nearly a transformed leader, projecting a tough image instead of the image of a president who backed down whenever challenged by Congress.[127]

The *Washington Post* praised Carter after the conclusion of what its editorial called, "The Jimmy Carter Conference."

He did a beautiful piece of work. He saw possibilities that few others saw, took risks that he did not have to take and set a model of disinterested dedication that let him call for concessions that were simply unforeseen. There will be a richly earned boost to his presidency and to the stature of the United States in the world.[128]

The national news weeklies appeared exuberant in their assessments of Carter after the Camp David summit. As with the news dailies, the discussion of a revived presidency prevailed. Tom Mathews' *Newsweek* report "Born Again!" observed:

His hideaway summitry had all but demolished the public perception that he was a well-meaning amateur who simply couldn't cope with the demands of the Presidency.

. . . the success of Camp David had restored the leaderly image he needed to get on with his job. He could no longer be taxed so heavily for clumsy handling of politicians, when he had dealt so successfully with Begin and Sadat. *His relish for immersing himself in minutiae no longer seemed quite so eccentric or misplaced. His reputation as the nation's quickest study had been redeemed overnight.* . . . If Carter can maintain the Camp David glow, he may indeed have a born-again hold on the White House.[129] (emphasis added)

In the same edition of *Newsweek* (October 2) Susan Fraker enthusiastically recounted Carter's "overnight" revival. Carter "erased his image as a can't cope amateur hopelessly out of depth in the White House." While inflation could diminish Carter's public standing, "for the moment, a born-again Jimmy Carter had won the long-in-coming esteem of his countrymen—and perhaps salvaged his own presidency in the process."[130] Tom Mathews agreed with Fraker's assessment concerning the role of inflation: "If inflation doesn't undo Carter, his new era of good feeling could last for quite a while."[131]

U.S. News described Camp David as "a turning point for Jimmy Carter's Presidency." The news report asserted that Carter established himself as a formidable leader:

As a result of the framework for Mideast peace he engineered between Egypt and Israel, the President has gained new respect in Congress and will win more legislative battles.

Internationally, Carter now will be taken more seriously as a tough bargainer who has the drive and the skills to get what he wants.

Politically, the President has reestablished himself as the leader of his party, sought after as a speaker. Potential challengers for the Democratic presidential nomination in 1980 may think twice about taking him on. Snipers within the party will hold their fire. . . .[132]

U.S. News's Jack McWethy described Camp David as Carter's "finest hour." McWethy attributed the achievement to the president's ability to work privately in negotiations with small groups of people: "Carter kept all the working groups small, the kind of close quarters where his intense, probing personality could have maximum impact."[133] In a following issue *U.S. News* declared the president an asset to congressional Democrats seeking reelection.[134]

Time magazine noted the importance of the summit to Carter. *Time* reported that "all the participants deserve high marks for the extraordinary effort the summit represented, and none more so than Jimmy Carter. Alone of the principals he should benefit at home from an unequivocal, sorely needed and well-earned rise in the esteem—and the opinion polls—of his countrymen. His summit . . . moved the troubled Middle-East a little closer to peace—and a little farther from war."[135] Noting a sudden rise in Carter's prestige and popularity, the magazine reiterated a common theme: "It was a born-again presidency for Jimmy Carter." *Time* predicted more legislative victories for the president and added that among our allies "Carter had acquired new stature." The news reporter attributed the summit achievement to Carter's "mixture of idealism, tenacity, and mastery of detail."[136]

Other *Time* magazine articles established the relationship between the Camp David achievement and subsequent votes in Congress favorable to the president.[137] Yet the magazine warned that inflation could undermine Carter's new popularity: "Carter had definitely staged a comeback since his summer of discontent. . . . If inflation is not brought under control, many of Carter's other accomplishments could be quickly—if unfairly—forgotten."[138]

The nation's opinion page writers also cheered Carter's Camp David achievement. Joseph Kraft, who initially feared the president would undermine the peace process by seeking a "comprehensive" solution,[139] proclaimed after the summit that Carter "had unsaid the charge that he is 'inept in foreign policy.'" Kraft added:

> He is in a far better position now to elicit support from Japan and the European allies. He can deal much more confidently with Russia, particularly in arms control. At the least, accordingly, the Camp David summit marks for Jimmy Carter a first, big step toward realizing the promise of his presidency.[140]

Economic affairs columnist Hobart Rowen believed that the treaty enhanced Carter's economic policy leadership:

> President Carter's spectacular success at Camp David not only gives his personal prestige a needed boost at a critical time, but also renews the image of the United States as a commanding world power.
> . . . by getting a framework for Mideast peace, Carter at one stroke has enhanced confidence in his ability to handle international and domestic economic problems, including the sagging dollar and persistent inflation.[141]

Evans and Novak declared the Camp David summit "a dramatic display of U.S. mediation unprecedented in American history." They charged Carter to expand the "promise of Camp David" into a lasting Mideast peace. The columnists noted that such an accomplishment would make Carter "a leader to be reckoned with."[142] By early November Evans and Novak declared Carter had, at least temporarily, "restored his presidency." In this view, "in these final days of the 1978 campaign, Carter exudes an image of presidentiality not visible in the darker days of summer."[143]

Marvin Stone of *U.S. News* proclaimed that the significance of "President Carter's extraordinary diplomatic achievement . . . is that, for all practical purposes, the tortuous 30-year Mideast war could be ended by Christmas." Stone saw the agreement as a signal of new hope for the Mideast and for the Carter presidency:

President Carter deserves high marks for starting a process that holds out the hope of ending the futile cycle of bloodshed. In achieving this impressive success, the President displayed a realism and diplomatic skill conspicuously lacking in the conduct of Administration foreign policy in the past.

. . . It is to be hoped that the Camp David summit may someday be remembered as the transformation of Jimmy Carter into a realistic and effective statesman.[144]

Tom Wicker described Carter as a "redeemed" president. According to Wicker, "not in modern history has so spectacular an achievement so quickly redeemed a President whose standing had been so low." Wicker continued:

[Carter now has] a renewed public sense of him as a forceful and courageous leader able to rise above the usual precautions and maneuvers of politics to fight for what he believes in. That is his real gain from the summit and other recent victories.[145]

David Broder changed his earlier assessment that Carter was a liability to congressional Democrats seeking reelection in 1978. Broder reported that congressmen who previously distanced themselves from the president began to associate more freely with him. Yet Broder complained that in the post–Camp David euphoria only President Carter was being modest about the summit achievement. The columnist asked Carter to forego that "down home" style and allow people to admire their leader openly. "Somebody should tell Carter it is not unconstitutional for people to look up to their president."[146]

Hugh Sidey agreed that the American tendency to admire our presidents "is a phenomenon as old as the Republic but mercifully just as valid today as 202 [sic] years ago." Sidey added:

A successful summit in the Maryland mountains is not a cure for Carter's leadership problem. But surely it is a kind of achievement at the critical time needed to bring people a little closer to their President, to silence for the moment a lot of petty grievances that grew bigger than they should have because of Carter's fumbling.

He will surely see as never before that it is the President and only the President who can give an Administration, indeed a nation, direction and force. As Americans cheer his Camp David achievement, Jimmy Carter with luck and wisdom could be born again a second time in a way that could lift this nation as well as himself. Men in public service are nourished by justified public acclaim. Carter's time has at last come.[147]

James Reston used the Camp David achievement as an opportunity to discuss the fickle nature of Washington-based opinion. Reston observed that "this city changes its mood almost as fast as it changes its clothes." The *Times* columnist pointed out the president's earlier fall in public opinion

. . . was clearly eroding his capacity to govern. If he couldn't get his major bills through a Congress dominated by large Democratic majorities and was challenged by these same majorities on the conduct of foreign and defense policy, how could he lead the nation at home or abroad?

His success at the Camp David Middle East conference . . . turned this around, but maybe this is a good time to recall Murphy's Second Law of Politics, namely, that nothing in Washington is ever quite as good or bad as the popular opinion of the moment.[148]

Robert G. Kaiser did not adopt an optimistic view of Carter's leadership after Camp David. The title of Kaiser's column reveals its substance: "Has Anything Changed—Except the Polls?" Kaiser assessed that "despite Camp David, Carter's record thus far is dominated by his failure to exercise effective political leadership."

Camp David demonstrated that Carter is an effective negotiator, a master of intricate detail and a man of nerve. Those are qualities that his associates have been attributing to him throughout his presidency, and the summit at least provided an opportunity for them to shine. All those skills could contribute to effective political leadership, but none of them guarantee it, alone or together. That is Carter's problem.[149]

This somewhat unfavorable evaluation of Carter proved the exception in the post–Camp David press assessments. Eventually, though, the unflattering press views of the Carter administration reemerged. In the press evaluations of Carter's leadership of the 95th Congress can be seen further evidence of how Camp David temporarily changed perceptions of the Carter presidency. The retrospective analyses of Carter's second year were generally less favorable than the earlier reviews of the 95th Congress. In the end of year assessments, generally three to four months after Camp David, the negative pre–Camp David perceptions of the Carter administration began to reappear.

Carter at Midterm

The 95th Congress

Journalists favorably assessed Carter's legislative relations at the end of the 95th Congress. Many of these assessments emphasized the view that the president succeeded in dealing with Congress because the Carter White House learned to work constructively with political Washington. Joseph Kraft, for example, argued that the Carter administration successfully concluded the 95th Congress because the president learned from earlier mistakes and abandoned the quest for far-reaching comprehensive solutions.[150]

Susan Fraker observed that after months of criticism of Carter as "an amateur politician unable to wheel and deal with Congress," the administration could claim several major victories in the 95th Congress. The president could claim a "most impressive record in foreign policy." Fraker assessed that "Carter has finally shown his willingness and ability to horse-trade, cajole and threaten his way to legislative victories."[151]

B. Drummond Ayres reported that while the Carter administration's record in the 95th Congress was not impressive, by the end of that session congressmen respected the president. Ayres credited Carter's new political tactics for the turnaround:

> [Carter] did not get along well with the 95th Congress. Most members considered his demand for action on a lengthy list of [issues] . . . far too ambitious for a single Congress. They were irked by his seeming unwillingness to compromise and by the sometimes amateurish efforts of the lobbyists.
> For the first 18 months of the two-year session, many members of the House and Senate . . . openly laughed at the President's efforts to get action on his agenda. By adjournment Sunday, the laughter had died. The President had learned in the final months to wheel and deal, and the House and Senate had come to respect his new found ability.[152]

Times columnist Terrence Smith gave Carter's legislative record high grades. "Looking back on the two sessions of the 95th Congress, Mr. Carter could take comfort in a record that clearly exceeded what he had been expected to achieve."[153] And Hedrick Smith declared the atmosphere in the nation's capital "transformed":

> . . . this fall . . . will probably become known as the period when Jimmy Carter strengthened his Presidency by exercising power with more robust self-confidence.
> . . . the first term of the Carter Presidency has now gained greater coherence and sharper definition.
> . . . the Carter White House has shown greater agility and dispelled some of the earlier charges of incompetence.
> . . . Mr. Carter has shaken the crippling image of incompetence by working out the Israeli-Egyptian accord at Camp David with his mediation.
> . . . the atmosphere here in Washington has been transformed. No longer do other politicians talk so glibly of a one-term Carter Presidency.[154]

U.S. News perceived a renewed sense of confidence within the Carter White House after Camp David, two successful vetoes, and legislative victories on civil service reform, tax, and energy policy. The news story added that "Carter is gaining enough stature to at least partially fill the leadership vacuum created on Capitol Hill."[155]

At the end of the 95th Congress the *Washington Post* reflected on Carter's earlier leadership difficulties and eventual successes:

> He came to Washington rather like an emissary . . . to a strange foreign capital on whose institutions and mores he intended to impose his own superior design. He found that the establishment was fragmented and parochial, resistant to designs not of its own hand. . . .

. . . he was able to turn events to his own advantage. The upshot is the hard-won respect in which he is basking now that the 95th Congress has gone home. He is widely perceived to be a "presidential" president at last.

Now, domestic performance—especially bargaining with Congress—is the chief measure by which Washington, if not the country at large, sizes a president.

He has stopped demanding that Congress overhaul just about every major social program simultaneously. It is not, however, that he has caved in entirely to the "old" politics. What ostensibly savvy politician would, for instance, have vetoed a public-works bill or undertaken a serious civil service reform? It·was in his own way that he finally came to terms with the 95th Congress.

His strong finish (in the 95th Congress) makes it possible, for the first time since Lyndon Johnson's political heyday, to imagine that the American system can enjoy the crucial element of a strong president.[156]

End of the Year Assessments

The assessments of Carter's presidency at midterm were generally consistent with the above analyses of the 95th Congress. Of the critics who perceived the president as becoming an effective leader many attributed this turnaround to Carter's newfound political skills including patronage politics, bargaining with Congress, and limiting the public agenda. It is interesting to note that Carter received very little, if any, credit for doing these things until after Camp David. And after Camp David, Carter received recognition for a number of legislative accomplishments that previously went unrecognized. *U.S. News*'s story, "Carter at Midterm: New Goals, New Tactics," reported:

> The Jimmy Carter starting the last half of his term is a vastly changed man from the fledgling President who entered the White House two years ago. Although intimates insist that his basic goals remain unaltered, Carter has yielded to blunt political realities by lowering his sights and drastically restraining the reformist zeal with which he first approached the task of leading the government.
>
> Carter now takes pains to pay homage to Congress—consulting, bargaining and bending—after a start in which he virtually ignored the wishes and sensibilities of lawmakers, with disastrous consequences to his legislative programs.
>
> The President even plays up to leaders of the Democratic Party these days.
> . . .
> The President's seeming endless list of high priorities has been scaled down to more realistic proportions.[157]

The *New York Times* also discussed approvingly the development of Carter's presidency over two years:

> In his freshman year, Mr. Carter behaved like any new student eager to conquer all subjects at once. He proclaimed policies for everything—energy, welfare, nuclear nonproliferation. There was an amateurish assumption that accomplishment lay in the quality of the analysis rather than in success on Capitol

Hill. The Administration soon learned the difficulty of the latter. In his Sophomore year, Mr. Carter thinned out his wish list—and achieved many of his goals.[158]

Dennis A. Williams of *Newsweek* offered a similar view of Carter as having grown into the job of president:

. . . though Carter may be largely unloved by Democratic regulars, he has dramatically improved his standing with the party. Six months ago, he did little fund raising, dispensed few patronage jobs and was widely viewed as out of his depth in the White House . . . His Camp David summitry and late legislative success defused the competency question, and Carter has been much more willing recently to play the party game.[159]

In separate December 31 columns Joseph Kraft and David Broder each portrayed Carter as a maturing president. Joseph Kraft noted: "In both domestic and foreign affairs, the Carter administration moved from losing positions that bred public doubt to winning positions that began to inspire confidence."[160] Broder noted signs of "growth" and "maturity" in the Carter administration. The columnist found a "transition from the mentality of campaigning to the consciousness of governing, from striking a pose to taking a stand."[161] Broder also noted that Carter's "skills have developed in the period of apprenticeship, and the priorities for him are perhaps clearer now than they were two years ago."[162]

Despite Camp David, by midterm a number of Carter's critics returned to earlier themes in the press assessments of the administration: Jimmy Carter was still an enigma; the administration still lacked a sense of policy priorities; the White House staff still had poor relations with political Washington. *Time* magazine recognized Carter's "impressive string of victories" yet perceived the president as "an enigmatic leader of uncertain political philosophy. He is not inspirational by nature, and is not likely ever to be a charismatic commander."[163] And the *Wall Street Journal* considered Carter to be "as much an enigma as when he took office. One might even say more of an enigma." The *Journal* continued: "It has been an administration of multiple confusions, reflective in part of the multiple confusions of our times."[164]

The most critical assessments of Carter's performance at midterm came from Hedrick Smith and Norman C. Miller. Smith acknowledged improvements in White House operations such as the addition of politically experienced individuals to the liaison staff and the limiting of policy priorities, yet still found Carter plagued by the kinds of problems journalists identified prior to Camp David:

. . . there is a feeling abroad and in Washington that Mr. Carter is often more at the mercy of events than he is their master.

With his engineer's penchant for problem solving, he has produced lists of solutions for lists of problems without generating broad political inspiration or framing a public philosophy for the country.

Personally, Mr. Carter has established a reputation as a decent, honest, intelligent, hardworking President with laudable instincts for good government. But he has yet to establish a rapport with the electorate. He appeals to reason rather than stirring public passions, perhaps because political evangelism is not his style. With his manager's eye, he has focused on process and structure but has not offered an inspiring vision.[165]

In a midterm assessment of the administration entitled "Carter's Failure," Norman C. Miller argued that the president lacked "the intangible gift of leadership that inspires people to think that he can make a difference." Among Carter's alleged leadership problems were: the president's poor speaking ability, his lack of a clear vision for the future, and inept White House public relations:

Mr. Carter is just a bland, even boring presence, intelligent, no doubt, honest, unquestionably, hard-working and well-intentioned, surely.

Such qualities are admirable, of course, but they are not enough. To be successful, a President or any political leader must somehow inspire people to believe that his efforts and policies will make a tangible difference in their lives. President Carter, so far, has failed to do this.[166]

Conclusion

By the end of 1978 some journalists again began to doubt the president's leadership abilities. A number of columns noted that without an economic recovery Carter's fortunes would decline. Journalists defined the president's ability to handle the economy as a major leadership test. In December 1978 *Time* reported that, "Jimmy Carter is preparing for what may be the biggest battle of his presidency. . . . Carter's political fortune largely depends on his success in curbing federal spending and the inflation it breeds."[167] Hugh Sidey declared that the inflation battle would make or break Carter's presidency:

Carter has been compelled to choose, the very crux of leadership. He has declared inflation the principal adversary of America.

. . . In a sense Carter seems at last to have experienced "his Bay of Pigs"— the kind of crisis that historians tell us bares the true stuff of Presidents, forcing them to search out the bedrock of their own convictions, to urge the nation toward the same conclusions, to make decisions that totally involve the presidential mind and heart; decisions that, if waffled later, could produce national trauma and personal eclipse.[168]

What is most evident in the 1978 assessments of the Carter presidency is their fluctuating nature. For several months (April through August) the critical commentaries on the "failing" presidency of Jimmy Carter seemed to prevail. Then came a revival of the Carter image after Camp David (September). Yet the negative evaluation of Jimmy Carter identified earlier, that of the politically inept and inexperienced leader, never disappeared completely. By the end of 1978 the generally negative assessments of the Carter presidency returned.

A number of critical commentaries can be attributed to journalists' expectations of Jimmy Carter. Again in 1978 can be seen the danger posed by a president explicitly establishing the criteria by which he should be judged. This danger was evident in the outcry over the firing of United States Attorney David Marston. Although the firing was not unusual and involved no wrongdoing by the administration, Carter was strictly held to a seemingly absolute standard he established for himself in the 1976 campaign: not to allow "political" considerations to influence decisions regarding the Justice Department.

The unsubstantiated allegations of staff aide Hamilton Jordan's improprieties provide additional examples. The press's expectation that Jimmy Carter would hold his staff to the strictest standards of ethical and personal conduct in office undoubtedly contributed to the strong reaction to seemingly trivial gossip-column innuendoes about Jordan's social behavior.

The Panama Canal treaties accomplishment is also revealing. Journalistic reactions to these legislative victories show that by publicly affirming an apolitical, uncompromising style Carter perhaps created for himself a no-win situation. Journalists initially condemned Carter for avoiding traditional legislative arm-twisting techniques. When it appeared to journalists that Carter abandoned his moral high ground to strike a few bargains with Senators wavering on the Canal vote, journalists condemned him for breaking a campaign position.

The more general expectations of presidential leadership and performance become easier to identify in 1978 than in Carter's first year. Journalists evaluated Carter's performance according to a set of expectations such as (a) the need for a coherent foreign policy approach influenced mainly by one rather than many minds; (b) the need for constant negotiation and compromise with members of Congress; (c) the need to adopt a limited, achievable policy agenda combined with a clear strategy of developing support; (d) the need to incorporate Washington "insiders" into the White House decision making process.

Journalists portrayed the Carter administration in 1978 as failing to fulfill the above expectations. Many journalists did acknowledge improvements in White House operations such as the inclusion of Democratic Party leader Robert Strauss in the decision making process and some personnel and tactical changes in the congressional liaison outfit. But for the most part, despite the temporary relief from criticism provided by Camp David, journalists maintained a negative view of the Carter presidency throughout 1978.

Notes

1. Joseph Kraft, "Appraising Carter's First Year," *Washington Post*, January 3, 1978, p. A17.

2. "In Congress the Mood Will Even Get Feistier," *U.S. News and World Report*, December 26, 1977/January 2, 1978, pp. 33–34.

3. "Winging His Way Into '78," *Time*, January 9, 1978, pp. 9–11.

4. David Broder, "A Battle Plan for the President," *Washington Post*, January 20, 1978, pp. A1, 15.

5. David Broder, "A Retreat From Vulnerable Positions," *Washington Post*, January 20, 1978, pp. A1, 15.

6. "The State of Mr. Carter's Country," *New York Times*, January 22, 1978, p. E18.

7. Hedrick Smith, "President's Address: Modest Proposals Along With Cautious Caveat," *New York Times*, January 20, 1978, p. 11.

8. "The State of the Union: A Theory of Limited Government," *Washington Post*, January 21, 1978, p. A16.

9. "That Mishandled Marston Affair," *Time*, February 6, 1978, pp. 30, 33.

10. Hedrick Smith, "Lower Carter Horizons May Raise Performance," *New York Times*, January 29, 1978, p. E1.

11. Norman C. Miller, "Ridicule Threatens to Erode Support for the President," *Wall Street Journal*, February 24, 1978, p. 10. See also on this issue, "The Marston Mess," *Washington Post*, January 23, 1978, p. A22.

12. Rowland Evans and Robert Novak, "The Marston Case: How to Make a Crisis," *Washington Post*, January 19, 1978, p. 25.

13. "The Marston Question," *Wall Street Journal*, February 2, 1978, p. 14.

14. Hugh Sidey, "A Mutation of the Cornpone Syndrome," *Time*, October 31, 1977, p. 15.

15. Ibid.

16. Meg Greenfield, "Georgians on My Mind," *Newsweek*, January 16, 1978, p. 88.

17. Meg Greenfield, "Peter Pan Politics," *Newsweek*, July 31, 1978, p. 76.

18. "Ham and Amaretto," *Newsweek*, March 6, 1978, p. 28.

19. George F. Will, "Hamilton On the Town," *Newsweek*, March 6, 1978, p. 108.

20. Hugh Sidey, "A Troublesome Question of Class," *Time*, March 6, 1978, p. 20.

21. "Tabulations of Harried Ham," *Time*, March 6, 1978, p. 19.

22. "Ham Jordan: Carter's Unorthodox 'Right Arm,'" *U.S. News and World Report*, February 27, 1978, p. 33.

23. Norman C. Miller, "Ridicule Threatens to Erode Support for the President," *Wall Street Journal*, February 24, 1978, p. 10.

24. David Broder, "Power, Glory—and 'Many Dangers,'" *Washington Post*, March 1, 1978, p. A23.

25. Rowland Evans and Robert Novak, "Hamilton Jordan: A Question of Competence, Not Arrogance," *Washington Post*, March 3, 1978, p. A23.

26. "Lay Off Jimmy Carter," *Wall Street Journal*, April 28, 1978, p. 16.

27. Hugh Sidey, "Does Congress Need a Nanny?" *Time*, March 27, 1978, p. 13.

28. "Carter's Panama Triumph," *U.S. News and World Report*, March 27, 1978, p. 27.

29. "After Carter's Panama Victory," *U.S. News and World Report*, May 1, 1978, p. 25. See also, "Carter's Panama Woes," *U.S. News and World Report*, April 24, 1978, p. 34.

30. "Carter Wins on Panama," *Time*, March 27, 1978, pp. 8–11.

31. "Carter's Balance Sheet: A Panama Plus, but Overall, There Are Still Too Many Minuses," *Time*, May 1, 1978, p. 11.

32. Richard Steele, "Heading For a Win," *Newsweek*, February 13, 1978, p. 18.

33. Peter Goldman, "Tough Talk From the Boss," *Newsweek*, May 1, 1978, p. 22.
34. "Panama: Some Second Thoughts," *Washington Post*, April 21, 1978, p. A20.
35. David Broder, "Will Carter Be Tough on Carter?" *Washington Post*, April 23, 1978, p. D7.
36. Ibid.
37. Rowland Evans and Robert Novak, "The Heated Debate Over the Neutron Bomb," *Washington Post*, March 31, 1978, p. A19.
38. "A Frightening Report," *Wall Street Journal*, April 5, 1978, p. A19. See also, "The Neutron Decision," *Washington Post*, April 6, 1978, p. A22; and "The Carter Neutron Statement," *Washington Post*, April 19, 1978, p. C6.
39. Rowland Evans and Robert Novak, "The Heated Debate Over the Neutron Bomb," *Washington Post*, March 31, 1978, p. A19.
40. "The Neutron Bomb Furor," *Time*, April 17, 1978, p. 10.
41. "A Shift in Tactics," *U.S. News and World Report*, May 1, 1978, p. 20.
42. Hugh Sidey, "Still Searching for a Formula," *Time*, May 1, 1978, p. 16.
43. Hugh Sidey, "The Perils of Giving 'Em Hell," *Time*, May 22, 1978, p. 20.
44. Peter Goldman, "The New/Old Jimmy," *Newsweek*, May 15, 1978, pp. 28–29; see also Goldman's "The Carter Revival," *Newsweek*, June 5, 1978, p. 26.
45. "A Shift in Tactics," *U.S. News and World Report*, May 1, 1978, p. 20.
46. James Reston, "Who Will Tell Jimmy," *New York Times*, April 16, 1978, p. A19.
47. Rowland Evans and Robert Novak, "The President Nobody Fears," *Washington Post*, March 30, 1978, p. A23.
48. James Reston, "Who Will Tell Jimmy," *New York Times*, April 16, 1978, p. A19.
49. Ibid.
50. William Safire, "The Floating Anchor," *New York Times*, April 20, 1978, p. A23.
51. Vermont Royster, "Carter's Troubles," *Wall Street Journal*, August 23, 1978, p. 12.
52. Allan L. Otten, "Tougher Than Expected," *Wall Street Journal*, August 3, 1978, p. 12.
53. Joseph Kraft, "Colliding Moral Decisions," *Washington Post*, June 20, 1978, p. A11.
54. George F. Will, "Hamilton On the Town," *Newsweek*, March 6, 1978, p. 108.
55. Tom Wicker, "Another P.R. Solution," *New York Times*, May 21, 1978, p. E21.
56. David Broder, "The President IS Learning," *Washington Post*, August 23, 1978, p. A15.
57. David Broder, "Carter at the Summit: A Cloud of Doubt," *Washington Post*, July 12, 1978, p. A19.
58. Ibid.
59. David Broder, "Will Carter Be Tough on Carter?" *Washington Post*, April 23, 1978, p. D7.
60. Hugh Sidey, "Black Holes and Martian Valleys," *Time*, April 10, 1978, p. 22.
61. Hugh Sidey, "The Perils of Giving 'Em Hell," *Time*, May 22, 1978, p. 20.
62. Ibid.
63. Hugh Sidey, "It's a Time of Testing," *Time*, June 12, 1978, p. 20.
64. Hugh Sidey, "The Politics of Amazing Grace," *Time*, July 24, 1978, p. 14.
65. "A Problem of How to Lead: Dissatisfaction is the Washington Mood," *Time*, July 31, 1978, pp. 10–11.
66. "Repackaged Again," *Wall Street Journal*, August 4, 1978, p. 8.

67. Joseph Kraft, "There's No Quick Fix," *Washington Post,* July 30, 1978, p. B7.

68. Meg Greenfield, "Jimmy the What?" *Newsweek,* August 14, 1978, p. 76.

69. Anthony Lewis, "Savaging the President," *New York Times,* April 24, 1978, p. A23.

70. Meg Greenfield, "Thinking Small," *Newsweek,* April 24, 1978, p. 112.

71. David Broder, "A Battle Plan for the President," *Washington Post,* January 8, 1978, p. D7.

72. "How Carter's Staff Plans to Avoid Another Round of Blunders," *U.S. News and World Report,* March 20, 1978, p. 21.

73. Ibid.

74. "A Bold and Balky Congress," *Time,* January 23, 1978, pp. 8–16.

75. "The Art of Saying No," *Wall Street Journal,* April 13, 1978, p. 24.

76. John W. Mashek, "Carter and Ford: A Study In Contrasts," *U.S. News and World Report,* February 13, 1978, p. 27.

77. Rowland Evans and Robert Novak, "Carter and the House: Are Relations Cooling?" *Washington Post,* February 16, 1978, p. A19.

78. "A Problem of How to Lead: Dissatisfaction is the Washington Mood," *Time,* July 31, 1978, pp. 11–14.

79. Richard Boeth, "Confronting Congress," *Newsweek,* July 3, 1978, pp. 21–22.

80. David Broder, "A Neglected Democratic Party," *Washington Post,* June 14, 1978, p. A27.

81. "Carter's Shredded Goals," *U.S. News and World Report,* August 14, 1978, pp. 13–14.

82. "Carter's 18 Months: What Went Wrong," *U.S. News and World Report,* July 24, 1978, pp. 17–22.

83. Jack McWethy, "Carter's Inner-Circle: Surviving Under Fire," *U.S. News and World Report,* August 7, 1978, pp. 27–28.

84. Another story in the same issue of U.S. News and World Report called Strauss "one of the very few non-Georgians around Carter who can be called key men." [*sic*] The article portrayed Strauss as a White House trouble-shooter "who could play the back-slapping rituals in the Capitol." See "Carter's Mister Fix-It," *U.S. News and World Report,* August 7, 1978, pp. 14–16.

85. McWethy, pp. 27–28.

86. Alan L. Otten, "Isolation," *Wall Street Journal,* May 4, 1978, p. 20.

87. Alan L. Otten, "Tougher Than Expected," *Wall Street Journal,* August 3, 1978, p. 12.

88. "Carter's Balance Sheet," *Time,* May 1, 1978, pp. 10–12.

89. "A Problem of How to Lead," *Time,* July 31, 1978, p. 11.

90. "A Presidential Test," *Washington Post,* February 13, 1978, p. 20.

91. "What's In An Urban Policy," *Newsweek,* March 28, 1978, p. A16.

92. Marquis Child, "All the President's (Illustrious) Men," *Washington Post,* May 2, 1978, p. A19.

93. David Broder, "An 'Unsettling' Way to Make Policy," *Washington Post,* July 16, 1978, p. B7.

94. Joseph Kraft, "The Foreign-Policy Tyro," *Washington Post,* June 13, 1978, p. A21.

95. Meg Greenfield, "The New Quagmire," *Newsweek,* June 5, 1978, p. 112.

96. Karen Elliot House, "Uneven Justice?" *Wall Street Journal,* May 11, 1978, pp. 1, 18.

97. "Why Carter Puzzles Europe," *U.S. News and World Report,* June 5, 1978, pp. 17–19.

98. "Tug Of War Over Foreign Policy," *U.S. News and World Report*, June 19, 1978, pp. 37–40.

99. "A Week of Tough Talk," *Time*, June 12, 1978, p. 17.

100. "Soft Words—and a Big Stick," *Time*, July 3, 1978, p. 12.

101. "A Sadness the World Feels," *Time*, July 24, 1978, pp. 8–10.

102. Rowland Evans and Robert Novak, "Carter's Summit Gamble," *Washington Post*, May 5, 1978, p. A19.

103. Rowland Evans and Robert Novak, "Ignoring the Dangers of the Afghan Coup," *Washington Post*, May 8, 1978, p. A23.

104. George F. Will, "Is Carter Sleepwalking On Foreign Policy?" *Washington Post*, March 30, 1978, p. A23.

105. "Happy Anniversary," *Wall Street Journal*, May 22, 1978, p. 22.

106. "Changing Course," *Wall Street Journal*, June 2, 1978, p. 14.

107. "Linkage Rigma Role," *Wall Street Journal*, June 12, 1978, p. 16.

108. "Pushed Around in Moscow," *Wall Street Journal*, July 5, 1978, p. 8.

109. "The Rafshoon Veto," *Wall Street Journal*, August 24, 1978, p. 14.

110. See "The Rafshoon Veto," and "The Rafshoon Veto Revisited," *Wall Street Journal*, August 28, 1978, p. 20; "Admiral Rafshoon," *Wall Street Journal*, September 7, 1978, p. 22; and "The Veto Victory," *Wall Street Journal*, September 11, 1978, p. 24.

111. "The Veto Victory," *Wall Street Journal*, September 11, 1978, p. 24.

112. Rowland Evans and Robert Novak, "Carter's Veto Politics," *Washington Post*, August 25, 1978, p. A19.

113. "Carter Fires a Salvo: He Hands Congress a Veto—and Threatens More," *Time*, August 28, 1978, p. 10.

114. "The Fight Over Fighters," *Time*, May 22, 1978, pp. 17–18.

115. "F-15 Fight: Who Won What," *Time*, May 29, 1978, p. 12.

116. "Back to Old-Fashioned Politics," *U.S. News and World Report*, May 22, 1978, p. 19.

117. "Testing, Testing, Testing: Jimmy Carter Has to Keep Proving Himself to Congress," *Time*, August 7, 1978, pp. 12–13.

118. "The Right Thing For America," *Time*, August 14, 1978, p. 8.

119. See Jack McWethy, "Carter's Inner Circle," *U.S. News and World Report*, August 7, 1978, pp. 27–28; "Carter's Shredded Goals," *U.S. News and World Report*, August 14, 1978, pp. 13–14; "What Carter Aides Really Think of Congress," *U.S. News and World Report*, August 14, 1978, p. 15; Tom Mathews, "Operation Recovery," *Newsweek*, August 7, 1978, pp. 18–19; Susan Fraker, "Carter's Tax Fiasco," *Newsweek*, August 7, 1978, pp. 20–21.

120. "An Unpretentious Summit," *Wall Street Journal*, August 11, 1978, p. 10.

121. "Mr. Carter's Achievement," *Wall Street Journal*, September, 19, 1978, p. 22.

122. "Washington Wire," *Wall Street Journal*, September 8, 1978, p. 1.

123. Karen Elliot House, "Begin and Sadat Sign Historic Agreement that Could Soon Bring Middle East Peace," *Wall Street Journal*, September 18, 1978, p. 3.

124. Karen Elliot House, "Strong Forces for Success of Accord but Problems Remain," *Wall Street Journal*, September 19, 1978, pp. 1, 34.

125. Norman C. Miller, "The Presidential Jimmy Carter," *Wall Street Journal*, September 20, 1978, p. 22.

126. "Twelve Days in September," *New York Times*, September 19, 1978, p. 92.

127. Hedrick Smith, Supplemental material from New York Times news service and the Associated Press, September 29, 1978, p. 60.

128. "The Jimmy Carter Conference," *Washington Post*, September 19, 1978, p. A20.

129. Tom Mathews, "Born Again!" *Newsweek*, October 2, 1978, pp. 24–27.

130. Susan Fraker, "Can the Magic Last?" *Newsweek*, October 2, 1978, pp. 22–23.

131. Tom Mathews, "Carter's Momentum," *Newsweek*, October 9, 1978, p. 42.

132. "Mideast Triumph: What It Does for Carter," *U.S. News and World Report*, October 2, 1978, p. 23.

133. Jack McWethy, "A Dogged Carter at Work," *U.S. News and World Report*, October 2, 1978, p. 29.

134. "Carter: Help or Hindrance," *U.S. News and World Report*, October 9, 1978, pp. 28–29.

135. "A Sudden Vision of Peace," *Time*, September 18, 1978, p. 18.

136. "Carter's Swift Revival: His Summit Triumph Brings Him New Stature and New Power," *Time*, October 2, 1978, pp. 8–11.

137. "We're Taking Control: The Hero of Camp David Keeps Pushing Congress," *Time*, October 9, 1978, p. 23; and "Hey, You Hear That Vote?: Carter Takes a Stand Against Spending and Wins a Surprising Victory," *Time*, October 16, 1978, pp. 30–33.

138. "With All Five Fingers," *Time*, October 30, 1978, pp. 32–33.

139. See Joseph Kraft, "A High Risk Mideast Summit," *Washington Post*, August 10, 1978, p. A23; and Kraft's, "Summit Without Pressures," *Washington Post*, September 7, 1978, p. A19.

140. Joseph Kraft, "The Summit: 'Carter Pounced on Peace,'" *Washington Post*, September 19, 1978, p.A21; see also Kraft's "Fighting Euphoria," *Washington Post*, October 1, 1978, p. C7.

141. Hobart Rowen, "The World Looks Anew at Carter," *Washington Post*, September 21, 1978, p. A25.

142. Rowland Evans and Robert Novak, "Mideast: Success Depends On Carter," *Washington Post*, September 20, 1978, p. A15.

143. Rowland Evans and Robert Novak, "Carter's New Confidence," *Washington Post*, November 3, 1978, p. A23.

144. Marvin Stone, "End of a 30-Year War," *U.S. News and World Report*, October 9, 1978, p. 92.

145. Tom Wicker, Supplemental material from the *New York Times* news service and the Associated Press, October 1, 1978, pp. 7–8.

146. David Broder, "Carter's Campaigning: With Coattails," *Washington Post*, September 27, 1978, p. A23.

147. Hugh Sidey, "The Sweet Fruits of Success," *Time*, September 25, 1978, p. 18.

148. James Reston, Supplemental material from the *New York Times* news service and the Associated Press, September 27, 1978, p. 103.

149. Robert G. Kaiser, "Has Anything Changed—Except the Polls?" *Washington Post*, September 30, 1978, p. A15.

150. Joseph Kraft, "The 95th Congress: A Strong Finish for Carter," *Washington Post*, October 17, 1978, p. A17.

151. Susan Fraker, "A Last Minute Rush," *Newsweek*, October 23, 1978, pp. 42–44.

152. B. Drummond Ayres, Supplemental material from the *New York Times* news service and the Associated Press, October 17, 1978, pp. 51–52.

153. Terrence Smith, "Congress Wound Up With New Respect for Carter," *New York Times,* November 6, 1978, p. 51.

154. Hedrick Smith, "Carter's New Image: Exercising Power With Confidence After A Period of Vacillation," *New York Times,* November 7, 1978, p. A24.

155. "Carter—Can He Tame Congress," *U.S. News and World Report,* January 1, 1979, p. 22.

156. "A Presidential President," *Washington Post,* October 18, 1978, p. 16.

157. "Carter at Midterm: New Goals, New Tactics," *U.S. News and World Report,* January 22, 1979, p. 33.

158. "Junior Year," *New York Times,* January 25, 1979, p. A18.

159. Dennis A. Williams, "Running All Alone," *Newsweek,* December 18, 1978, p. 28.

160. Joseph Kraft, "Carter's Year: The Turnarounds . . . ," *Washington Post,* December 31, 1978, p. B7.

161. David Broder, ". . . and the Surprises," *Washington Post,* December 31, 1978, p. B7.

162. David Broder, "Breathing Space for the President," *Washington Post,* November 8, 1978, p. A15.

163. "A Rough Apprenticeship, a New Beginning," *Time,* January 1, 1979, p. 40.

164. "Carter at Halftime," *Wall Street Journal,* January 22, 1979, p. 20.

165. Hedrick Smith, "At Midterm, Tests Await a Stronger Carter," *New York Times,* January 25, 1979, p. B9.

166. Norman C. Miller, "Carter's Failure," *Wall Street Journal,* January 18, 1979, p. 16.

167. "Carter's Cutters vs. the Bulge," *Time,* December 4, 1978, p. 33; see also "War on Inflation: Stage II," *Time,* November 6, 1978, pp. 18–22; and "To Rescue the Dollar," *Time,* November 13, 1978, pp. 18–30.

168. Hugh Sidey, "The Crux of Leadership," *Time,* December 11, 1978, p. 44.

5

Carter's Third Year: 1979

In the first two years of the Carter presidency a negative press portrait of the president developed. The image of Carter as an inexperienced and ineffective leader emerged early in the term when Carter experienced difficult relations with Congress. By the end of 1977 this negative press portrait became widespread.

Despite Carter's legislative and diplomatic successes in 1978 journalists still reviewed his leadership negatively. Journalists responded to successes like the Panama Canal treaties vote with attempts to explain *why* Carter triumphed. Only the Camp David triumph inspired a fundamental, albeit temporary, revision of Carter's press portrait.

1. *Timing.* The evaluations of Carter's third year followed a similar pattern. After somewhat optimistic early assessments the negative base evaluation of Carter returned and was interrupted by particular events. The first major deviation from the negative base evaluation occurred after Carter's successful diplomatic intervention in the Middle East peace process in March.

The most important deviation in press assessments occurred during the July events surrounding Carter's domestic summit. For many journalists the retreat to Camp David appeared timed to deflect the criticism that was crippling Carter's image. Two days after the favorably received July 15 Crisis of Confidence speech, 34 members of Carter's Cabinet offered their resignations. Journalists portrayed the Cabinet shake-up as a Nixon-like "massacre" and a "great purge." While the Cabinet shake-up was the kind of "take charge" action journalists frequently advised Carter to pursue, the unusual timing of the event led the press to perceive Carter's administration as in a state of crisis and even a "state of siege" mood.

The end of 1979 assessments also must be evaluated in light of particular events taking place at that time. The Iranian hostage takeover (November 4) and Soviet invasion of Afghanistan (December 25) became the focus of evaluations of Carter's presidency. Journalists also assessed the timing of White House decisions according to their relevance to forthcoming strawpolls, caucuses, and primaries.

2. *Rhetoric/Symbolism.* The assessments of Carter's rhetoric and symbolism began in 1979 with the State of the Union address. Journalists found this address characterized by a "restrained" and "moderate" tone. Once again

journalists criticized the president for his "spare" vision of the future and for his discussion of what government was not capable of doing. As with the 1978 State of the Union address a number of journalists treated Carter's discussion of the limits of government's ability to solve problems as a new theme for this presidency.

Throughout most of the year journalists portrayed Carter's presidency as symbolizing weakness and lack of resolution. Many commented on Carter's lack of stature or lack of an "aura of decisive leadership." Journalists regarded Carter's effort in the State of the Union address to establish a theme for his presidency (the "New Foundation") as ineffectual.

The major turnaround in the press's assessments of Carter's rhetoric and symbolism occurred immediately after the Crisis of Confidence speech. For many journalists this speech epitomized what they had expected all along from President Carter. Journalists praised the speech for its "passion" and "eloquence" finding it reminiscent of Carter's "spirit of '76." In David Broder's words, "Jimmy Carter found his voice" again. Predictions of a "reborn presidency" did not last. In the wake of the Cabinet shuffle the earlier press view of Carter as lacking a flair for rhetoric and an ability to inspire returned.

3. *Agenda.* In early 1979 journalists expected Carter to adopt a relatively limited policy agenda. They perceived Carter's increasingly focused agenda as a prudent effort to improve the administration's chances for legislative victories.

Some journalists judged the specific agenda items rather than the scope of the agenda. The conservative journalists criticized Carter's energy program as long gasoline lines in April focused attention on this issue. A number of journalists held the energy program in high regard while lamenting Carter's efforts to enact his policies. In these reviews we see the continuation of the journalistic distinction between the assessments of Carter's agenda and the assessments of Carter's efforts at policy development.

Carter's foreign policy priority item in 1979—SALT II—came under increased press criticism. Carter perceived the securing of such a treaty as potentially one of the major accomplishments of his presidency. Most conservative journalists consistently denounced the arms control process. But two events in particular—the disclosure of a Soviet troop presence in Cuba and the invasion of Afghanistan—resulted in widespread criticism of the arms control process.

By the end of 1979 foreign policy crises dominated the Carter agenda. Journalists assessed the administration according to its ability to handle a number of highly complex and uncontrollable foreign policy problems.

4. *Policy Development.* The most persistent journalistic criticism of the Carter presidency in 1979 concerned the administration's efforts at policy development. Journalists depicted Carter's foreign policy approach as incoherent and confusing. Many journalists attributed the alleged lack of direction and coherence in foreign policy to the belief that the administration relied upon too many foreign policy spokesmen. Journalists continued to

make much of the philosophical differences between Secretary of State Cyrus Vance and National Security Adviser Zbigniew Brzezinski.

There was some fluctuation in this negative assessment of Carter's foreign policymaking approach. Carter's March trip to Jerusalem to redeem the Israeli-Egyptian peace treaty somewhat redeemed the president's image as an astute foreign policy leader. Carter succeeded, some journalists claimed, because he relied on the prestige of the American presidency to bring about this "diplomatic triumph." A few journalists portrayed the Middle East trip as the kind of "bold gamble" presidents are supposed to take.

A second deviation from the negative assessments of Carter's foreign policy approach occurred at the beginning of the Iranian hostage crisis. Journalists portrayed Carter's seizing of over $9 billion in Iranian assets as another example of what presidents should do: take direct, immediate action in a foreign policy dispute. Amid predictions of a Carter "revival," a number of journalists praised Carter for taking direct action without losing his sense of restraint. The hostage crisis was not resolved quickly and journalistic reviews of Carter's leadership eventually became negative.

The negative portrayal of Carter's domestic policy leadership became overwhelming in 1979. Journalists assessed that Carter's domestic agenda ran into difficulties in Congress because of the president's apolitical nature. In this view Carter did not know how to persuade, coerce, cajole, "wheel and deal." Journalists portrayed Carter as a problem solver, an "engineer president," a "rationalistic" thinker, but not an effective legislative or public opinion leader. In George F. Will's revealing phrase, Jimmy Carter was not a "muscular politician" capable of leading a "muscular nation."

There was almost no deviation in 1979 from this press image of Carter. Some journalists perceived a potential comeback for Carter's domestic agenda after the July 15 Crisis of Confidence speech. Yet this interpretation did not prevail. After the Cabinet shake-up a few days later the image of Carter as weak, indecisive and incapable of leadership prevailed.

5. *Staff.* Journalists subjected Carter's White House staff to continual criticism in 1979. The major press themes were that Carter's staff was "undisciplined," contemptuous of Washington's political norms, too insular, and too limited in their previous experiences and geographic origins.

Perhaps the most devastating indictment of Carter's White House staff came from former Carter speechwriter James Fallows. Fallows' controversial *Atlantic* magazine articles criticized Carter's leadership and the competence of the White House staff. Fallows' thesis that the president and the White House staff lacked political acumen and did not care about the norms of political Washington appeared to confirm journalists' worst suspicions.

After the mid-July Cabinet shake-up a good deal of journalistic criticism focused on the White House staff. Some journalists portrayed the event as a "purge" of independent thinkers in the administration and as the formal elevation of the "Georgian insiders." The promotion of Hamilton Jordan to Chief of Staff invited considerable criticism. For many journalists Jordan symbolized Carter administration "disdain" for the political establishment.

Moreover, for 30 months Carter steadfastly resisted the temptation to adopt a formal Chief-of-Staff position. The abuses in that position during the Nixon presidency led Carter to believe that the lack of such a position indicated a desire to reject the Nixon-model of White House staffing. Carter's eventual turnaround on this position invited press analogies between presidents Carter and Nixon.

Early Evaluations: January–February

The Carter administration's foreign policy achievements in 1978 generated favorable reporting of the president's leadership. Terrence Smith's *New York Times* story on the January 5–6 summit of Western nation leaders at St. Francis, Guadaloupe was an example of such favorable reporting. During that summit Western nation leaders agreed to deploy in Europe new missiles capable of striking Soviet territory. Smith attributed the collegial atmosphere of this summit to Carter's enhanced status: "As a result of the diplomatic progress of the last six months, Mr. Carter seems to have established himself as an effective member of the exclusive club of world leaders. Certainly he cuts a more authoritative figure today than he did six months ago in Bonn."[1]

Hugh Sidey attributed the administration's 1978 foreign policy achievements to Carter's new tactics in the international realm. According to Sidey, the president abandoned the campaign promise of an open foreign policy and the administration's major accomplishments were "nurtured in secrecy." Sidey asserted that "it is commonly believed around the capital that his decisiveness and the smooth execution of his plans have shored up his leadership, and that his new strength will soon be reflected in more public respect for the President."[2]

President Carter's 1979 State of the Union address inspired a new round of critical commentaries. Many critiques focused on the president's moderate tone and lack of any major call for public action against a problem. Yet many journalists praised Carter for limiting the administration's policy priorities. A *New York Times* editorial asserted that in his address Carter seemed "at pains to respond to the needs and mood of the times." The editorial reminisced:

> In his freshman year, Mr. Carter behaved like any new student, eager to conquer all subjects at once. . . . In his sophomore year, Mr. Carter thinned out his wish list—and achieved many of his goals. . . . Now for his third year he has narrowed his goals even more. He has decided to major in inflation and to minor in SALT. Neither concern is new, but Mr. Carter's emphasis is. Even a President can claim only so much public attention. For Mr. Carter so to select his issues is welcome—and Presidential.[3]

A *U.S. News and World Report* news story agreed with this view of Carter's speech:

Jimmy Carter is telling Americans to expect a year of prudence and moderation—a period of less, not more, from the federal government.

The new approach is a sharp turnaround from the evangelical fervor with which Carter began his term—preaching about a "new spirit" in the land at his inauguration and ambitiously pledging to lead the nation into far-reaching reforms of both government and society.[4]

Peter Goldman of *Newsweek* also assessed Carter's State of the Union address:

At mid-passage in his Presidency, Jimmy Carter is summoning America this week to a reduced new vision of its future—a vision suddenly dominated by what cannot be done.

Carter's steel-belted budget and his spare State of the Union Message may be, in spirit if not cost, the most conservative any Democrat has offered since the New Deal.[5]

A *Time* magazine news story observed that the speech's message would incite difficulties between the president and "traditional" Democrats in favor of higher social welfare spending.[6] *Time* magazine also assessed the state of the Carter administration:

In failing to achieve real leadership of the nation, Carter has so far proved unable to break through the post-Viet Nam, post-Watergate mood of bitterness and distrust that, in part, brought him to office.

. . . Carter has exacerbated many of the difficulties he has faced. His most damaging weakness in his first two years has been a frequent indecisiveness, strangely accompanied by a failure to anticipate the effects of his actions.

. . . In addition there seems to be a growing, perhaps dangerous longing for a leader who is larger than life. By the indications of Carter's first two years, he will never be an inspirational leader.[7]

The *Wall Street Journal* disliked Carter's speech and criticized its lack of a theme: "Indeed, the message was so lacking in theme that it might be better described as a stew."[8] The *Washington Post* criticized Carter's "omission [of] any serious discussion of energy policy."[9] Even though Carter appeared to accept the advice to "scale-down" the list of administration priorities, the *Post* was displeased with his selection of priorities.

The Failing Presidency: February–March

During February and part of March journalists gave considerable attention to Carter's leadership difficulties. *U.S. News and World Report* inquired: "Iran, Indochina, energy, inflation. It's one battering after another for Carter. Question now: Is there time for yet another comeback?" The news report assessed that "Carter increasingly is seen . . . as indecisive and irresolute, a leader who not only hesitates to act but who actually shrinks from using the levers of power."[10] *Time* also characterized Carter as an indecisive leader unable to control events:

> The basic trouble seems to be that Jimmy Carter after two years in office, is still unable to project a sense that he is in control of events. . . . His foreign policy has come to seem primarily reactive, responding to events that he did not anticipate. And his response has tended to be indecisive.[11]
>
> No one event, no single mistake, produced this new season of political depression for Carter. The President's loss of stature is both a cause and effect of his handling of foreign policy. There is a pervasive sense at home and also abroad that Carter is not in command.[12]

Journalists offered these negative views of Carter's foreign policy leadership in response to a series of events. By late February, Peking's incursion into Vietnam obscured the diplomatic achievement of normalizing relations with China. The Camp David triumph was shadowed by the difficulties that the signatories were having abiding by the treaty provisions. Revolutionaries toppled the Shah's regime in Iran. The murder of a United States ambassador by Afghan police endangered Carter's SALT campaign. Journalists portrayed the administration's responses to these events as weak and ineffective. David M. Alpern of *Newsweek* noted that while "bold strokes are not [Carter's] style . . . as a result he often fails to project the aura of decisive leadership that is expected from the President." Alpern characterized Carter's leadership "style" and inability "to strike dramatic postures" as part of the problem:

> But critics traced Carter's irresolute image to a fundamentally chaotic system of formulating foreign policy, and to a still undisciplined staff whose conflicting opinions . . . further undercut the President.
> . . . The people closest to Carter say that he remains as tough as ever, but that is hardly the impression he has communicated—particularly in the field of foreign policy. Some critics say it is too late for the President to alter the impression of weakness and incoherence in his conduct of foreign affairs. That is probably a premature reading, given Carter's quick turnaround in the polls after Camp David. But time is running out.[13]

The *Washington Post* found Carter's foreign policy confusing because the administration appeared to be juggling "Two Washington Triangles." The *Post* argued:

> Jimmy Carter looks foolish for the questionable management of two critical Washington triangles, Moscow-Peking-Washington and Carter-Vance-Brzezinski. He leaves a lot of anxious Americans and foreigners alike right back where they were in mid-1978, wondering just who's in charge.[14]

Some journalists criticized the president for being too willing to accommodate the Soviet leadership. Evans and Novak claimed that a lack of realism plagued the president's world view: "Jimmy Carter sees a relatively stable world, as it was perceived in Dwight D. Eisenhower's day, not the place of dangers demanding heroism painted by John F. Kennedy."[15] Carter's world view allegedly contributed to Soviet adventurism abroad:

> A president who predictably will turn the other cheek—for reasons of theology, policy, or both—makes life more certain for the gentlemen in the Kremlin. They never were quite sure whether Kennedy, Johnson, Nixon and Ford would suddenly choose force, they can be certain—on the experience thus far—that Carter will not.[16]

The *Wall Street Journal* frequently attacked the president's commitment to a SALT treaty with the Soviets.[17] The *Journal* warned the administration against neglect of Soviet worldwide activities as a means of ensuring a new SALT treaty. Peter Goldman concluded that Carter's inability to control world events became a political liability:

> What the public tensions over SALT signaled was a deeper malaise spreading among Democrats over foreign policy Carter style—a sinking feeling, as one friendly congressman put it "there is something to be said after all for experience."[18]

Hugh Sidey pointed out that "most of those who express concern blame no single party or single President for the end of an era in which America was predominant. But it is now President Carter's job to deal with the situation."[19] Sidey subsequently criticized the president's rhetoric of American decline and the limitations of American power. "Carter, perhaps, seems too ready to endorse second best."[20] Sidey raised additional doubts about Carter's foreign policy leadership:

> The increasingly personal nature of his leadership sometimes seems to be a protective device designed to give him room to maneuver but also keeping him from seeing the real world. Sincerity and warmth, changes of language and diversionary drama replace substantive progress. . . . [Carter's] actions emerge as a series of emotional responses rather than the work of an integrating intelligence, which is a crucial quality for leadership on a globe so intricately and tightly bound.[21]

Meg Greenfield revitalized some common criticisms of Carter's leadership. She characterized Lyndon B. Johnson's leadership approach as the standard by which other Democratic presidents should be assessed and concluded that Carter's leadership fell short of expectations:

> Johnson had a feeling for managing those personal political struggles that made more sense than Carter's fresh-eyed technique—and that Carter in battling some of the unhappy results of the LBJ era could do worse than to borrow some of the former President's wiles.[22]
> . . . [Carter] is predominantly a rationalist, an analyzer, a man who believes that somewhere out there in the realm of objective reality there is a best analysis of what can and should be done.

Jimmy Carter presumes a world of enlightened self-interest, rationality, intelligence, and at least minimal goodwill. And given these attributes, people can be expected to understand certain things as we in this country understand them—or as Jimmy Carter understands them—and to submit, eventually, to the blandishments of good sense and the dictates of wisdom.[23]

The Middle East Gamble: A Brief Revival? (March)

The faltering Middle East peace process contributed to the negative assessments of Carter's leadership. As a *Washington Post* editorial observed in late February, "the search for a peace treaty between Egypt and Israel is in a state of extraordinary fragility."[24]

On March 7 President Carter flew to the Middle East to salvage the stalled peace talks between Israel and Egypt. This intervention in the negotiations prompted the *Post* to comment that, "Plainly, President Carter is giving peace in the Mideast his very best effort."[25] The *Wall Street Journal* praised Carter's "gamble": "Foreign policy almost always involves gambles but there is no chance of success unless the risks are accepted."[26] Karen Elliot House predicted renewed characterizations of the president's "ineptness" if he returned from the Middle East without a treaty agreement.[27]

By March 13 the president achieved a breakthrough in the peace process as Begin and Sadat agreed on all substantive points of a treaty. Some journalists proclaimed Carter's presidency revived by the Mideast intervention. *Time* magazine's reporting on the president's "bold peace mission" reflected other evaluations in its praise of Carter. *Time* declared Carter's effort "one of the most startling and swiftly executed diplomatic initiatives in years."[28] The news magazine proclaimed that Carter's effort "was masterful. . . . He has taken a tremendous risk and won."

Carter achieved a victory of presidential diplomacy that has brought Egypt and Israel to the threshold of peace after 30 years of enmity and four brutal wars. By his daring and persistent personal intervention, Carter fundamentally altered the geopolitical equation in the volatile Middle East. He also strengthened his own standing both at home and overseas. . . . Carter's achievement will probably help him most in silencing those who accuse him of feckless leadership.[29]

Karen Elliot House portrayed Carter's presidency as revived by the negotiations which, she believed, would enhance his popularity, prestige, and chances for favorable congressional action on administration programs.[30] Yet House added that the treaty signing did not guarantee a lasting Middle East peace but was just one step in a long, difficult healing of historic animosities.[31] *U.S. News* hailed Carter's efforts as a "diplomatic triumph" that did not assure a lasting peace in the region.[32] Hugh Sidey, who one week earlier chastised the president for a lack of realism, praised Carter's "soothing touch of realism":

The President has abandoned another piece or two of that image of himself as the barefoot boy with a smile. That may be one of the best signals yet for his troubled leadership. Along with the Bible, he carried to the Middle-East a new sensitivity to the world's historical realities. He displayed an eloquence that until now he has resolutely choked. He showed it all, a soothing touch of realism that has barely been allowed.

. . . Just as Carter finally conceded to himself the realities of congressional manipulation and started to make some headway on the Hill, it could be that after more than two years of training he is learning the ropes of world power.[33]

Rowland Evans and Robert Novak unreservedly praised Carter's achievement:

The world . . . is applauding Carter's courage and tenacity in taking his peace campaign to the Mideast at immense personal risk. He surely merits such applause.

Magic was the principal ingredient of Carter's formula. . . . It was extraordinary because no clear solution—only hope—was in sight. Besides risking more of his fading personal prestige, Carter was also risking the fading reputation of this country.[34]

David Butler of *Newsweek* noted that Carter's "hard-won achievement would go a long way toward restoring some sadly lacking luster to his Presidency."[35] After the conclusion of Carter's trip to the Middle East, Butler asserted that "the cliff-hanging nature" of the "negotiations in which Carter played a major role flowed directly from the fact that he *was* involved: persistently, passionately—and riskily—capitalizing on the prestige of the Presidency."[36]

Many journalists portrayed Carter as gifted at dealing with small groups of people. Journalists simultaneously portrayed Carter as unable to communicate to large audiences. For example, the *Washington Post* was so impressed with Carter's ability to negotiate with small private groups that it advised Carter to pack up and hide out at Camp David to mediate with congressional leaders an agreement on energy policy.[37] Angus Deming of *Newsweek* also portrayed Carter as an effective negotiator. Deming believed that Carter's negotiating style was more suited to sessions with leaders of foreign nation-states than to sessions with congressmen:

. . . many of those who have seen Carter in action in small gatherings or meetings with another head of government, say that the President achieves results with his low-key personal style—a blend of transparent sincerity, friendliness and unpretentiousness. Carter also gets high marks for doing his homework and for pursuing his objectives with unflagging determination.

. . . he often succeeds in putting foreign leaders at ease by displaying a trait that some Carter critics find maddening: a refusal to act overly Presidential.

Because he can appear to be an aloof outsider, Carter may always have trouble winning friends and influencing people in the U.S. Congress. It is possible that his understated style is more effective abroad. . . . [Carter's] strengths seem to be just those qualities that Middle East peace negotiations demand: careful preparation, sincerity and determination.[38]

Joseph Kraft also contrasted Carter's ability to stage foreign policy successes with his failure to generate support for domestic programs: "Can foreign policy spectaculars save the Carter presidency? Only with difficulty . . . [Carter] seems to have so little else going for him." Kraft added that no solid public and congressional support for the administration's domestic policies existed and that "foreign policy issues, which are most fit for presidential leadership, cannot carry the day."[39]

Failing Again: April–Early July

Joseph Kraft summarized the difficulties Carter would have maintaining momentum after the Middle East peace treaty success: "They loved the peace treaty ceremony in the White House because it showed Jimmy Carter being 'presidential.' But what can he do for an encore?" Kraft offered an assessment that became commonplace in journalistic circles: the president was capable of periodic foreign policy accomplishments but could not "run the railroad when it comes to domestic affairs."

> The true trouble is that Carter has not imposed himself or a surrogate on the decision making process in domestic affairs. He is not master of his own advisers. Still less in the Congress. Strained efforts to look "presidential" in these conditions only betray the self-doubts that forced the efforts in the first place.[40]

In early and mid-April of 1979 gas lines in America became long and citizens became impatient with government's inability to resolve the fuel shortage. Journalists scorned Carter's efforts to deal with energy policy. Peter Goldman referred to Carter's 1979 proposals for gasoline rationing and windfall profits taxes on oil companies as "MEOW II" and "second-stage MEOW."[41] Goldman borrowed this description of the administration's proposals from Russell Baker's humorous discovery of an acronym for Carter's first energy speech proclaiming the "moral equivalent of war."

The *Wall Street Journal* was in the forefront in criticizing Carter's energy proposals. Even when Carter cleared the way for crude oil decontrol, a policy the *Journal* favored, the editors offered faint praise and lamented the administration's "Soft, Soft Sell" of the policy. The editors added that they would have applauded the initiative if they believed Carter actually understood why decontrol was "wise and necessary."[42] The *Journal* complained that Carter's statements that greedy oil millionaires would benefit most from the decontrol of crude oil undermined support for a much needed policy.[43] The *Journal* accused Carter of using "childish rhetoric" in his attacks on oil companies for achieving large profits during the energy crisis and declared Carter's attacks "demeaning" to the presidency.[44] The *Washington Post* declared Carter's criticisms of "Big Oil" unconvincing and added:

Instead of making a reasoned case for a reasonable policy, Mr. Carter is indulging in bad-tempered accusation and terms like "kickback." That kind of rhetoric has a great capacity to sour the process of negotiation and compromises that lies ahead of any tax bill. The president will certainly get his windfall tax, but the holy war, and the passions it arouses, can only make it more costly.[45]

In mid-April James Reston summarized his perception of the majority opinion in Washington about the president. According to Reston, Washingtonians believed that Carter was a one-term president who "doesn't look like a world leader—a good man but not quite up to the job." Reston offered "A Minority Report" arguing that these evaluations were correct only if the magnitude of the problems Carter faced was ignored.[46] Reston offered this assessment several days before the publication in *Atlantic* magazine of a former insider's report on the administration's problems.

Carter's former speechwriter James Fallows published an essay highly critical of the Carter administration in the May issue of *Atlantic*.[47] On April 27 Reston described Fallows' critique as "the talk of Washington these days."[48] The *Atlantic* article depicted Carter as "arrogant, complacent, and insecure." Fallows described Carter as a man who "believes fifty things but no one thing." Fallows reported that the president believed he owed his election to no one except the inner circle of "Georgians":

At the start of the Administration, as in the general election campaign, Carter and his captains felt omniscient: they had done what no one else had been known to do. Why should they take pains to listen to those who had designed the New Deal, the Fair Deal, the Great Society? The town was theirs for taking; it would have required nothing more than allowing the old warriors a chance to help. But Powell and Jordan and Carter let those people know that they could go to hell.[49]

Concerning Carter's tactics in dealing with Congress, Fallows appeared to confirm journalists' worst suspicions:

[Carter's] skin crawled at the thought of the time consuming consultation and persuasion that might be required to bring a legislator around. He did not know how congressmen talked, worked, and thought, how to pressure them without being a bully or flatter them without seeming a fool.[50]

Many columnists commented on Fallows' insights. Reston praised the Fallows critique "as an honest effort" to understand Carter's strengths and weaknesses.[51] William Safire summarized Fallows' assessments and concluded that the former presidential speechwriter offered insights on the president's character:

These judgments of a saddened admirer cast light on the general disillusionment with President Carter. He offered apparent goodness without effectiveness; the secret of Carter is that he wanted, above all, to *be* President, and had no clear idea of what he wanted to *do* as President.[52]

David Broder summarized Fallows' criticisms of Carter's staff. Broder attributed the elevation of political amateurs to major White House staff positions to a presidential selection process which encourages intense loyalty to individual candidates rather than loyalty to political parties. In Broder's view, only young, inexperienced individuals committed to a particular candidate are willing to make the personal and family sacrifices necessary to engage in a two-year long campaign. Party professionals are slighted by such a process since successful candidates feel obligated to hire their "amateur" campaign advisers.[53]

U.S. News's Marvin Stone asked whether there was "Still Time for Carter?" Stone cited Fallows' columns as evidence of the administration's problems:

> Leadership. Almost by definition it is the talent for inspiring people to follow, to sacrifice if need be.
> ... It is still conceivable that Carter has the capacity for this more immediate type of leadership, if only he better understood the powers—and yes, responsibilities—of a President. James Fallows, in his well publicized articles for the *Atlantic* magazine, blames Carter for failing to inspire his own staff with a sense of mission. The "laid back" atmosphere of the White House today is a far cry from the ferment under Franklin Roosevelt, John Kennedy or Lyndon Johnson.[54]

The *New York Times* was almost alone in criticizing Fallows' columns. A *Times* editorial reported that, "When Jimmy Carter came out of nowhere to win the Presidency, it was conventional wisdom to regard him as a brilliant politician, but lacking substantive knowledge." With reference to the Fallows stories the *Times* added: "That view has surfaced again." The *New York Times* editors disagreed with what they perceived as Fallows' major thesis—that Jimmy Carter was an astute politician lacking substantive knowledge:

> On the contrary, the President's substantive positions seem to us generally sound. The failure has been that of Jimmy Carter, politician.
> Anyone can be an analyst; the President must be, in the first sense, a politician.
> Where is Jimmy Carter the explainer, cajoler, reassurer? The President seems to shrink from the bully pulpit, to act as though being apolitical demonstrates integrity.[55]

Many journalistic evaluations during May and June portrayed the Carter presidency as deeply in trouble. On May 29 Hedrick Smith wrote that "the Carter Administration is suffering its worst malaise since taking office."[56]

In a June 4 article, "Carter: Song of Woe," *Time* magazine portrayed the Carter presidency as on the verge of faltering.[57] One week later *Time* presented a most gloomy analysis of Carter's plight, "The Sky Is Falling

On Washington!"[58] Tom Mathews of *Newsweek* reported that the administration's public standing was so low that Carter would have to abandon his "Why Not the Best" slogan in 1980 for "a more modest slogan: 'Consider the rest.'"[59] Peter Goldman asserted in early June that the Carter administration was in a "state of seige mood." In discussing the defeat in Congress of Carter's proposed oil-price decontrol plan Goldman defined the president's existing leadership problem:

> His defeat was in turn symptomatic of his larger weakness on the Hill—a debility that has brought his program to something near stasis. His own political gifts are held in light regard in Congress. Respect for his staff is low and sliding; O'Neill has lately reverted to his old habits of calling Carter's man Hamilton Jordan "whatzisname—Hannibal Jerkins." And now, in his reduced state, Carter no longer frightens congresspeople with his ultimate threat—to go over their heads to the countryside.[60]

Journalists offered several explanations for the alleged failings of the Carter presidency. Joseph Kraft, rejecting the comparisons by some of Jimmy Carter to former president Richard M. Nixon, defined the administration's problems in this way:

> . . . the troubles of the Carter administration spring not from abuse of personal power but from nonuse of power on impersonal issues. . . . Jimmy Carter, by contrast, qualifies for sainthood. His administration has been open to a fault. Far from indulging himself or his colleagues in privilege, he has driven good people from government by the rigor of his standards for personal behavior. . . . The case of Mr. Carter demonstrates that good intentions are almost irrelevant, and perhaps even downright harmful.[61]

Evans and Novak diagnosed Carter's problems as stemming from a tendency to appease the political left. Efforts by a non-ideological president to appease the political left only contributed, they argued, to the image of Carter as an "indecisive" leader.[62] The *Wall Street Journal* also placed blame for the president's problems on liberal ideology, rejecting for the most part arguments proclaiming incompetence or the ungovernability of the nation as responsible for the administration's difficulties:

> [Carter] is his party's President at a time when the party's traditional stance has lost favor with the voters.
> In essence, Mr. Carter has been trying to mediate between his party's liberals, still a powerful force in Congress, and the public at large. It is not working, simply because those liberal initiatives of a few years ago have run aground on reality. There is no more money for government to spend; indeed, what it's spending now has saddled us with serious inflation. The public wants tax and inflation relief, not more social programs.[63]

James Reston differed with his colleagues as to where to assign blame for fuel shortages, inflation, and an inefficient bureaucracy. According to

Reston these problems were too large for any mortal to overcome. "The truth is that the nation is in the midst of a vast transformation seemingly beyond the control of Mr. Carter or any of his opponents."[64]

The *New York Times* also doubted the president's responsibility for inflation and gas lines. The editors questioned the assumptions of Carter's critics, including the view that Carter should emulate a former Democratic president:

> One factor in the discontent seems to be a remembered sense of mastery among past Presidents, notably Lyndon Johnson. How much of that is romantically selective? Plenty of us were uncomfortable indeed when LBJ was picking up dogs, and Congressmen, by the ears and insisting on having their votes and their, well, loyalty, in his pocket.
> . . . Surely a major source of discontent is the very intractability of the nation's problems. Inflation and energy are not problems of Jimmy Carter's making. The responses he has proposed have not brought notable results, in part because Congress has not let him try them. But they have been sensible. We have not heard from any economist or expert, let alone candidate, with better ones.
> . . . There is still a stronger and more troubling explanation for present discontents: officials and citizens everywhere are less willing than ever to subordinate parochial interest to national need. . . . No one can govern a free society that thus refuses to be governed. . . .[65]

Most critics of Carter were less sympathetic than the *Times*. Many critics blamed the president for the nation's problems while downplaying other factors contributing to these ills. By early July, Martin Schram of the *Washington Post* described the mood of the Carter White House: ". . . a feeling has set in that is far gloomier than emptiness. It is despair."[66]

Carter's SALT achievement did not revitalize journalists' faith in his presidency. On June 18 Carter and Soviet Premier Leonid Brezhnev signed in Vienna a Strategic Arms Limitations Treaty (SALT II) intended to limit each superpower to 2,250 strategic weapons. The president's leadership in the five-day long conference received mixed press reviews.

A few months prior to the June summit meeting between Carter and Brezhnev the administration's foreign policy came under increased press criticism. Marvin Stone summarized a common sentiment that differed from the *Times*'s view that Carter, to a great extent, was a victim of uncontrollable events:

> Jimmy Carter did not get us into the troubles, but he has not gotten us out, either. And that was the job he said he wanted—to set things right—and it was the job we elected him to do.[67]

Stone was not alone in this regard. Other commentators attributed foreign policy problems then facing the United States to the president's alleged "lack of resolve" and policy inconsistencies:

David Broder: The nasties in the world are getting the dangerous notion that the United States is easy picking. . . . It is time for the United States to show the flag and Carter to show some backbone.

Joseph Kraft: It is no accident that Carter has recently been getting lumps from the Russians, from the Chinese, from the Mexicans and from practically everybody else. He comes on weak, and whatever the merits of this or that policy, it seems beyond dispute that under his stewardship the country is very poorly prepared to meet a challenge as difficult as any we have faced since World War II.

New York Times: Mr. Carter long ago foresaw the right responses to these challenges but he has not defined them as overriding requirements. . . . If these are priorities, why not hammer at them when the nation so obviously yearns for action?

Wall Street Journal: In the world of geopolitics, if you lose in one place you will be tested in another. If you lose successively you will be tested in more and more ways. If you start not even to put up a fight, everyone will start to bully you.[68]

Based on these perceptions of Carter as unwilling to project American power abroad many journalists harbored low expectations for the Carter-Brezhnev summit. Joseph Kraft, for example, perceived Carter as in a weak position for negotiations, lacking threats or inducements to offer the Soviets. In Kraft's view the administration put the United States in a poor position in the geopolitical struggle because "some of the president's advisers, grouped around the secretary of state, seem to suffer guilt about the Vietnam War."[69] The *Washington Post* offered a similar view:

Mr. Carter has not built much confidence in either his personal bargaining abilities or his vision of how the United States should adjust to a world in which it is no longer undisputed No. 1 and the Soviet Union is coming on strong.[70]

The *Wall Street Journal* blasted the SALT process in general and Carter's dedication to securing a new peace treaty in particular. The *Journal* argued that "preoccupation with a dubious arms agreement erodes broader American security interests," and lamented "the imbalance that SALT has introduced into American diplomacy."[71] The *Journal* disapproved of Carter's pledge to abide by a Strategic Arms Limitation Treaty even if rejected by the Senate. The editors portrayed Carter's pledge as an example of a dangerous "Imperial Presidency."[72]

David Broder offered a hopeful view of the summit. Despite earlier criticisms of Carter for allowing the Soviets to gain the upper hand in the superpower struggle, Broder wrote:

The president is anything but naive about the Russians. He is an Annapolis graduate and former submarine officer, trained to estimate the capability of an adversary—not to assume his goodwill. . . . He is going to Vienna, not because he assumes he can trust the Russians, but because he knows it is vital to seek verifiable arms agreements that, if enforced, will make this world a slightly safer place in which to live.[73]

George F. Will found the president "naive" about the Soviet leaders' intentions. Will proclaimed Carter to be from the "revisionist" wing of the Democratic party. Through his association with this group of foreign policy elites whom Will characterized as overly trusting of the Soviets, Carter "provide[d] himself with the narrowest range of foreign policy advice of any modern President."[74]

Finally, the *Washington Post* offered a retrospective on the superpower summit which summarized the ambivalent nature of the press's assessments of Carter's role in the negotiations:

> It was, in all, a satisfactory performance that, if it failed to generate unexpected accord or public electricity, apparently did not generate further tension or significant misperception of undue euphoria either.
>
> But Mr. Carter did not seem to emerge with the notably enhanced stature as an international statesman that would have helped smooth SALT's Senate way.[75]

A Crisis of Confidence: July

By July 1979 journalists regarded the Carter presidency as doomed. Carter stood lower in opinion polls than Richard Nixon during the height of Watergate.[76] A CBS/New York Times poll showed that self-identified Democrats favored Senator Edward M. Kennedy (D-Mass.) over Carter 53%– 13% for the 1980 Democratic presidential nomination.[77] Inflation reached an annual rate of 13% and Americans waited in long lines to purchase gasoline as the price of imported oil continued to rise.

Carter retreated in early July to Camp David to confer with aides about his scheduled national address on energy policy. Despite objections from Vice-President Mondale and some White House staff Carter cancelled the television address. The speech would have been the president's fifth major energy address to the nation. The national audience for Carter's addresses had dwindled from 80 million viewers for the first speech to just 30 million for the fourth. The president decided he was going to learn why the American people had lost faith in his leadership. In an unprecedented act of presidential self-reflection Carter remained at Camp David for over a week to confer with aides, business leaders, academicians, religious leaders and public officials about the state of the country and how the administration should respond to the nation's ills.[78]

Carter's retreat to Camp David caused a public stir. In a *New York Times* column "Carter Agonistes," Hedrick Smith described the energy speech cancellation and move to Camp David as "one of the most extraordinary spectacles of any recent Presidency." Smith noted that Carter exposed "his presidency yet again to charges of incompetence."[79] Timothy D. Schellhardt lamented the "new confusion" nationwide with the president's actions.[80]

The *Washington Post* asked: "Now the President is confusing the imagery. Is he Moses or Heidi's Alm Uncle—a supplicant ascending the mountain in search of wisdom or a brooding, vaguely ominous presence already there?"[81] *U.S. News* asked in a headline story, "Is Time Running Out for Carter?"[82] Even less restrained (but very much in character) was the *New York Post*'s boldest black front-page type screaming out: "WHAT THE HECK ARE YOU UP TO, MR. PRESIDENT?"[83] *Time* regretted that Carter "seemed so mired in indecision." Carter's retreat "seemed to be nothing more . . . than a spectacular display of White House ineptitude."[84] Peter Goldman assessed that Carter's "pallid habits of leadership is no longer in question."[85] And Tom Wicker offered a depressing view of the president's leadership problems:

> President Carter has reached the low point not only of his Administration but perhaps of the postwar Presidency. That is bad for the man and worse for the country; either he pulls things together in the immediate future or the rest of us are stuck with a virtual lame duck in the White House for the next 18 months.
> . . . One of Mr. Carter's signal weaknesses has been a preoccupation with the details of program and policy, for which a more confident President would have been willing to rely on hired thinkers; and a concurrent disinterest in the vital politics of winning public acceptance of what he proposes. But Presidents are elected fundamentally to carry the country; and however high-minded Mr. Carter may be in eschewing politics, arm-twisting, jawboning and all other acts of persuasion, he is only recoiling from the first duty of a political office.[86]

Carter's energy speech cancellation prompted William Safire to accuse the president of "lies" for asserting that no staff divisions resulted over the speech decision. Safire characterized Carter's staff as "petty and disloyal" and said the president "is a political zombie."[87] Safire also foreshadowed a major theme in the post–Camp David assessments of Carter:

> . . . the President will try to transfer the wide dissatisfaction with his own performance into a "national malaise," and late in '79 will seek to recapture his own spirit of '76.
> . . . [One can] admire the stunt that focuses our attention on his good intentions rather than on his dreary record.[88]

Joseph Kraft believed Carter's leadership problem stemmed from a tendency to favor the interests of "Little America" rather than "Big America." In Kraft's view, Little America was a coalition of "militant feminists, consumer advocates and minority and environmental leaders" who "took over the Democratic party in 1972 and the government in 1976." Big America included the corporations, unions and urban agglomerations that dominated national political life for years. Kraft perceived an "affinity between outsiders" that led the Carter White House to form an alliance with Little America. Kraft concluded that, "Little America can't run Big America. That is why the president and the country are currently in such trouble." Kraft believed that Carter needed to bring into the White House "prestigious figures with close ties to Big America. The requirement is that these men commit the administration to a different way of doing business and a different set of priorities."[89]

Meg Greenfield believed that most pundits praised Carter for having accepted the conventional wisdom of Washington by consulting the nation's leaders about the administration's problems. Regardless of the correctness of this claim, Greenfield disagreed with the alleged views of her colleagues and characterized the summit a typical Carter response:

> In the Catoctins, the President was re-creating the circumstances in which he clearly prefers to lead, learn and—in his terms—govern: dealing directly with individuals and spokesmen, engaging personally, one on one, with constituents, circumventing (or fleeing or ignoring) the machinery of government itself.
>
> . . . It is a highly personal, anti-institutional method, and it combines in some odd proportions humbleness and notions almost of royalty.
>
> . . . I have never seen any evidence that he enjoys or relishes governing in the more conventional sense of grappling with individuals and institutions, wheeling, dealing, compromising, enticing, threatening and, finally, making the *machine* make things happen. I think that sloppy process is what he is trying to reorganize out of government—and to lift himself beyond as well.[90]

Hugh Sidey concluded that the essence of presidential leadership in difficult times was a capacity to inspire people to think and behave differently toward their own plight. Only a president, Sidey argued, is positioned "To Push a Nation Beyond Itself." Sidey noted:

> . . . last week, as he had before, Carter seemed to falter and slip back, hesitant and uncertain about how to lead the nation into a future that grows darker each day. The chilling conclusion was echoed even in the ranks of his friends and supporters: he may not be up to the challenge. . . . A growing number of both politicians and scholars believe that because of the energy and economic crises, this nation needs a kind of revolution in thought and way of life. The principal executive of such an effort of inspiration and organization must be the President. Yet the size of the challenge and the power he has at his command seem too great for his comprehension or use.
>
> . . . If history is a guide, there really is no one who can tell Carter how he should lead. It must come from within him. That is the worry. He has little sense of history, nor has he proved himself to be an imaginative man. These may be fatal flaws.[91]

Hedrick Smith pointed out that on the symbolic level the retreat and invitation of 130 discussants, as well as Carter's meetings with two American families, evoked the themes of openness and accessibility that once gave the Carter presidency great appeal. Smith called the discussions at Camp David a "rotating town meeting," the kind of forum in which Carter excels. While Carter succeeded in capturing the nation's attention for the speech, Smith warned, he risked creating high expectations with these actions.[92]

David Broder agreed that Carter's summit created high expectations. Yet Broder did not perceive the president as harboring any illusions about the effects of the retreat and national speech which the *Post* columnist proclaimed a potential "turning point" for the administration:

The extraordinary events of the past 10 days, unparalleled in the history of the modern presidency, probably have created an exaggerated sense of anticipation. If there is a national malaise, as Carter believes, he is realistic enough to know it will not be cured by a single presidential speech. He does not see himself as a Moses coming down from the mountain.[93]

On July 15 (the day of Carter's speech) Broder reported that Carter planned to address the national "malaise" that evening. Broder perceived the domestic summit as Carter's effort to reach out to the "American leadership elite." Carter, according to Broder, had "belatedly" acknowledged the legitimacy of the nation's "elites."[94]

The July 15 *Washington Post* editorial attempted to predict the president's message to the nation that evening. The *Post* attributed to Carter a word that would eventually be used to caricature the president's message:

The President has made malaise a household word. . . . Mr. Carter is widely reported to believe that the nation's energy and economic troubles are part of a larger skein of troubles, that they help cause and are also intensified by what he has identified as a national malaise. . . . It is this larger dissatisfaction of the spirit which Mr. Carter intends substantially to address in his speech tonight.

. . . some part of the disaffection may be not so much more than impatience and frustration growing out of [Carter's] own performance in office.[95]

On July 15 President Carter addressed the nation about the crisis of confidence in our major institutions. As Carter revealed in his memoirs: "I tried to express to the American people what I had learned at Camp David. I spoke . . . about the need to have faith in our country—not only in the government, but in our own ability to solve great problems. There was a growing disrespect for our churches, schools, news media, and other institutions; this change had not come suddenly or without cause."[96] Carter closed the speech with a brief discussion of the administration's new energy proposal. The following day Carter announced his six-point program to reduce oil imports and create alternative energy supplies.

Over 100 million Americans viewed the Crisis of Confidence speech. It was the largest audience for any speech by the president. The public responded favorably to Carter's address. A number of journalists proclaimed the address the beginning of Carter's political "rebirth." Others saw the speech as a rekindling of that spirit of '76 which led Carter from political obscurity to the White House. Hedrick Smith reported:

In what was part sermon, part program, part warning, the President returned to homilies and populist rhetoric of his 1976 campaign in an effort to save his Presidency and to try to restore what he feels is lost contact with the American people. . . . Speaking easily, naturally and confidently, he portrayed himself as a people's President who had lost touch with the people and had begun to regain it in the past 10 days at Camp David. . . . Implicit in the President's approach tonight was an attempt once again to cast himself in the outsider's role that proved to be such an effective campaign tactic in 1976. . . . He spoke of Washington critically, almost as if he were not a part of the Washington establishment.[97]

Martin Schram wrote on July 17 of the "rebirth of the Carter presidency" and Carter's political "turnaround":

> Jimmy Carter is a man given to rebirths. He is a man who has the capacity to stop in mid-crisis, take stock and set out on a new course with a different purpose.
> . . . He has disdained repeated staff suggestions that he use a speech coach to improve his oratory style. He had stuck in the first years of his presidency to that Southern churchy style, where he would let his voice tail off at the end of every sentence, a habit that connoted reverence but not confidence. Carter even disdained suggestions that he at least practice what he preached, fixing a scowl on anyone who dared suggest a rehearsal. But that was the first Carter presidency, not the one that was inaugurated last night.[98]

David Broder affirmed after the president's speech that, "Jimmy Carter found his voice again." The televised address may not save the Carter presidency or solve the energy crisis, Broder reported, "But it will surely go down in history as one of the most extraordinary addresses a chief executive has ever given." Broder continued:

> It was a speech that only Jimmy Carter could have given—the kind that made him so distinctive and effective a candidate in the early months of 1976. It was the kind of speech he failed to give in his first 30 months as president.
> . . . in this most critical speech of his presidency, he delivered his text more effectively than he has ever done before. He avoided the sing-song rhythm, the misplaced stresses, and the falsetto squeaks that have marred past performances.[99]

Broder acknowledged that energy could be the "most divisive issue" on which to stake a presidency. "A more cautious politician would probably have chosen another issue—almost any other issue—by which to be judged." In this speech, Broder concluded, Carter successfully conveyed the urgency of the energy crisis to a skeptical nation.[100] Broder also portrayed the speech as an extraordinary effort to salvage a faltering presidency:

> Whatever the outcome of this desperate gamble to recoup his fortunes on the energy issue, Carter has won new respect for his honesty with himself.
> He managed to do what few people in positions of power . . . can do: Step back from a situation in which they have an enormous investment of ego and appraise their own performance.[101]

Peter Goldman assessed that Carter delivered the Crisis of Confidence speech "with an urgency, a passion and an eloquence rare in his or in any other recent Presidency." Goldman added:

> He did not spare himself or his diminuendo style of leadership from a share of the blame for the malaise he described. . . . His implicit pledge was nothing less than a fundamental renovation of his Presidency with a clear agenda headed by energy and with a forcefulness of bearing he has rarely revealed. . . . [Carter] felt he had to do something to shake the nation free of its malaise.
> . . . What Carter contemplated at Camp David reached far beyond the issue agenda to a fundamental redesign and redirection of his Presidency—a turn away from the engineered twelve-point programs of his first two and a half years to a kind of sawdust trail revivalism more nearly akin to his 1976 campaign.[102]

U.S. News and World Report referred to the speech as "an extraordinary effort by a U.S. Chief Executive to rally a nation—and save a Presidency." The news story reported: "As the President's effort went into high gear, no one could say if it would pay off for him and for the country. But there was an almost universal feeling that Carter had to try something, and try it fast, to rescue his Presidency."[103]

Tom Wicker doubted that the Crisis of Confidence speech would revive Carter's standing. After asking whether Carter "[came] across as a stronger leader" Wicker answered:

> The rhetoric and manner were more forceful than usual with him, and few will doubt the sincerity of his words. But after more than two years of a President constantly giving the appearance of amateurish ineptitude, *more than an effective speech will be required to make Jimmy Carter resemble FDR.*[104] (emphasis added)

Although many journalists praised Carter's speech, some criticized his diagnosis of the national condition. The criticisms fell into three categories: (1) the speech was a public relations ploy to direct attention away from the president's inability to lead; (2) Carter's energy proposals were the wrong medicine; and (3) Carter was blaming others for problems his administration either created or could not solve.

George F. Will referred to the Camp David retreat as "a satire of media politics, a broad-brush caricature of leadership."[105] Will disparaged Carter's "war" on the energy crisis and, like Tom Wicker, held up Franklin D. Roosevelt as a model of crisis leadership:

> When FDR wanted to galvanize the nation, he went on a 100-day dash, doing things like closing the banks. Bang! Three days after taking office his impact was visible on Main Street.
> Carter flinches from the one obvious action that would have an immediate bite of seriousness: He will not decontrol gasoline prices.[106]

Will appeared concerned about the favorable public reaction to Carter's speech. In Will's view Americans expected too little of their president. He predicted that voters would embrace Carter in 1980 because no matter how ineffectual a leader, they knew "Carter at least will not steal the White House silverware." Will believed that citizens were preoccupied with the private virtues of public leaders while not sufficiently concerned with public virtues such as the "ability to lead."[107] Will also disagreed with Carter's diagnosis of the national condition. Will's rebuttal to the president's assessment offers insight into his views on the nature of leadership:

> Carter, who longs for wartime unity, is repelled by the sight of Congress "twisted and pulled" by "special interests." But what repels him is the essence of politics in a free, commercial, continental nation.
>   . . . This is a big, muscular nation full of muscular "factions," and the nation cannot be governed by other than muscular politicians. It cannot be governed by someone who is not good at . . . "wheeling and dealing."[108]

Hugh Sidey perceived the domestic summit as "a devastating indictment of [Carter's] own advisers." Sidey pointed out that the summit would never have been necessary had the Carter White House been doing its job properly. Sidey also discussed the president's leadership problems:

> In Carter's approach to leadership, he has from the start differed markedly from his predecessors. He has been almost as much a supplicant as an authority, a man searching for an elusive consensus in town halls and along Main Street. He has walked more among the people than ahead of them.
>   . . . He may overwhelm himself with too many facts, to the point that he cannot finally make a decision with vision and conviction.[109]

Norman C. Miller called the Camp David retreat "action for the sake of action." Not certain of what needed to be done, the president opted for a "do-something strategy." Miller argued that such drastic action not accompanied by a strategy to resolve the nation's plight further called into question the president's leadership ability.[110]

The *Washington Post* was unenthused about the president's diagnosis of the nation's ills: "The politics of it were devilishly clever, if not angelically attractive—a down-in-the polls president laying off his own unpopularity on the mental health, or lack thereof, of the people." The *Post* believed that Carter's "boomerang rhetoric against the very government he administers" undermined the administration's efforts to achieve a sensible energy policy.[111]

Not surprisingly, the *Wall Street Journal* was one of the president's strongest critics:

> Mr. Carter has reacted to the public's low opinion of his administration by "getting tough" and proposing a further suspension of private freedoms. He justifies this on grounds that it is the American people, not his administration and the Congress, who deserve the blame for our economic problems.

The two key problems that provoked [Carter's] rhetorical outburst—inflation and gasoline lines—are clearly and directly attributable to the policies of the Carter administration.[112]

The *Journal* accused Carter of exploiting public prejudices to divert attention from the administration's inability to solve the energy crisis. In an editorial "From Homily to Demagogy," the *Journal* accused Carter of "scapegoating" OPEC when the war in Iran was responsible for the energy shortage:

But it's far easier to attack dark-skinned foreigners . . . than to admit that one's own policies and administrators have failed.
. . . When the first flush of support dies down, it will become clear that President Carter's strategy for energy war will produce disasters that no amount of demagogy can conceal.[113]

The *New York Times* was more disappointed than the *Journal* in the president's energy proposal. The *Times* agreed with the president's definition of the problem but not with his prescription:

Once again, President Carter has defined the problem, boldly and correctly. Once again he proposes a "war" to rescue the country from crippling dependence. . . . He finds the people ready to sacrifice to "win" this war.
So what does the President prescribe? A collection of measures that, at best, will keep the crisis from getting worse in the next five years.
If there is such an urgent danger to the nation's security and economy, then why does the President not propose a clear and present antidote? Why does he not capitalize on the people's willingness to follow his lead? If he is right about the peril and the opportunity, then he must be judged timid in his response. He simply can't have it both ways.[114]

Joseph Kraft also found Carter's speech excessive in comparison to the substance of the administration's proposals:

The Jimmy Carter who came off the mountain Sunday night wasn't a president ready to make decisions, bite bullets and cut Gordian knots. He was a candidate currying favor with his constituency. So even as he announced the country was at a "turning point in our history," he missed the turn.
Once again . . . Carter shrinks from decision. He says nothing about the truly hard task of pulling a sick industrial system out of the dumps. He ducks when it comes to raising prices and deferring environmental objectives.
Far from governing, far from paying out popularity to make hard things possible, Carter is now moving to accumulate popularity by doing easy things.[115]

In mid-August, Anthony Lewis accused Carter of raising public expectations too high. Lewis also believed that Carter misdiagnosed the country's situation. The *Times* columnist criticized Carter for allowing Congress to recess for a month before taking action on the administration's energy proposals:

The Carter program is largely exhortation and sand castles. It lacks the concrete policy changes that could really make a difference, and be the focus of meaningful public discussion. . . . The President shied away from steps that would have been bold in reality, and politically painful.

. . . the decent, quiet, thoughtful character of the man has somehow not translated itself into the leadership techniques that make Washington work. It was an unhappy symbol when Carter, after all the noise about energy, let Congress go home for a month without a murmur. Can you imagine Franklin Roosevelt missing that chance to make a point?[116]

Two of the most representative advocates of the view that Carter caused the so-called national "malaise" were William Safire and Joseph Kraft. Safire's column "Tricks of the Trade" characterized Carter's speech as a clever device to shift blame from the administration's incompetence to the American people:

. . . the "crisis" is not of the nation's spirit, it is of the Carter Administration's eptitude. The American people have not lost confidence in themselves, they have lost confidence in Mr. Carter. The way he turned that around was neat.
. . . He seems not to care if his tough demeanor and slap-dash decisions have weakened the dollar and shaken the institution of the Presidency. To save his political life, the President has been willing to plunge the nation into an artificial crisis; to meet that crisis, he has created a false and unnatural personality. And that is quite a trick.[117]

Finally, Joseph Kraft contemplated whether Carter contributed to the "national malaise":

In many ways, Carter sows discord and works against a return to national harmony.

For one thing, he is a genuine outsider. As a rural Southerner he is not at home in what I have called Big America—the world of the main corporations, unions, cities and universities. Not only did he come to power by challenging the established structure of authority in the country, but he stays in power by renewing the challenge.

[Carter] lacks the natural attributes of leadership. He has neither the heroic stature of an Eisenhower nor the glamor of a Kennedy. Not even the governing skills of Nixon or Johnson.[118]

These criticisms of the president's speech and energy proposal could not match the enormity of the reaction against Carter's Cabinet shakeup. On July 17, two days after the Crisis of Confidence speech, thirty-four top officials submitted their resignations to the president. The following day Carter named Hamilton Jordan as White House Chief of Staff. On July 19 through 21 Carter accepted the resignations of Secretaries Michael Blumenthal (Treasury), Joseph Califano (Health and Human Services), James Schlesinger (Energy), and Attorney General Griffin Bell. These officials were replaced, respectively, by William Miller, Patricia Harris, Charles Duncan, and Benjamin Civiletti. Soon after Carter accepted the resignation of Secretary Brock Adams

(Transportation). While Carter called the changes "constructive" the print media portrayed the event as a Nixon-like "massacre." In his memoirs Carter conceded:

> I handled the Cabinet changes very poorly. . . . [W]ith all the Cabinet involved in the process, the changes were portrayed as a great governmental crisis and negated some of the progress we had made during the past two weeks in reestablishing better relations with the public. I made the changes rapidly and formed a very strong team with the new appointments, but the same decisions could have been made in a much more effective manner.[119]

The press's reaction to the Cabinet shake-up was less tame than Carter's self-criticism. *U.S. News* labeled the event "Jimmy Carter's 'July Massacre' . . . a desperate gamble to save his beleaguered Presidency."[120] *Time* called the Cabinet shake-up "the most thoroughgoing and puzzling purge in the history of the U.S. presidency."[121] Peter Goldman called the acceptance of Cabinet resignations "a purge as complete and bloody as any in recent Presidential history."[122] William Safire characterized Carter's actions as "Nixon-like."[123] Meg Greenfield added that such a drastic measure coming in the middle of a congressional session, about one year from the elections, appeared "mad."[124]

Journalists portrayed the Cabinet shake-up as a desperate move by a faltering president. They questioned Carter's commitment to a Cabinet of independent thinkers. Jordan's elevation to Chief of Staff was viewed as an effort to restrict control over White House decision-making to the so-called "Georgia mafia."

The *Wall Street Journal's* "Washington Wire" column reported on July 20 that, "Loyalty to Carter now is the test for survival in [Carter's] administration. . . . Staff chief [Hamilton] Jordan had long gunned for [Joseph] Califano and [Michael] Blumenthal because of their independent ways."[125]

That same day James Perry and Albert Hunt of the *Journal* also reported on "one of the messiest power transfers the capital has ever seen." The *Journal* reporters believed that the Cabinet shuffle signaled the tightening of the reins of the "Georgia Mafia" in the administration.[126] The *Post's* Martin Schram expressed a similar view:

> They have pulled the wagons into a circle at the White House in the name of leadership, and all that is certain is that the Georgian insiders are safe— and all the rest are just Indians.
> The message behind yesterday's Cabinet firings is get along or get out. Get along with Hamilton Jordan, Jody Powell and Frank Moore, because they are staying, or get out of the Cabinet.
> President Carter, whose autobiography was called, "Why Not The Best?" has opted to stress personal loyalty and political necessity.[127]

Schram concluded that the Cabinet incident negated all of the positive effects of the Crisis of Confidence speech.[128] The *Journal* predicted that Califano and Blumenthal "would be difficult to replace, particularly now that Mr.

Carter has so obviously turned to the callow and shallow advice of his campaign teammates."[129] Marvin Stone added:

> The President wielded an uncertain tomahawk and ended up scalping more people than he needed to, failing to anticipate, as he has before, the consequences of his actions.
>
> . . . Shake-ups in government are inevitable and sometimes salutary. But the motives and moves this time leave questions. Regardless of the argument over who said what to whom, the chief complaint against Joe Califano was that [he] was not completely loyal—however that is to be interpreted.
>
> . . . [Blumenthal was fired because he] spoke up in the Cabinet meetings and told the President how he saw things. . . . This is one of the most disturbing factors. We would hate to see Carter retreating into a soundproof room, as did some previous Chief Executives who heard nothing that they didn't want to hear.[130]

Peter Goldman's discussion of "Jimmy Carter's Cabinet Purge" focused on the suspicion that Carter made loyalty the key criterion for survival in the administration. Goldman assessed that Carter's "midsummer massacre" had

> . . . gutted his domestic policy team of some of its strongest players, signaled survivors that political loyalty has priority over professional competence and sent a seism of anxiety around the world about the stability of his reign.
>
> . . . The suspicion remained that Carter's White House was passing into the wagons-in-a-circle configuration common to the unhappy recent history of the office—a time in which the courtiers draw in the reins of power and view their ablest colleagues as potential traitors.
>
> . . . The danger for Carter lay in that state-of-seige insularity that has overtaken every Presidency at least since Lyndon Johnson's—a garrison mood in which dissent is perceived as disloyalty and the whisper of the courtiers is mistaken for the voice of America.[131]

In its July 30 issue *Time* magazine carried two articles on the Cabinet incident. The first, "Carter's Great Purge," emphasized the same themes as the above assessments. The second story, "Here Comes Mr. Jordan" focused on the role of the new Chief of Staff. From the former article comes the following analysis of "Carter's wholesale slaughter approach":

> Everywhere, loyalty had become the watchword. A President who had entered office promising that associates could speak their minds freely . . . had clearly heard enough. With the exception of Bell, Carter removed non-Georgian dissenters and replaced them with men who had already demonstrated their loyalty to the Carter team. . . . In effect, the President and his men had done little more than try to shift blame for their troubles to the Cabinet and draw up the wagons in a circle for the 16 month political seige that will end with the 1980 election.[132]

The second article questioned Jordan's fitness for the role of Chief of Staff and challenged the competence of Carter's "White House Georgians":

The staff Carter transplanted to 1600 Pennsylvania Avenue from his Georgia-based presidential campaign was from the start young, inexperienced and fundamentally disorganized. Worse, its members came to Washington with chips on their shoulders about the city's entrenched political establishment. Jordan himself refused even to meet most of the Democratic congressional leadership.[133]

Joseph Kraft concluded that Carter was "bleeding from a thousand self-inflicted wounds. He has lost the respect of Congress and made financial markets skittish." Kraft found it difficult to understand why mass Cabinet resignations were required "in order to make a few, not very significant changes. Even harder to understand is the extreme reliance he places on two persons—Rosalynn Carter and the new White House Chief of Staff Hamilton Jordan—whose strengths are not so much substantive as psychological." In Kraft's view the president's actions put the administration in a poor position to deal with the problems of energy and inflation. "The president's political hold is tenuous. He has become the candidate 16 months before the election, and it is a question whether he can govern effectively."[134]

The *Washington Post* editors regarded the changes in the Carter administration as overdue. In a July 19 editorial the *Post* stated:

A first conclusion is this: Some of Mr. Carter's moves are probably not only right, but also overdue. He should have a chief of staff and Hamilton Jordan as his senior trusted aide should be it. A more normally structured and less collegial White House staff (and atmosphere) is likely to improve the efficiency of the Carter presidency.

. . . And there ends the good news. Now for the part that doesn't look so good. At the simple human level, this thing . . . is likely to have the demoralizing effect that sudden unkindnesses always do. . . . [And] a 2 1/2-years-into-the-term revelation that things are going very badly implies, first, that the president has been far from attentive to his business and, second, that he—not just a bunch of others—has been derelict.[135]

According to the *New York Times* Carter had returned to the role that he was most comfortable with—that of the political candidate running against the establishment. Carter's problem was running against the establishment while leading it:

. . . he seems to have reverted to the stance that won him the White House in the first place, that of the Washington outsider challenging the Washington insiders—Candidate Carter taking some jabs at the leadership of President Carter. It looks as though he wants to be both the omnipotent shah and the triumphant ayatollah; as though he wants to take the family picture and be in it, at the same time.

. . . political agility is not the same thing as masochism. And when it came to actually shuffling half his Cabinet, there was Mr. Carter running against himself again; and also running into himself. All the theatrics on energy had barely sunk in before he upstaged himself with all the Cabinet news.[136]

U.S. News reported that Carter was "coming through as a trapped leader striking out in panic." The news report identified the most scathing comparison of Carter's actions: "Comparisons are being drawn with the Nixon White House, with allusions to a besieged staff pulling the wagons into a circle to stand off the 'enemy.'"[137] David Broder perceived the events leading up to, and including, the Cabinet resignations as a desperation play by Carter to restore an image of leadership: "Reduced to its political essence, it is a bold—almost desperate—bid to buy time in a rapidly eroding situation."[138]

Two articles by Hedrick Smith also portrayed the Cabinet shakeup as (1) an attempt to put stronger White House control over department operations; (2) an effort to cut loose individuals who were political liabilities; and (3) a return by Carter to the anti-Washington themes of the 1976 campaign.[139] William Safire claimed that by rejecting the Nixon model of leadership Carter "gave up much of the authority and purposefulness" of the presidency.[140] And Norman C. Miller's criticisms of Carter for being "insecure" and "isolated" were reminiscent of common perceptions of President Nixon.[141]

The extraordinary events of July 1979 exhibit the propensity of journalistic assessments of the president to vary widely in a short period. The initial speech cancellation and withdrawal to Camp David brought more criticism than usual of the administration. These events appeared to confirm for many journalists the image of the president as indecisive and not in control of his office.

Many journalists initially hailed the Crisis of Confidence speech as one of Carter's finest moments in office. Most assessments focused on the rhetorical and symbolic aspects of Carter's speech which many journalists found reminiscent of Carter's 1976 campaign.

Journalists portrayed the Cabinet shake-up as a governmental crisis created unnecessarily by the president. They perceived the incident, after Carter's successful speech, as an ill-timed and desperate attempt to restore a beleaguered presidency. Once again journalists accused Carter of incompetent leadership and seeking to maintain a "Nixon-like" insular White House.

Continuing Problems: Late July–November

The belief that Carter's presidency would not receive an opportunity for a second term became widespread in late 1979. Carter's difficulty working with Congress was a continuing saga. In mid-August *U.S. News and World Report* reported that "Senators and representatives in overwhelming numbers give Jimmy Carter flunking grades as President." The magazine based this statement on opinion polls of congressmen that revealed that eight of ten members graded Carter's congressional relations as "poor." By October 1, a *U.S. News and World Report* news story observed that in any attempt to recapture the leadership image Carter could not count on much help from Congress. The article concluded that Carter's bargaining powers with Congress were being eroded by the Kennedy challenge and Carter's low public opinion ratings.[142] Tom Morgenthau of *Newsweek* offered a similar view:

> The President, Congressional veterans said, is caught in a self-perpetuating bind: widespread perceptions of his weakness before a Kennedy candidacy have already undermined his clout in Congress—and his inability to get his way on the Hill makes any political recovery all the more difficult.[143]

Terrence Smith found the president unable to maintain a healthy relationship between the political branches. Smith asserted that Carter's problems with Congress

> . . . are fundamentally a reflection of his own low standing in the public opinion polls and the doubts about his prospects for renomination, much less re-election. As a consequence, few Congressmen feel indebted to Mr. Carter or under much compunction to heed the wishes of the White House. He still lacks a cadre of trusted "agents" in Congress who do his bidding out of a sense of personal loyalty.[144]

The Andrew Young controversy plagued the Carter presidency in mid-August 1979. U.S. Ambassador to the United Nations Andrew Young, in defiance of government policy, met privately with representatives of the Palestine Liberation Organization (PLO). Young resigned his position under pressure after it was revealed that he failed to inform the State Department about the meeting with the PLO representatives. Angus Deming of *Newsweek* noted that, "The Young affair once again raised the specter of an Administration in disarray and a President unable to control his own people." Deming concluded "it was evident that Carter had suffered yet another embarrassment that he could ill afford."[145] According to *U.S. News and World Report* the Young resignation damaged Carter's credibility.[146] The *Washington Post* perceived this event as an example of the president's inability to act decisively and diffuse controversy.[147]

As the opening presidential straw poll approached in late 1979, journalists assessed Carter's actions against the backdrop of his political ambitions. The president whom journalists so frequently portrayed as an anti-political leader became regarded as a full-time politician in the White House. On many occasions journalists alleged that federal grants and jobs were directly related to Carter's single-minded desire to defeat Senator Edward M. Kennedy (D-Mass.) in forthcoming straw polls, caucuses and primaries. As *Time* magazine noted:

> Though Carter rebuked Gerald Ford for using his patronage powers in the 1976 campaign, the President has lately resorted to the same practice. He has

made scores of influential appointments in the states where early caucuses and primaries are being held. He has deluged deserving Democrats with invitations to official functions.[148]

On October 29 both *U.S. News and World Report* and *Newsweek* reported on Carter's supposedly newly discovered political astuteness. John W. Mashek, White House correspondent for *U.S. News and World Report,* assessed that Carter "is prepared to exploit every advantage of his office in the months ahead." Mashek noted that Carter demonstrated a recognition of "the popular effect of announcing bundles of 'goodies'—including federal grants for housing, transportation, health and public works" before the Florida caucuses.[149] In a report on Carter's October 20 dedication of the John F. Kennedy library in Boston, Peter Goldman observed:

> As he demonstrated yet again during the week, Carter is learning to exploit the powers and perquisites of his office—to quote the utterances of his recent guest the Pope; to crowd into the victory pictures in a World Series championship locker room; even, as his satisfying mini victory in Florida suggested, to use his incumbency to win elections.[150]

A Failing Presidency

From the Cabinet upheaval until the seizing of the American hostages in Iran on November 4 the press devoted considerable attention to the failed presidency theme. The following articles reveal journalists' views on the essence of public leadership. All of these evaluations, except James Reston's, argue that Carter lacked the attributes of a national leader. A good starting point is *Time* magazine's Lance Morrow, who wrote that "Carter has often seemed an inadequate and dispiriting figure. . . . Carter has not been able to find within himself the passion, the spiritual heat, to inspire. . . . Carter utterly lacks the sheer exuberance of power." Morrow noted that America's "era of great individualists" ended with Lyndon B. Johnson: "It was with LBJ that the U.S. crisis of leadership began." Morrow added that Americans want a leader who is larger than life, who can inspire confidence and solve the nation's many problems.[151]

The *Wall Street Journal* blamed the president's leadership problems on his having "co-opted" the left-wing of the Democratic party. The *Journal* argued that Senator Edward M. Kennedy, ironically, had a chance to win his party's nomination because Jimmy Carter adopted Kennedy's ideas which resulted in a failed presidency.[152] The *Journal* added: "Mr. Carter has been a weak leader because, far from being out in front of the people, he has had to be led kicking and screaming to go in the directions the nation needs to go and wants to go." The *Journal* concluded that Carter's leadership problem could not be defined as an inability to get favorable action on the administration's proposals. Rather, the *Journal* believed, the proposals were wrong. The editorial implied that the nation would be worse off if Carter was, in George F. Will's words, a "muscular leader" capable of moving fifty-dollar rebates and the elimination of three-martini lunches through an otherwise unwilling Congress.[153]

The *Journal's* editorial opinion was almost unique. More often than not commentators subscribed to theories of presidential leadership defining the purpose of the Chief Executive as moving the nation in a particular direction— the "muscular leader" who compels respect and congressional acquiescence. For example, David Broder wrote:

> What we need are people . . . who understand the need for coalition building. We need people who have demonstrated the skills of negotiation and compromises, the insights, the articulateness and the boldness to overcome the centrifugal forces tugging at government in this hyper-pluralistic age.
>
> Amateurs and outsiders, however well motivated, are not likely to possess these qualities or to have honed them to any degree.[154]

Hugh Sidey offered a glorified view of the Chief Executive's purpose: "Only the President can define the national purpose and galvanize his people to pursue it. He is the only person who can move fleets and make diplomatic challenges."[155] Yet, Sidey defined Carter's leadership problem as stemming from "The Compulsion to Excel." In Sidey's view Carter tried to achieve too much: the president woke up earlier and worked later than previous occupants of the Oval Office. In this column, rather than defining a president's role as single-handedly moving fleets and galvanizing public support, Sidey charged Carter to adopt a more humble, Truman-standard of achievement.[156] James Reston argued similarly that Carter's best attributes included hard work, determination, and the ability to absorb detailed information. Reston also believed Carter was in trouble "because of his good qualities. He is trying to go everywhere and do everything."[157]

Meg Greenfield offered some ideas on how a president should lead. These views offer insight into Greenfield's assessment of Carter as lacking leadership attributes:

> The leader is the one who knows how to build [power], activate it, maintain it and use it. He needs to be "tough" in the sense of being serious and consistent and aggressive in the way he exercises this power, and that includes making it costly for those who oppose him and worthwhile for those who comply. But finally and always the blunt instrument will depend on some measure of public support.[158]

Some commentators considered the Carter presidency to be at a crucial turning point. In reaction to the Kennedy challenge and U.S.-Soviet conflict the *Washington Post* noted President Carter was

> . . . being assaulted and pushed, but in a measured and selective way, by his most feared political competitor at home and the country's most feared political competitor abroad. Whatever else these developments may mean, they surely reflect an assumption about the condition of the Carter presidency—that it is malleable and weak.

. . . We are about to see in more ways than one whether the rationalistic, low-key, what's-all-the-fuss-about and—yes—rather passive and mechanistic presidency of Jimmy Carter has the strengths that he and its other promoters say it has.[159]

Peter Goldman reported in August that Carter had a brief time in which to reestablish the viability of the administration. Goldman believed that the prospects for a Carter revival were slim:

Carter's Son of Jimmy revival opened under a cloud of suspicion, shared even in the White House, that he has between 60 days and six months in which to reverse his failing fortunes or be ground under.
. . . Carter's people agree that he will have to produce in what could be prohibitively short order—that he must show real leadership in the three-front war against inflation, recession and the energy bind, or, as one aide concedes, "it's all over."[160]

A *Newsweek* article one month later by Tom Morgenthau also assessed that "Carter has no more than 60 days to somehow revive his faltering presidency. . . . [Carter] faces the real possibility of turning into a lame duck even before the first primary vote is cast."[161]

These criticisms of President Carter reflect a number of the themes in the journalistic assessments discussed so far. Among the criticisms made at this time was the view that Carter was not an inspirational leader. Rather, he was "low-key," "rationalistic," "mechanistic," and lacking the "exuberance of power." Carter allegedly did not understand the necessity of coalition-building. Journalists perceived the president as moving haphazardly from issue to issue, from crisis to crisis, rather than defining a vision for the nation's future.

Foreign Policy Crises: September–January 1980

Foreign policy problems consumed the latter stages of Carter's third year. These problems included the seizure of American diplomats in Teheran by Iranian students and the Soviet invasion of Afghanistan. An earlier, less serious problem was the revelation of the presence of 2,000 Soviet troops in Cuba.

In early September, Senator Frank Church (D-Idaho), Chairman of the Senate Foreign Relations Committee, revealed publicly his knowledge of the Soviet troop presence in Cuba. Church's knowledge of the Soviet brigade was based on privileged information from U.S. intelligence reports that were revealed to some congressional leaders. While campaigning in Idaho, Church called a press conference to report his plans to cancel SALT II hearings pending clarification by the administration of the status of the Soviet troops in Cuba. The Church statement caused a public furor. The press portrayed the event as a major test of Carter's crisis leadership. *Time* magazine reported the Soviet presence in Cuba was a "test" of the Carter administration's resolve,[162] and of Carter's "leadership ability." The magazine noted that this was "potentially the most explosive" issue faced by the Carter administration.[163]

The *Washington Post* portrayed the Soviet presence in Cuba as a test of Carter's resolve and added that the affair occurred because Carter was "malleable and weak."[164] In the *Post*'s view the Cuba crisis "was produced in good measure by the administration's own ineptitude."[165] Tom Wicker agreed that in this event "Mr. Carter underlined the ineptitude of his administration and reinforced the widespread impression that the President doesn't know what he's doing."[166] Joseph Kraft criticized Carter's response to the Soviet presence in Cuba:

> The Russians must now be under the impression that President Carter needs SALT so badly that it doesn't matter how recklessly they behave in areas of confrontation. Worse still, the same estimate is probably being made by countries that base their actions on assessments of the balance between Washington and Moscow.[167]

In light of the Cuba controversy Marvin Stone assessed the SALT debate as a referendum on Carter's ability to deal with a growing Soviet military threat:

> The crisis of confidence in Carter's ability to deal with the Soviet threat comes as no surprise to those familiar with the President's record. With rare exceptions, his actions have engendered doubts among America's allies as well as among defense authorities in this country about his judgment and his leadership.
>
> At the outset he packed his administration with officials who seemed more interested in pursuing arms control negotiations with Moscow than in countering Russia's massive military buildup. All too frequently, the President has tended to play down the Soviet threat and question the utility of military power. The administration has lacked a coherent strategy to underwrite the nation's overall security and to protect America's interests overseas.[168]

President Carter eventually diffused the furor over the Soviet presence with a speech to the nation and a session with congressional leaders. It became evident that the Soviet troops were a portion of a larger brigade that had been in training in Cuba for a number of years. The *Washington Post*, which earlier declared the Carter presidency "malleable and weak" because of its acceptance of the Soviet presence in Cuba, offered an editorial— "The Crisis that Wasn't."[169] *Time* magazine's story, "Carter Defuses a Crisis," referred to "the inflated fuss over the Soviet combat brigade in Cuba" and added that Carter's speech to the nation "was one of the most important of his career." Yet the *Time* report noted that Carter's handling of the incident failed to "add any much needed decisiveness to his image as a leader."[170]

On November 4, 1979, exactly one year prior to the 1980 elections, a group of Iranian militants seized the United States embassy in Teheran taking more than 50 diplomats hostage. As Carter revealed in his memoirs, the administration at first was unaware of the potential for the hostage affair to last long:

> We were deeply disturbed, but reasonably confident that the Iranians would soon remove the attackers from the embassy compound and release our people. We and other nations had faced this kind of attack many times in the past, but never, so far as we knew, had a host government failed to attempt to protect threatened diplomats.[171]

When it became apparent that the hostage crisis was not to be resolved quickly and that the Iranian militants were acting with the support of their government, the Carter administration adopted a variety of responses including a ban on importation of Iranian oil and the freezing of nine billion dollars of Iranian bank assets in the United States. The president also ordered a crackdown on Iranian students in the United States who possibly had violated the terms of their visas. The public reacted favorably to the president's actions. Opinion polls showed by December 4 the largest one-month gain by a United States president in polling history. Amid this public acclaim Carter announced on December 4 his plans to run for re-election.

Print-media opinion of Carter's handling of the Iranian crisis was mixed. Some journalists praised Carter's "leadership" in handling the international incident. Others simply reported that Carter benefited in opinion ratings from the hostage takeover. Many writers criticized the president's response to the hostage seizure.

The early reaction to Carter's policy of restraint was reserved. A *Time* magazine report noted that Carter recognized that patience would "reinforce the public's perception of the President as a poor leader. Carter must have recognized the potential damage to his candidacy, but concluded that he had little choice but to act as he did."[172]

U.S. News and World Report also reported initially on the importance of the events in Iran to Carter's stature both domestically and abroad:

> Freedom for the Americans was Jimmy Carter's major goal. But the President had other crucial stakes riding on negotiations with Iran. Among them: To avoid further deterioration of his image, already that of an indecisive leader, at home and abroad. This was important in the wake of what critics believed was his weak-kneed response to the presence of a Soviet combat brigade in Cuba.[173]

George F. Will characterized the administration's sanctions against Iran as ineffectual and guaranteed "to keep the United States immobile." Will accused Carter of "treating the crisis as a media event and . . . offering as policy a stream of gestures." According to Will, the administration's response accelerated "the erosion of respect for this nation." Will added that "the kinds of policies that brought on the crisis—right-mindedness, supplications and the scrupulous avoidance of conflict—are failing to resolve it."[174]

Marvin Stone's editorial "Iran—and After" also attributed the hostage takeover to the president's "abhorrence of power." After implying that there was "a link between the outrages against American diplomatic missions and the past performance of this administration in world affairs," Stone added:

> The U.S. has projected an image of weakness, indecision and vacillation. For the past three years, there has been a pattern in every international test of strength—tough talk followed by a shrinking from action. . . . Throughout, Carter has demonstrated a penchant for responding to challenges and rebuffs by turning the other cheek. . . . The cumulative effect of the Carter administration's behavior has been to debase the prestige of the United States and to invite insults—and worse—even from the pygmies of the international community.[175]

A *Washington Post* editorial found Carter willing to accommodate international enemies. In reference to Khomeini's assertion that Carter lacked the "guts" to engage a military operation against Iran the *Post* replied: "The taunt is not entirely unfounded. . . . His diplomacy, in general, has relied on a premise of the other person's reasonableness that, to put it mildly, has not always been in evidence."[176]

Joseph Kraft initially charged the administration "to play it cool" so as not to endanger the lives of the hostages. He criticized the president for rhetoric which supposedly led to a hardening of the Ayatollah's position.[177] Only several days after making this observation Kraft's enthusiasm for "cool" headed responses had waned. Kraft implied that Carter's alleged lack of resolve prolonged the hostage crisis.[178] Kraft assessed that Carter's renunciation of force "weakens the American stance around the world." He observed that "public abandonment of the military option deepens the plight of the hostages."[179]

Some journalists portrayed Carter as basking in undeserved public acclaim. Terrence Smith wrote that the Iranian crisis gave Carter a second political life. That crisis, Smith added, detracted from Carter's leadership problems, the Young affair, the Cabinet shakeup, the Cuban crisis, and other incidents affecting the president's public esteem.[180]

Joseph Kraft implied that Carter's political standing would improve even with a prolonged hostage affair: "The hostages get Jimmy Carter's best shot—compassion for people in trouble. So, as long as they are center screen, the Iran crisis promotes the political fortunes of the President."[181]

Some critics' views were compatible with public sentiments about Carter's response. A *Time* magazine news article found Carter to be projecting a leadership image: "After months of floundering and indecision, Carter has appeared both prudent and dynamic—in short, a leader."[182] *Time* responded approvingly to Carter's first press conference since the crisis began: "[Carter] spoke in determined and sometimes angry tones, projecting with considerable success the sense of leadership that he often seemed to lack."[183] And in its end of the year issue *Time* issued a report on "Carter's Rousing Revival":

This was Jimmy Carter, President, leading the U.S. in a way that, until the Iranian crisis erupted in November, the former Governor of Georgia had not managed in his three years in the White House. Through those first thousand days, Carter had stumbled and tripped, scored some victories, but lost his way many times. Under his Administration, the economy had worsened, with inflation moving to levels higher than any since the end of World War II and with the threat of a serious recession growing more on balance, the American people had judged Jimmy Carter to be inept. . . . All that has now changed.[184]

Attempting to convey how he and other benevolent critics of Carter would react if the hostage situation dragged on very long, William Raspberry wrote:

Concern for the well-being of the hostages made patience seem an attractive choice. Concern for image, for the danger of communicating a sense of weakness to the world and for the prospect of triggering additional insult, suggested the need for a strong, military response.

Carter, who might have opted for some saber-rattling reaction, knowing that he would have had our support, opted instead for restraint. It was a wise choice.

But there is a fine line between restraint and timidity, and the danger for Carter is that, if the Iranian situation drags on much longer, those of us who have been praising him for refusing to act rashly will be damning him for refusing to act.[185]

This view proved correct. An early example of the almost fickle nature of public discourse on Carter's handling of the crisis was the *Washington Post*'s editorials. After characterizing the Ayatollah's assertion that Carter had no "guts" as a reasonable claim, the *Post* wrote on December 4:

The irony of Jimmy Carter's presidency is that he has never seemed so presidential as he has in these last terrible 30 days. He has demonstrated leadership in a uniquely difficult situation in stark contrast to the political amateur hour that describes much of his administration's relations with Congress, the Democratic Party and large parts of the political world.[186]

By the end of December the *Post* raised questions about Carter's leadership "quality" and "almost reticent" responses to international crises:

It is not so much that he is letting the nation's defenses slip, or that his crisis management skills are not up to snuff. It is that he has not yet found the right voice in which to speak to the American people about the perils they face in the world. . . . There is in his tone and his message an apparent absence of urgency, a surfeit of let-us-be-patient, day-at-a-time resignation.[187]

The changing assessments of many of Carter's critics reflected more than the hostage crisis. In late December 1979 the Soviet Union moved troops into Afghanistan and installed a puppet ruler. Carter referred to the Soviet invasion as a "grave threat to peace" yet appeared unable to influence the

Soviets' behavior. Carter's initial reply, to invoke the principles of international law, was spoofed by George F. Will: "Quick, find that rulebook and notify the referee. President Carter says the Soviet invasion of Afghanistan violates 'accepted international rules of behavior.'" Will complained that Carter's rules were those of the international community: "But that community is . . . [a] fiction."[188] A *Washington Post* editorial agreed that the diplomatic realm was not a serious forum for resolving the Afghanistan crisis:

> If the administration finds something unacceptable in Soviet policy in Afghanistan, it should take its protests out of the code of diplomatic signals and put the issue in a forum where the American voice will be clearly heard. Otherwise, everybody, including the Russians, may conclude that Mr. Carter doesn't really care.[189]

Marvin Stone believed that a weak foreign policy encouraged Soviet adventurism. Stone, lamenting the "stench of weakness that hangs over Washington," believed that the Soviet invasion of Afghanistan "further exposed to ridicule the Carter policy of appeasing the Soviet dictatorship."[190]

In early January 1980 Carter responded by imposing a grain embargo on the Soviet Union, requesting a Senate delay of consideration of the SALT II treaty, and boycotting the Olympic games in Moscow. Carter announced these moves in a nationally televised address. The press response was mixed. Joseph Kraft noted the action came too close to the Iowa caucuses to be considered anything but political:

> Even though I favored the actions announced by the President, it was impossible not to feel that the sudden rush to the screen was totally political, was motivated heavily by a wish to out flank the Republican debate in Des Moines. . . . Unless the president is prepared to take himself out of the race, being nonpolitical in the midst of a campaign comes hard. But there is a good test. Anything announced dramatically on national television smacks of domestic politics.[191]

Time magazine emphasized that the embargo "violated all Jimmy Carter's instincts—his political instinct for the charitable gesture, his personal instinct for compassion." The report concluded that by demanding sacrifices at home to confront a threat abroad, the Carter administration "carries out, in the most fundamental way, the demands and obligations of world leadership."[192] This view is understandable given the magazine's belief that earlier "U.S. policy led Moscow to conclude that it might be able to take advantage of a President who appeared so unsure of himself. Another element that may have contributed to the current crisis is the Administration's declining ability to use force."[193]

Journalists perceived the administration's response to the Soviets' action as a fundamental policy reversal after three years of seeking negotiated settlements to international disputes. This theme pervaded the assessments of Carter's foreign policy after the 1980 State of the Union Address. The following quotes from Robert Dudney's analysis in *U.S. News and World*

Report foreshadowed this theme and appropriately concludes the journalistic assessments of Carter in 1979:

It's not just strategy toward Russia that is being reversed. Almost every international goal set by the President three years ago is up for grabs.

. . . Nearly every international theme unveiled with great fanfare by the President three years ago has been abandoned or altered beyond recognition—from human rights to downgrading the Russian threat, from arms control to austerity in defense spending.

An ardent pursuit of detente and arms-control agreements with Russia has given way to a tough new approach to Soviet expansionism backed by military muscle flexing.[194]

Notes

1. Terrence Smith, "Carter at Summit Talks: A Gain in Stature," *New York Times,* January 8, 1979, p. A3

2. Hugh Sidey, "The Virtues of Secrecy," *Time,* January 1, 1979, p. 61.

3. "Junior Year," *New York Times,* January 25, 1979, p. A18.

4. "Carter to Nation: Don't Expect Too Much," *U.S. News and World Report,* February 5, 1979, p. 31.

5. Peter Goldman, "The Politics of Austerity," *Newsweek,* January 29, 1979, p. 20; see also, Peter Goldman, "Carter's 'New Foundation,'" *Newsweek,* February 5, 1979, p. 25.

6. "The State of the Union: Austere," *Time,* February 5, 1979, pp. 8–9.

7. "The State of Jimmy Carter," *Time,* February 5, 1979, pp. 10–12.

8. "A Pudding Without a Theme," *Wall Street Journal,* January 25, 1979, p. 24.

9. "Mr. Carter's Omission," *Washington Post,* January 25, 1979, p. A22.

10. "Presidential Seige," *U.S. News and World Report,* March 5, 1979, p. 19.

11. "Surprise and Confusion," *Time,* February 26, 1979, pp. 14–15.

12. "Carter: Black and Blue," *Time,* March 5, 1979, p. 11.

13. David M. Alpern, "Feeling Helpless," *Newsweek,* February 26, 1979, pp. 22–25.

14. "Two Washington Triangles," *Washington Post,* February 12, 1979, p. A18.

15. Rowland Evans and Robert Novak, "How Carter Views the World," *Washington Post,* January 31, 1979, p. A19.

16. Rowland Evans and Robert Novak, "Watchword at the White House: 'Restraint,'" *Washington Post,* February 21, 1979, p. A15.

17. See, for instance, "The Last Ditch Argument," *Wall Street Journal,* January 30, 1979, p. 16; and "Where Have You Been Senators?" *Wall Street Journal,* February 28, 1979, p. 22.

18. Peter Goldman, "Small-Stick Diplomacy," *Newsweek,* March 5, 1979, p. 39.

19. Hugh Sidey, "The Flood Tides of History," *Time,* February 19, 1979, p. 16.

20. Hugh Sidey, "How to End Up No. 2," *Time,* March 12, 1979, p. 16.

21. Hugh Sidey, "A Touch of the Healing Grace," *Time,* March 19, 1979, p. 29.

22. Meg Greenfield, "Giving Billy Abzug [sic] the Treatment," *Newsweek,* January 29, 1979, p. 88.

23. Meg Greenfield, "What Carter Thinks He's Doing," *Newsweek,* February 26, 1979, p. 100.

24. "Lurching on the Mideast Road," *Washington Post*, February 28, 1979, p. A22; see also, "Camp David II," *Washington Post*, February 22, 1979, p. A16.

25. "Toward Peace in the Middle East . . . ," *Washington Post*, March 6, 1979, p. A18. See also, "Not Yet Peace in the Mideast," *Washington Post*, March 13, 1979, p. A16.

26. "The Cairo Gamble," *Wall Street Journal*, March 7, 1979, p. 20.

27. Karen Elliot House, "Carter to Put Prestige On Line in Trip to Mideast Described as Do-Or-Die Effort," *Wall Street Journal*, March 6, 1979, p. 3.

28. "The Final, Extra Mile," *Time*, March 19, 1979, p. 14.

29. "Peace: Risks and Rewards," *Time*, March 26, 1979, pp. 12, 18.

30. Karen Elliot House, "Key Carter Triumph: Israeli Cabinet Clears Compromises But Mideast Tensions Are Still Seen," *Wall Street Journal*, March 15, 1979, p. 2.

31. Ibid; and Karen Elliot House, "Risks of Peace," *Wall Street Journal*, March 23, 1979, pp. 1, 26.

32. "Middle East: The Price Carter Paid," *U.S. News and World Report*, March 26, 1979, pp. 21–24.

33. Hugh Sidey, "A Soothing Touch of Realism," *Time*, March 26, 1979, p. 24; see also Hugh Sidey's "In Celebration of Peace: For Carter, Begin and Sadat, a Joyous Signing in Washington," *Time*, April 9, 1979, pp. 30–35.

34. Rowland Evans and Robert Novak, "To Buttress 'Innocent' Statesmanship," *Washington Post*, March 16, 1979, p. A19.

35. David Butler, "The Extra Mile," *Newsweek*, March 19, 1979, p. 33.

36. David Butler, "How Carter Did It," *Newsweek*, March 26, 1979, p. 32.

37. "On the Mountaintop," *Washington Post*, March 20, 1979, p. 25.

38. Angus Deming, "Jimmy the Persuader," *Newsweek*, March 19, 1979, p. 25.

39. Joseph Kraft, "No Domestic 'Miracles,'" *Washington Post*, March 18, 1979, p. D7.

40. Joseph Kraft, "Being Presidential," *Washington Post*, April 1, 1979, p. B7.

41. Peter Goldman, "Carter's New Energy Plan," *Newsweek*, April 2, 1979, pp. 27–28; and Peter Goldman, "The Energy Triangle," *Newsweek*, April 16, 1979, pp. 27–28.

42. "Decontrol's Soft, Soft Sell," *Wall Street Journal*, April 9, 1979, p. 20.

43. "A Revenue Measure," *Wall Street Journal*, April 16, 1979, p. 22.

44. "Demeaning Rhetoric," *Wall Street Journal*, April 25, 1979, p. 22.

45. "Declaring War on Big Oil," *Washington Post*, April 25, 1979, p. A28.

46. James Reston, "A Minority Report," *New York Times*, April 15, 1979, p. E17.

47. James Fallows, "The Passionless Presidency," *Atlantic*, May 1979.

48. James Reston, "Leaders of Men," *New York Times*, April 27, 1979, p. A31.

49. James Fallows, "The Passionless Presidency," *Atlantic*, May 1979.

50. Ibid.

51. James Reston, "Leaders of Men," *New York Times*, April 27, 1979, p. A31.

52. William Safire, "The Secret of Carter," *New York Times*, April 26, 1979, p. A23.

53. David Broder, "Government by Campaign Junkies," *Washington Post*, May 23, 1979, p. A23.

54. Marvin Stone, "Still Time for Carter?" *U.S. News and World Report*, June 25, 1979, p. 72.

55. "Shrinking From Politics," *New York Times*, May 25, 1979, p. A28. James Fallows in a letter to the editor of the Times (June 4, 1979, p. A16) claims that he never argued that Jimmy Carter should remain "above politics" but rather, that the president should be knowledgeable about what to do with political power. Fallows,

in fact, complained a number of times that commentators were taking his quotes out of context in order to portray the president and White House staff as negatively as possible. See "Fallows' Fracas: How to Enrage Ex-Colleagues," *Time*, May 7, 1979, p. A25. See also on the Fallows articles, "Ex-Speech Writer Views Carter as 'Arrogant, Complacent and Insecure,'" *New York Times*, April 23, 1979, p. A16; and Martin Tolchin, "Ex-Speechwriter Asserts Carter Doesn't Inspire Staff Confidence," *New York Times*, May 19, 1979, p. 48.

56. Hedrick Smith, "Carter Aides Showing Toll of Attacks From All Sides," *New York Times*, May 29, 1979, pp. A1, 20.

57. "Carter: A Song of Woe," *Time*, June 4, 1979, p. 16.

58. "The Sky Is Falling On Washington!" *Time*, June 11, 1979, pp. 20–21.

59. Tom Mathews, "On the Offensive," *Newsweek*, May 7, 1979, p. 31.

60. Peter Goldman, "State of Seige," *Newsweek*, June 4, 1979, pp. 20–21.

61. Joseph Kraft, "To Call it 'Lancegate' Is Ludicrous," *Washington Post*, May 27, 1979, p. C7.

62. Rowland Evans and Robert Novak, "The Peril Carter Sees On the Left," *Washington Post*, May 11, 1979, p. A15.

63. "The Presidential Puzzle," *Wall Street Journal*, June 6, 1979, p. 24.

64. James Reston, "Mr. Carter On His Critics," *New York Times*, May 30, 1979, p. A23.

65. "Underdog Carter," *New York Times*, June 3, 1979, p. E18.

66. Martin Schram, "Gas Crisis: Color the White House Blue," *Washington Post*, July 1, 1979, pp. A1, 5.

67. Marvin Stone, "Carter vs. a Dangerous World," *U.S. News and World Report*, March 5, 1979, p. 88.

68. The following quotes from Broder, Kraft, the *New York Times* and the *Wall Street Journal* are cited in Stone's article.

69. Joseph Kraft, "A Modest Summit," *Washington Post*, June 14, 1979, p. A19.

70. "The Second Vienna Summit," *Washington Post*, June 14, 1979, p. A18. See also, "For a Summit of Achievement," *Washington Post*, May 13, 1979, p. A18.

71. "Destabilizing Turkey," *Wall Street Journal*, May 31, 1979, p. 24.

72. "Policing Power Abuse," *Wall Street Journal*, June 4, 1979, p. 18.

73. David Broder, "At the Summit: An Open-Eyed President," *Washington Post*, June 13, 1979, p. A17.

74. George F. Will, "The SALT Crisis Was Optional," *Washington Post*, July 5, 1979, p. A19.

75. "Down From the Summit," *Washington Post*, June 20, 1979, p. A14. Additional articles about the summit not discussed here are "Atmosphere of Urgency," *Time*, May 14, 1979, pp. 12–13; Jack McWethy, "Carter vs. Brezhnev," *U.S. News and World Report*, June 18, 1979, p. 20; "'Khorasho,' Said Brezhnev," *Time*, June 25, 1979, pp. 10–15; "Signed and Sealed . . . But Not Delivered," *Time*, July 2, 1979, pp. 28–29, 32.

76. Elizabeth Drew, "A Reporter at Large," *The New Yorker*, August 27, 1979, p. 53.

77. "CBS/New York Times Poll," *New York Times*, July 13, 1979, p. 1.

78. Timothy D. Schellhardt, "Carter's Crossroads: His Future May Rest On Camp David Acts," *Wall Street Journal*, July 9, 1979, pp. 1, 18.

79. Hedrick Smith, "Carter Agonistes," *New York Times*, July 8, 1979, p. E1.

80. Timothy D. Schellhardt, "Carter's Crossroads: His Future May Rest On Camp David Acts," *Wall Street Journal*, July 9, 1979, pp. 1, 18. See also Schellhardt's "Do WE Expect Too Much?" *Wall Street Journal*, July 10, 1979, p. 22.

81. "Because It's There," *Washington Post*, July 11, 1979, p. A22.

82. "Is Time Running Out for Carter," *U.S. News and World Report*, July 9, 1979, p. 13.

83. Quoted in "Carter Was Speechless: Both His Friends and Foes Talked of Lack of Leadership," *Time*, July 16, 1979, pp. 8–11.

84. Ibid., p. 8.

85. Peter Goldman, "Carter's Secret Summit," *Newsweek*, July 16, 1979, p. 20.

86. Tom Wicker, "Carter on the Precipice," *New York Times*, July 10, 1979, p. A15.

87. William Safire, "Carter's 4th of July Panic," *New York Times*, July 9, 1979, p. A17.

88. William Safire, "All the Help He Can Get," *New York Times*, July 12, 1979, p. A21.

89. Joseph Kraft, "Tilting Toward 'Big America,'" *Washington Post*, July 15, 1979, p. E7.

90. Meg Greenfield, "A Government In Exile," *Newsweek*, July 23, 1979, p. 26.

91. Hugh Sidey, "To Push a Nation Beyond Itself," *Time*, July 16, 1979, p. 11.

92. Hedrick Smith, "Carter, Conscious of Risks, Seeks Wider Audience," *New York Times*, July 14, 1979, pp. 1, 6.

93. David Broder, "Carter Seeking Oratory to Move an Entire Nation," *Washington Post*, July 14, 1979, pp. A1, 8. Broder also wrote on July 15, the day of the Carter speech, that the President "will be addressing what he sees as a malaise in the country. . . . " In, "Carter Faces Tough Audience at End of Summit," *Washington Post*, July 15, 1979, pp. A1, 10.

94. Ibid.

95. "Changing the Way Things Are," *Washington Post*, July 15, 1979, p. E6. See also, "A Crisis of the Spirit," *Time*, July 23, 1979, pp. 20–29.

96. Jimmy Carter, *Keeping Faith* (New York: Bantam, 1982), p. 120.

97. Hedrick Smith, "Part Homily, Part Program," *New York Times*, July 16, 1979, pp. A1, 10.

98. Martin Schram, "Carter: Back on Track and Eager to Take the Lead," *Washington Post*, July 17, 1979, p. A14.

99. David Broder, "After 30 Months, Self-Criticism, Sense of Purpose," *Washington Post*, July 16, 1979, pp. A1, 15.

100. Ibid.

101. David Broder, "The Wife's Eye," *Washington Post*, July 18, 1979, p. A19.

102. Peter Goldman, "To Lift a Nation's Spirit," *Newsweek*, July 23, 1979, pp. 20–26.

103. "Down from the Mountain," *U.S. News and World Report*, July 23, 1979, p. 16; see also, Stephen Rosenfeld, "A Special Strain of Nationalism," *Washington Post*, July 20, 1979, p. A15.

104. Tom Wicker, "After the Thunder," *New York Times*, July 17, 1979, p. A17.

105. George F. Will, "The Virtues of Boldness," *Newsweek*, July 23, 1979, p. 92.

106. George F. Will, "The Silverware Criterion," *Washington Post*, July 22, 1979, p. D7.

107. Ibid.

108. George F. Will, "A Reluctant Broker," *Washington Post*, July 19, 1979, p. A19.

109. Hugh Sidey, "A Man Searching for Consensus," *Time*, July 23, 1979, p. 22.

110. Norman C. Miller, "The Carter Enigma," *Wall Street Journal*, July 19, 1979, p. 14; see also James Perry and Dennis Farney, "Carter's Fate May Hinge On Where Voters Place Blame for Nation's Ills," *Wall Street Journal*, July 17, 1979, p. 2.

111. "The Right Commitment," *Washington Post*, July 17, 1979, p. A16.

112. "The Real Jimmy Carter," *Wall Street Journal*, July 17, 1979, p. 18.

113. "From Homily to Demagogy," *Wall Street Journal*, July 17, 1979, p. 18.

114. "Riding Casually to War," *New York Times*, July 17, 1979, p. A16.

115. Joseph Kraft, "Carter: A Candidate Again," *Washington Post*, July 17, 1979, p. A17.

116. Anthony Lewis, "The Carter Mystery: II," *New York Times*, August 16, 1979, p. A23.

117. William Safire, "Tricks of the Trade," *New York Times*, July 19, 1979, p. A19.

118. Joseph Kraft, "A Genuine Outsider," *Washington Post*, July 19, 1979, p. A19.

119. Jimmy Carter, *Keeping Faith* (New York: Bantam, 1982), p. 121.

120. "Behind the White House Purge," *U.S. News and World Report*, July 30, 1979, p. 14.

121. "Carter's Great Purge," *Time*, July 30, 1979, p. 10.

122. Peter Goldman, "Jimmy Carter's Cabinet Purge," *Newsweek*, July 30, 1979, p. 22.

123. William Safire, "Through the Dark, Glassily," *New York Times*, July 23, 1979, p. A17.

124. Meg Greenfield, "Post-Surgical Care," *Newsweek*, July 30, 1979, p. 84.

125. "Washington Wire," *Wall Street Journal*, July 20, 1979, p. 1.

126. James Perry and Albert Hunt, "Carter Shakeup Stirs Tension and Disarray—Just as He Tries to Lead," *Wall Street Journal*, July 20, 1979, pp. 1, 24.

127. Martin Schram, "A Ring Around the White House," *Washington Post*, July 20, 1979, p. A1.

128. Ibid., pp. A1, 9.

129. "The Cabinet Shuffle," *Wall Street Journal*, July 19, 1979, p. 14.

130. Marvin Stone, "Carter's Uncertain Tomahawk," *U.S. News and World Report*, August 6, 1979, p. 72.

131. Peter Goldman, "Jimmy Carter's Cabinet Purge," *Newsweek*, July 30, 1979, pp. 22–23.

132. "Carter's Great Purge," *Time*, July 30, 1979, pp. 10–11.

133. "Here Comes Mr. Jordan," *Time*, July 30, 1979, p. 22.

134. Joseph Kraft, "Self-Inflicted Wounds," *Washington Post*, July 29, 1979, p. D7.

135. "Reinventing the Administration," *Washington Post*, July 19, 1979, p. A18.

136. "Running Against Himself," *New York Times*, July 22, 1979, p. E18.

137. "Behind the White House Purge," *U.S. News and World Report*, July 30, 1979, p. 14.

138. David Broder, "Buying Time," *Washington Post*, July 22, 1979, p. D7.

139. Hedrick Smith, "Edgy Capital Sifts Rumors," *New York Times*, July 19, 1979, pp. A1, 17; Hedrick Smith, "Dismissals Taken as Pre-Campaign Move by Carter," *New York Times*, July 20, 1979, pp. 1, 10; and Tom Wicker's "Carter's 'Different Road,'" *New York Times*, July 22, 1979, p. E19.

140. William Safire, "Through the Dark, Glassily," *New York Times*, July 23, 1979, p. A17.

141. Norman C. Miller, "Carter's Insecurity," *Wall Street Journal*, August 2, 1979, p. 10.

142. "Congress Tells Carter How He Rates," *U.S. News and World Report*, August 13, 1979, pp. 21-23; and William L. Chaze, "Little Help for Carter in Congress," *U.S. News and World Report*, October 1, 1979, p. 23.

143. Tom Morgenthau, "Carter Can't Get Up the Hill," *Newsweek*, October 1, 1979, p. 19.

144. Terrence Smith, "Carter and Congress: The Last Picture," *New York Times*, September 9, 1979, p. E1.

145. Angus Deming, "The Andrew Young Affair," *Newsweek*, August 17, 1979, p. 16.

146. "Goodbye Andy (Young)," *U.S. News and World Report*, August 27, 1979, p. 16.

147. "A Belated Intervention," *Washington Post*, September 2, 1979, p. C6.

148. "Kennedy: Ready, Set . . . ," *Time*, September 24, 1979, p. 15.

149. John W. Mashek, "As Carter Flexes Muscles of the White House," *U.S. News and World Report*, October 29, 1979, p. 38.

150. Peter Goldman, "Jimmy in Camelot, " *Newsweek*, October 29, 1979, p. 34.

151. Lance Morrow, "A Cry for Leadership," *Time*, August 6, 1979, pp. 24–27.

152. "Kennedy and Carter," *Wall Street Journal*, September 19, 1979, p. 20.

153. "On Leadership," *Wall Street Journal*, October 26, 1979, p. 20.

154. David Broder, "The Leading Question," November 18, 1979, p. A23.

155. Hugh Sidey, "The Forge of Leadership," *Time*, November 19, 1979, p. 23.

156. Hugh Sidey, "The Compulsion to Excel," *Time*, October 1, 1979, p. 23.

157. James Reston, "In Praise of Fishing," *New York Times*, September 19, 1979, p. A25.

158. Meg Greenfield, "Leadership Chic," *Newsweek*, October 22, 1979, p. 132.

159. "Kennedy, Cuba and Carter," *Washington Post*, September 9, 1979, p. B6.

160. Peter Goldman, "On the Revival Circuit," *Newsweek*, September 19, 1979, p. 21.

161. Tom Morgenthau, "Teddy Gets Ready," *Newsweek*, September 17, 1979, pp. 28–29.

162. "The Storm Over Cuba," *Time*, September 17, 1979, p. 15.

163. "Search for a Way Out," *Time*, October 9, 1979, pp. 24-25.

164. "Kennedy, Cuba and Carter," *Washington Post*, September 9, 1979, p. B6.

165. "Mr. Carter and Cuba," *Washington Post*, September 30, 1979, p. B6.

166. Tom Wicker, "Out of the Closet," *New York Times*, September 18, 1979, p. A25.

167. Joseph Kraft, "Reverse Linkage," *Washington Post*, October 4, 1979, p. A22.

168. Marvin Stone, "Real Issue in SALT Debate," *U.S. News and World Report*, September 17, 1979, p. 88.

169. "The Crisis That Wasn't," *Washington Post*, October 3, 1979, p. A22.

170. "Carter Diffuses a Crisis," *Time*, October 16, 1979, p. 43.

171. Jimmy Carter, *Keeping Faith* (New York: Bantam, 1982), p. 457.

172. "Blackmailing the U.S.," *Time*, November 19, 1979, p. 15; see also "Iran: The Test of Wills," *Time*, November 26, 1979, pp. 20–32; and "Angry Attacks on America," *Time*, December 3, 1979, pp. 24ff.

173. "Nightmare in Iran," *U.S. News and World Report*, November 19, 1979, p. 23; see also, "Test of U.S. Resolve," *U.S. News and World Report*, November 26, 1979, p. 29; "Islam in Ferment," *U.S. News and World Report*, December 10, 1979, pp. 27–30; and "A Nation Aroused," *U.S. News and World Report*, December 17, 1979, pp. 23–24.

174. George F. Will, "Gestures, Gestures," *Washington Post*, December 30, 1979, p. D7.

175. Marvin Stone, "Iran—and After," *U.S. News and World Report*, November 26, 1979, p. 108.

176. "No Guts?" *Washington Post*, November 22, 1979, p. A22.

177. Joseph Kraft, "Riding Out the Islamic Wave," *Washington Post*, November 27, 1979, p. A17.

178. Joseph Kraft, "Running From Crisis," *Washington Post*, December 2, 1979, p. D7.

179. Joseph Kraft, "Responding Less Than Forcefully," *Washington Post*, December 13, 1979, p. A19.

180. Terrence Smith, "Carter's Second Chance: Political Benefits in Iranian Crisis," *New York Times*, December 5, 1979, p. A26.

181. Joseph Kraft, "The OPEC Test," *Washington Post*, December 18, 1979, p. A19.

182. "The Hostages in Danger," *Time*, December 17, 1979, p. 21.

183. "The Storm Over the Shah," *Time*, December 10, 1979, p. 27.

184. "Carter's Rousing Revival," *Time*, December 31, 1979, p. 12.

185. William Raspberry, "Running Out of Patience and Luck?" *Washington Post*, December 28, 1979, p. A17.

186. "As Mr. Carter Announces," *Washington Post*, December 4, 1979, p. A20.

187. "Voice of the President," *Washington Post*, December 30, 1979, p. D6.

188. George F. Will, "Ruling Out Detente," *Washington Post*, January 3, 1979, p. A19.

189. "Moscow Versus Islam," *Washington Post*, December 26, 1979, p. A12.

190. Marvin Stone, "Meaning of Afghanistan," *U.S. News and World Report*, January 14, 1979, p. 84.

191. Joseph Kraft, "No Time for Prime Time," *Washington Post*, January 10, 1980, p. A19; see also, Joseph Kraft, "Crisis on Hold," *Washington Post*, January 13, 1980, p. B7.

192. "Grain Becomes a Weapon," *Time*, January 21, 1980, pp. 21–22.

193. "Squeezing the Soviets," *Time*, January 28, 1980, p.13.

194. Robert Dudney, "Carter's U-Turn in Foreign Policy," *U.S. News and World Report*, January 28, 1980, pp. 23–26.

6

Carter's Final Year: 1980

1980 was pure hell—the Kennedy challenge, Afghanistan, having to put the SALT Treaty on the shelf, the recession, Ronald Reagan, and the hostages . . . always the hostages! It was one crisis after another.
— Jimmy Carter to Hamilton Jordan, January 22, 1981[1]

The above quote inspired the title of Hamilton Jordan's *Crisis*, a book detailing his impressions of the final year of the Carter presidency. For the Carter administration it was a year notable mostly for its disappointments and frustrations. The press's treatment of the administration's handling of 1980s crises grew increasingly unsympathetic. The tone of a great deal of news reporting and commentary in 1980 was hostile to the Carter administration. The president who so frequently was called caring, honest and compassionate was portrayed during the 1980 campaign as "mean" and vindictive. Once perceived as a leader committed to principle above political expediency, Carter was portrayed in 1980 as the complete politician, skillfully dispensing federal grants and jobs where all the critical primaries were.

1. *Timing.* In 1980 the negative press assessments of Carter became increasingly prevalent. Brief reassessments, somewhat more favorable than usual, occurred after Carter's State of the Union address (January 23), a meeting with Western alliance leaders in Venice (June 22–23), and a televised press conference by Carter explaining the White House staff's knowledge of Billy Carter's involvement with the Libyan government (August 4).

The dominant theme in the journalists' assessments in 1980 was that President Carter's actions were motivated by his single-minded desire to be reelected. Journalists accused Carter of exploiting the Iranian hostage crisis and other issues for short-term electoral gain. These allegations reflect an important perception of Carter in the press: that of the astute electoral politician. It appears strange that journalists who previously portrayed Carter as apolitical suddenly referred to him as the complete politician. An important distinction between two types of assessments must be made. First, throughout the term journalists criticized Carter's political skills in developing public and congressional support for administration policies. Second, in 1980 journalists who discussed Carter's political acumen usually referred to the president's campaign-related activities. Therefore, journalistic accusations that Carter's activities and decisions were timed with political considerations in mind do not contradict earlier portrayals of Carter as an apolitical president.

2. *Rhetoric/Symbolism.* Carter's 1980 State of the Union address was highlighted by a commitment of the United States to use armed forces if necessary to repel any Soviet attempt to disrupt Persian Gulf oil supplies. Carter also called for large defense spending increases and military draft registration. In this speech many journalists perceived a change in the president's philosophy of how to deal with the Soviet threat. In the aftermath of the Soviet invasion of Afghanistan there was considerable press support for an aggressive United States foreign policy. For many journalists, Carter's apparent commitment to containment of the Soviet threat brought needed coherence to a foreign policy which for three years seemed to be lacking a sense of direction.

The strongest criticism of Carter's rhetoric came during the 1980 campaign. Journalists accused Carter of conducting a "smear" campaign against Republican nominee Ronald Reagan. The so-called "meanness issue" dominated a good deal of journalistic criticism of Carter in 1980. In the views of many journalists, during the 1980 campaign Carter engaged in "mean spirited" attacks, "gutter politics," "ugly smears," and "strident personal attacks." These comments were reactions to Carter's campaign statements which portrayed Reagan as belligerent in the foreign policy realm and unconcerned with civil rights issues at home. Journalists generally interpreted Carter's harsh attacks against Reagan as part of a desperation strategy of an incumbent president lacking a strong record of achievement.

3. *Agenda.* A great deal of the assessments of Carter's 1980 agenda focused on the perception that political crises established the administration's policy priorities. Two general impressions emerged from this realization: first, some journalists believed that many of Carter's misfortunes were forced upon him by events the administration could not control. Second, some journalists agreed with this view but were more forthcoming in criticizing Carter for reacting to events rather than changing the course of events.

On a few occasions journalists credited Carter with taking control of the agenda. The first occasion was the State of the Union address where journalists perceived the president as taking the initiative in defining a foreign policy agenda that would focus on Soviet worldwide adventurism while downplaying the administration's desire for arms control negotiations. This favorable impression was reinforced by the June 22–23 meeting of Western alliance leaders in Venice, Italy, where Carter appeared to receive a commitment from allied nations to take a unified stance against the Soviet invasion of Afghanistan.

There was little debate over Carter's major agenda items in 1980—Iran, Afghanistan, and the domestic economy. The major press complaints concerned the effects of Carter's policies. As the hostage crisis dragged on, journalists became increasingly critical of the administration's policies. Carter set an arbitrary deadline (February 20) for the Soviets to withdraw from

Afghanistan. Once that date passed many journalists blamed United States "weakness" for the continuation of this crisis. Finally, inflation soared to 18% in 1980, inviting strong criticism of the administration's economic policies.

4. *Policy Development.* In 1980 journalists continued to criticize Carter's efforts at building public and congressional support for administration programs. Journalists also faulted Carter's efforts at implementing the administration's policies. For example, while many journalists liked the tone of the State of the Union address, they complained that Carter's foreign policies remained unclear.

Criticisms of Carter's foreign policy followed three incidents, each of which appeared to confirm journalists' beliefs that Carter's foreign policy lacked clear goals and direction. The first incident was a March 1 United Nations Security Council vote to condemn Israeli settlements on the West Bank. Two days later Carter disavowed the vote and asserted that the United States intended to veto the measure. Poor communication was the official explanation for the vote mishap. Journalists used phrases such as "official incompetence," "rampant incompetence," "disjointed" policymaking, and "incoherent character of American foreign policy" to characterize the administration's role in the Security Council vote mishap.

The second incident was the April 24–25 military mission to rescue the American diplomats held hostage in Iran. Some journalists blamed the president for the mission's failure, which resulted in the deaths of eight American soldiers. The supposedly chaotic foreign policy process in the Carter administration was the target of this criticism. In the aftermath of the rescue mission and the Vance resignation journalists again raised such issues as the competence question, Carter's support for the military, and the apparent lack of a single voice directing foreign policy.

The third event was the influx of Cuban refugees into the United States in May. On May 6 Carter authorized $10 million to aid refugees from Cuba coming into the United States. The decision was controversial given Cuban leader Fidel Castro's policy of allowing "undesirable" citizens to seek refuge in the United States. Eight days later Carter ordered an end to the boat lift. This incident was, for some journalists, additional proof of Carter's foreign policy vacillation.

The following themes dominated journalistic assessments of domestic policy developments in 1980: (a) the president failed to communicate to the nation his vision for the future and his administration's policy priorities; (b) the administration had "frequent dramatic policy shifts" and "confusion over priorities"; and (c) Carter was "indifferent to strategy" and failed to push hard enough for administration programs. According to this view Carter simply announced worthy goals and expected enactment of his policies because they were "right."

5. *Staff.* The press image of the White House staff in 1980 was one of general incompetence and political inexperience. Journalists blamed Carter for relying too heavily on the so-called "Georgian insiders" for advice.

Criticism of the staff was most severe during the controversy surrounding Billy Carter's connections with the Libyan government. In addition to portrayals of a "hapless administration," staff "incompetence" and "insularity," there were many more serious accusations of "lying" and "cover-ups." These accusations disappeared when investigations revealed no White House wrongdoing. The indictments of Carter's staff as incompetent and isolated continued nonetheless.

Foreign Policy Crises

State of the Union: A "Carter Doctrine"

In early 1980 President Carter stepped up efforts to display a new foreign policy approach. On January 20 Carter appeared on Sunday television's "Meet the Press" to affirm United States resolve to deal with the Iran and Afghanistan crises. Carter proposed in his State of the Union address what became known as the "Carter Doctrine"—a commitment to use United States armed forces to repel any Soviet attempts to disrupt Persian Gulf oil supplies. In this speech the president also requested defense budget increases and called for a registration for the draft by 18 to 26 year olds.

A number of journalists portrayed the speech as the culmination of an evolving reversal in United States foreign policy priorities from human rights and arms control negotiations to containment of the Soviet threat. There were two other common assessments. One view expected Carter to revert to earlier foreign policy postures. The other view interpreted Carter as simply reading and reflecting the political climate, not being committed to the goals outlined in the State of the Union address.

In the aftermath of the Soviet invasion of Afghanistan a *Time* magazine news story considered that Carter "might be faulted for sending unclear signals to Moscow and frequently changing direction." The report contended that Carter's unwillingness to use force combined with "the fumbling U.S. policy" may have "led Moscow to conclude that it might be able to take advantage of a President who appeared so unsure of himself."[2] Carter's "tough" State of the Union address changed the news weekly's view of the president's foreign policy leadership. Praising the "sense of decisiveness that Carter projected in this speech," *Time* favorably reviewed the change in Carter's foreign policy approach. "All in all, it was one of the best received speeches of Carter's presidency. It was firm, measured, strongly felt." *Time* remained uncertain of Carter's ability to repel future Soviet aggression and concluded that Carter's policy did not reflect the sternness of his rhetoric.[3]

Hedrick Smith portrayed Carter's State of the Union address as a "forceful" speech which drew the line with the Soviets in the Persian Gulf.[4] A *Washington Post* editorial complimented Carter for making "some sense of the chaos that has overwhelmed both international life and his own foreign policy."[5] The *Post* added that it was perplexing that the president was prepared to go to war to protect oil routes yet would not impose a tax on gasoline to limit oil imports.[6] And *U.S. News* added that Carter had "committed this country to a policy of military containment that harks back to the coldest days of the Cold War."[7]

The *Wall Street Journal* favorably reviewed Carter's address. Two days prior to the speech the *Journal* asserted that Carter's foreign policy record caused the Soviet action in Afghanistan: "In fact we have been weak, and this weakness has invited the current Soviet boldness." Attempts by Carter to strengthen the nation's defenses "were anything but the result of Mr. Carter's leadership. Rather, each of them had to be wrung out of him by the pressure of events and public opinion."[8] After the 1980 State of the Union address the *Journal* was pleased with the apparent new direction in United States foreign policy:

> With President Carter's State of the Union message, we are starting to feel that he has really turned a corner on foreign policy. For the first time we have the sense that his administration really wants to do something about the Soviet Union, rather than merely to placate and dampen an aroused public opinion.[9]

Joseph Kraft called the Carter Doctrine "a breathtaking progression from the dream world to the world of reality." Like many critics Kraft did not believe that Carter's proposed actions reflected the severity of the rhetoric of the State of the Union address. The reason for this apparent disparity, Kraft noted, was Carter's political ambitions:

> So what Carter has done is to build up a crisis without declaring the cost. He has presented a menu but not the bill. That may be the ideal tactics for a president seeking reelection. But as a strategy for traversing a truly dangerous period, it is only a first installment.[10]

Martin Schram admired the president's political savvy in announcing a Carter Doctrine. Schram asserted that politically Carter had outflanked all of his rivals—hardliners focusing on "weakness" and liberals focusing on leadership problems—by enunciating a strong foreign policy response. Schram added, "what Carter did in his address Wednesday night was to build, for his policies and his politics, a New Foundation of his own."[11]

James Reston found Carter's new emphasis on foreign policy problems an astute political move to divert attention from the administration's domestic problems.[12] Reston blasted Carter's draft registration plan and argued that Carter was "sorely in need of both" a sense of history and a sense of humor. Reston did not believe that threats from the Soviets and Iran required war-like preparations.[13]

George F. Will compared the debate over Carter's handling of the Soviet threat to debates in the 1930s over the resolve of British and French leaders to handle the German threat. Like the 1930s, he insisted, 1980 was a time to replace irresolute leaders with "conservative nationalists." Will added that "habits die hard, and governments rarely change so markedly unless leaders are replaced."[14] Will later blamed Carter's defense policies for

America's foreign policy problems. Will accused Carter of feckless leadership and blasted the president for having "savaged" the American military services.[15]

Joseph Kraft argued that Carter's policy toward the Soviet threat in Afghanistan failed because of the president's unwillingness to use military force. Kraft shared Carter's outrage toward Soviet foreign policy yet found the Carter administration's actions lacking in substance. Kraft criticized Carter for failing "to commit American power on the spot":

> Without such a commitment, without engaging the deterrent, all the actions so far taken are a disservice to this country, its friends and even the Soviet Union.
> . . . the Carter administration has not yet faced up to its responsibility as a superpower. It has not accepted an obligation to maintain order in an area now critical to international stability. Neither has it put American ships or planes or soldiers on the spot in the threatened area.[16]

Rowland Evans and Robert Novak added similarly:

> President Carter's Pattonesque rhetoric about beefing up U.S. defense in response to the Soviet takeover of Afghanistan is being undermined by his failure to follow through where it counts: persuading Congress, his European allies and the Kremlin that he means business.
> . . . Failure to request adequate manpower and aircraft makes the Carter Doctrine to defend the Persian Gulf so much rhetoric. The question naturally arises: is the electioneering president playing games with defense?[17]

Iran: The Continuing Crisis

In the wake of the Iran and Afghanistan crises came an outpouring of public support for the administration. Carter's popularity as measured by opinion polls rose dramatically immediately after the seizure of the American hostages in Iran. In the Iowa caucus on January 21 Carter soundly defeated Senator Edward M. Kennedy (D-Mass.). And after the State of the Union address a *Time* magazine article enthusiastically declared the beginning of a "New Mood on Capitol Hill":

> Through nearly all of last year, Jimmy Carter seemed to Congress so lacking in clout with the voters that his legislative program could with impunity be delayed, hacked to bits or ignored. But when Congress reconvened last week, the President looked more like a political Charles Atlas, transformed by foreign crises from a 97-lb. weakling into a muscleman whose wishes had to be respected.[18]

These favorable reactions were undoubtedly in part displays of patriotism during a time of adversity. Patriotic emotions during the early stages of the crisis translated into support for the president. Tom Mathews correctly reported that "Carter's step-softly approach has met the approval of most Americans. But the longer the crisis in Iran drags out, the tauter nerves are likely to become."[19] In fact, as the hostage crisis dragged on, journalists became increasingly critical of Carter. Many critics even believed Carter exploited and prolonged the crisis to enhance his reelection chances. Norman C. Miller declared on January 31 that

> . . . the free ride on foreign policy is over for President Carter, and it should be. Ironic and undeserved political benefits have flowed to the President from the seizure of American hostages in Iran and the Soviet invasion of Afghanistan.
> . . . It is at least arguable that Iranian fanatics wouldn't have seized and held American hostages for 89 days if they had not believed President Carter lacked the will to retaliate. And it is arguable that the Russians wouldn't have invaded Afghanistan if they had not concluded that the Carter administration was weak.[20]

Joseph Kraft argued that Carter's wisest alternative to dealing with the "mess" in world affairs was to eliminate the administration's foreign policy team. In Kraft's view: "New men for new measures are required not merely as a gauge of the president's serious intentions. The fact is that the United States is starting to traverse a dangerous zone."[21]

A February 27 *Wall Street Journal* editorial alleged that Carter manipulated public emotions over the hostage situation to enhance his own reelection quest. Reacting to Carter's assertion that the public should not swing from "extreme optimism to extreme pessimism" the *Journal* blamed Carter for creating extreme optimism in an effort to help his campaign.[22]

Joseph Kraft's March 13 column "Who's Conning Whom?" offered some advice for Carter. Kraft believed Carter should break negotiations with Iran, threaten ominous action, and make *them* worry about *our* next move. Kraft added that "such a move would compromise the con game that has served Jimmy Carter's political interests so well." Kraft concluded that the administration's policy was one of "appeasement" and that "[Carter] has been the principal dupe of the Iranian con game."[23]

U.S. News and World Report observed that by April the administration's foreign policy toward Iran had shifted "from conciliation to coercion" to assist Carter's political needs:

> The President's policy of hanging tough seemed calculated at least in part to help redress his domestic political problems. Polls show a sharp increase in support for stronger action against Iran and a growing discontent with Carter's handling of the crisis.[24]

Rather than impugn Carter's motives many writers complained that the policy wasn't working and, in the *Washington Post*'s words, a "new approach is needed." On April 6 the *Post* complained: "Restraint has served the radicals' claim that it is not only safe but profitable to take advantage of the United States."[25] The *Wall Street Journal*'s April 1 editorial, "Enlisting in Humiliation," offered a similar assessment:

What is at stake in Iran is not merely the hostages, who have not been helped by Mr. Carter's policies, but the perception of the American position in the world. With each American humiliation, there is a new reason for other Persian Gulf states to seek what accommodation they can find with revolutionaries, religious fanatics and the Soviet Union.[26]

Time commented on the Carter administration's inability to receive agreement from Western European nations to impose sanctions against Iran:

Probably no factor has more impeded America's ability to lead the alliance in the current crises than the disdain that allied leaders have for Jimmy Carter. He is generally regarded as being inept and naive.[27]

In late April a series of events heightened criticism of Carter's policy toward Iran. On April 24–25 Carter canceled a hostage rescue mission due to equipment problems. Carter approved the cancellation on the advice of Colonel Charles Beckwith, commander of the rescue mission. During the withdrawal eight American servicemen died in a helicopter accident over an Iranian desert. Two days after this tragedy Iranian militants displayed the bodies of the dead American soldiers, adding further humiliation. On April 28 Secretary of State Cyrus Vance, who opposed the rescue mission, resigned his position.

In light of the tragic deaths a number of critics withheld judgment of the military mission. This restraint was evidenced by the *Washington Post*'s editorial, "In the Aftermath" and especially in Meg Greenfield's column, "Let's Avoid Scapegoats."[28]

Yet many critics did not withhold judgment of Carter's actions. Some journalists criticized the president's actions while others renewed old questions of Carter's leadership abilities. *Time* magazine's article "Debacle in the Desert," in discussing "the embarrassing" incident noted: "While most of Carter's political foes tactfully withheld criticism, his image as inept had been renewed."[29] Allan J. Mayer of *Newsweek* raised the eptitude question most directly:

. . . the curious timing and humiliating outcome of the ill-fated rescue mission distressed many of America's allies abroad—and, in an election year, seemed almost certain to revive the question of Carter's competence and consistency in the minds of many voters.

. . . the competence issue already weighs heavily on him; this latest failure is bound to take its toll. And public frustration over his Administration's inability to free the hostages can only increase as the weeks drag on.[30]

Joseph Kraft attributed the rescue mission failure and the hostage situation to "the sanctimonious moralism of Jimmy Carter." Kraft characterized Carter as unwilling "to sully his hands to save the shah or foster a military regime." And Carter "deluded himself in the conceit that he and Khomeini, as men of God, could make accommodation." Kraft criticized Carter for carrying out the rescue mission in a "half-hearted, second-best spirit." Kraft called Carter "unfit to be President at a time of crisis."[31]

George F. Will partly attributed the failed rescue mission to the Carter administration's alleged failure to support adequate defense budget increases. Will exclaimed that "the military had been ill-served by the president and his appointees. . . . You could hardly expect conviction in the use of military assets by a president who struggles to decrease those assets."[32]

The resignation of Secretary of State Cyrus Vance fueled press criticism of the president. Tom Wicker blasted the president for approving the rescue mission—"a reckless roll of the dice"—and asserted that the mission's failure proved Vance's reservations correct. Wicker proclaimed Vance the most distinguished member of an otherwise "undistinguished Cabinet."[33] A *Time* news report added: "The reasons behind Vance's quitting raised doubt about nothing less than President Carter's methods and judgment in forming foreign policy."[34]

Peter Goldman provided a gloomy picture of the effects of Vance's resignation on the Carter presidency:

> The departure of Vance laid bare the dissonance of policymaking Carter-style, fed the widespread suspicion that the hawks have taken over and left the President to break in a new Secretary of State at what may be the most perilous hour in world affairs since the Cuban missile crisis.
>   . . . a sense of impermanence has indeed stolen over the Administration with the slide in Carter's polls, and part of Muskie's price for hiring on was the pledge that he will be *the* voice of U.S. foreign policy. Carter assented, in part, because a voice as resonant as Muskie's might bring some coherence to the staticky expression of America's aims.[35]

Journalists questioned how the Vance resignation affected Carter's foreign policy. Tom Wicker believed that Carter's inability to establish a clear sense of foreign policy priorities made it difficult for Vance to excel as Secretary of State.[36] Hedrick Smith characterized Vance as a source of stability and moderation in the Carter administration.[37] *U.S. News* wondered whether the new secretary of state would be the "one voice" to speak for United States foreign policy:

> This point is made: Despite his exceptional lack of experience in international affairs, the President has insisted on more-extensive control over the day-to-day management of U.S. foreign policy than any other Chief Executive in modern times. . . . Will Carter delegate to his new Secretary of State the authority that is considered essential to pursue a coherent and consistent strategy? . . . [Muskie] will be rated a success if he can restore a measure of confidence in American leadership by insuring that the U.S. speaks with a single voice in foreign policy—a voice that can be understood and respected.[38]

Anthony Lewis claimed there was a lack of consistency in United States policy toward Iran and the Soviet Union. The *New York Times* columnist added that "being Secretary of State to Jimmy Carter is difficult because he does not provide . . . a steady sense of purpose, priorities."[39]

The *Wall Street Journal's* editorialists agreed with Vance's convictions in resigning and appeared pleased to see him out of power.[40] The *Journal* pointed out that Carter's foreign policy problems stemmed from Vance's conviction to avoid using force at all costs. The *Journal* approved of replacing Vance with Edmund S. Muskie even if that decision was motivated by the desire to enhance the administration's congressional relations.[41]

Other Foreign Policy Incidents

While Iran and Afghanistan dominated the discussion of Carter's foreign policy in 1980 journalists gave considerable attention to other foreign affairs issues. Most important was Carter's June trip to Venice, Italy for an economic summit of Western alliance nations. Amid increasing talk of the "dump Carter" movement within the Democratic party many journalists viewed this trip as an opportunity to enhance the president's prestige. Prior to the summit *U.S. News and World Report* asked whether it was still possible for Carter to overcome alliance doubts about "American leadership."[42]

When allies pledged to support measures against the Soviets, some critics commented that Carter accomplished what he set out to do. A *Time* news article commented that at the summit Carter showed "signs of statesmanship" previously lacking. The news report added that "the farther he is from home, the better he is able to act truly presidential."[43] Hugh Sidey observed: "His stubborn effort to unite the allies against the Soviet invasion of Afghanistan gave Carter a direction and force heretofore lacking."[44]

Journalists strongly criticized the president's handling of the influx of refugees from Cuba into the United States. After Cuban leader Fidel Castro gave permission to many "undesirable" citizens to leave his country over 120,000 Cubans entered America. The Carter administration provided approximately ten million dollars of aid to the refugees. Carter eventually ordered an end to the "boatlift" leading some journalists to criticize him for "another dramatic policy turnaround."[45] The *Wall Street Journal* called the administration's policy of erecting tents in Puerto Rico to house Cuban refugees "colonialism" and an "ugly abuse of the powers of incumbency."[46]

The *Journal* also strongly criticized the Carter administration's advocacy of the sale of uranium fuel to India for its Tarapur reactor. The president's support for this sale, according to the *Journal*, "runs counter to our non-proliferation objectives and also his own campaign rhetoric."[47] The *Journal* perceived Carter's policy as yet another indication of his weakness in facing challenges from abroad:

> Having failed to face down communism in Afghanistan or Ayatollahs in Iran, President Carter has just struck an ecumenical note by caving in to the Hindus. Despite Indira Gandhi's adamant refusal to accept safeguards against the diversion of nuclear material for military purposes, Mr. Carter has decided the U.S. will continue to ship uranium to India.[48]

The *Journal* complained that India "double-crossed the U.S. by using nuclear materials for weapons purposes." Such a deceit witnessed internationally along with Carter's continued support of India's claims, the *Journal* added, invited other international actors to take advantage of the United States.[49]

Less than one week before the 1980 elections the *Journal* challenged Carter administration claims of having succeeded over four years in limiting the spread of nuclear weapons worldwide. In its editorial "Proliferating Confusion" the *Journal* retorted: "The non-proliferation issue is in fact the perfect microcosm of the confused and unserious Carter foreign policy that has led us into trouble all over the world."[50]

Leadership "Failures"

Journalists attributed a number of issues and crises in 1980 to Carter's leadership "failures." Two foreign policy related incidents—a controversial United Nations vote and the Billy Carter-Libya connection—will be discussed in detail. I then consider some assessments of Carter's handling of the domestic economy.

A Voting Mishap

On March 1 the United Nations Security Council unanimously condemned Israel's policy of creating settlements on the West Bank of the Jordan River. After a major controversy ensued at home over the United States' "anti-Israeli" vote, the president on March 3 disavowed the action of two days earlier. Secretary of State Cyrus Vance accepted responsibility for the improperly cast vote which he attributed to a "communications failure." Journalists attributed the vote mishap to Carter's failure to establish a clear foreign policy decision making process.

The *Wall Street Journal* observed that the repudiated United Nations vote "tells a convoluted tale of rampant incompetence."[51] Tom Wicker implied that the president's explanation for the vote mishap was a politically motivated lie.[52] Joseph Kraft blamed the incident on "the disjointed, almost incoherent character of American foreign policy" in the Carter administration.[53]

The news weeklies also raised the eptitude question. Allan J. Mayer wrote for *Newsweek* that the White House statement disavowing the United States' United Nations vote had "revived nagging questions of Jimmy Carter's competence."[54] A *Time* magazine article, "Flip-Flops and Zigzags," assessed that the United Nations vote incident "was a remarkable example of official incompetence. . . . Carter's explanation was not only lame but incredible."[55]

George F. Will implied that Carter's explanation of the United Nations vote mishap was dishonest and, therefore, violated Carter's 1976 pledge to never lie as a president. Will did not attribute the United Nations' vote incident to administrative incompetence. Rather, Will blamed the incident on the "administration's recurring itch to compromise an ally." With the United Nations Security Council vote and questionable disclaimer, Will asserted, "the administration has taken another step toward turning the United States into an active adversary of Israel."[56]

Billy Carter and Libya

The so-called "Billygate" controversy of July and August created a storm of press criticism of President Carter's handling of the affair. President Carter's brother Billy accepted $220,000 from the Libyan government after having staged a public relations campaign on that nation's behalf. Billy Carter claimed that the large cash amount constituted "loans" and that he had committed no wrongdoing. Under the threat of legal action Billy Carter registered as a Libyan foreign agent on July 14. The matter became serious when it was revealed that Billy Carter received the loans after being singled out by First Lady Rosalynn Carter and National Security Adviser Zbigniew Brzezinski to make contact with the Libyans and request the assistance of that government in resolving the hostage crisis. It was also revealed that White House counsel Lloyd Cutler and President Carter may have become involved in Billy Carter's consultations with the Justice Department.

While the Libya affair mostly concerned the actions of Billy Carter, the press looked to the Carter administration for some explanation. Many journalists blamed the president for not controlling his brother's behavior. *U.S. News* reported that "Jimmy Carter appears to have shown poor judgment in allowing a member of his family to cash in on influence peddling that may have been unwittingly aided by the White House itself."[57] Ed Magnunson of *Time* added in the magazine's second consecutive cover story on Billy Carter that the president had failed "to deal decisively with an intimate who was callously abusing his ties to the Oval Office. And he had once again made it possible to ask troublesome questions about his judgment."[58]

Allan J. Mayer wrote that the Billy Carter affair "raises disturbing questions about the President and the Administration at a vulnerable moment."[59] The *New York Times* raised questions about the president's involvement in the Billy Carter affair and called for congressional hearings to resolve the controversy.[60] The *Times* observed:

> As we see it, an American President has not only tolerated but abetted his brother's conspicuous, protracted, tactless and illegal pandering to a Middle East power dedicated to trouble.[61]

> . . . maybe behind the smoke there is enough ineptitude or influence peddling to constitute fire.[62]

The *Wall Street Journal's* initial editorial on the Billy Carter affair focused more on the question of common sense than on possible illegal or unethical behavior on the part of the White House staff:

> . . . we're offended by the combination of this beer-swilling, Snopesian yahooism, on the one hand, and the born-again, moralistic preachiness, on the other, that pervades the Carter administration. We're amazed that such allegedly

sophisticated and resourceful men as Lloyd Cutler . . . and Zbigniew Brzezinski
. . . didn't have the sense to steer clearer of Billy Carter than they did.

Just the same, as far as we can determine the improprieties here are being
committed by Billy, not Jimmy.[63]

William Safire got the most journalistic mileage out of the Billy Carter
affair. From June 26 to October 20 Safire penned no less than twelve
columns for the *New York Times* on the topic. The tone of each column was
generally the same: that the White House covered up wrongdoings by Billy
Carter and the administration staff; that White House officials purposefully
lied about their activities; that Billy Carter deserved to be prosecuted; and
that the president generally allowed family and friends to profit from their
close association with him.[64]

Joseph Kraft wrote: "So why did it happen? Because Jimmy Carter is an
essentially weak president who does not deal with problems until they hit
him in the face." Kraft added that the affair also occurred because Carter
relied too much on family and on a "yes-man" staff of "Georgians" who
were "unable to make sound judgments."[65]

Several journalists argued that Billy Carter's actions did not constitute
the kind of political scandal identified by William Safire. Tom Wicker, in a
column entitled "A Watergate Parallel?" affirmed that the Carter administration's behavior was in no sense comparable to the offenses committed
by the Nixon White House. Yet Wicker affirmed that President Carter's
integrity was damaged by the less than candid White House disclosure of
what the president's advisers knew about Billy Carter's activities.[66]

Anthony Lewis also affirmed that this incident was not another "Watergate." In Lewis's view, "The reality is that Billy Carter is a pathetic
character who has no influence on his older brother. Everyone knows that."
Lewis perceived the accusations against the administration in the Billy Carter
affair as calculated efforts to make President Carter politically vulnerable.[67]

On April 4 President Carter held a televised press conference to answer
questions concerning his brother's Libya connection and any possible White
House wrongdoing. The public reacted favorably to Carter's press conference.
The news conference also removed almost all press suspicion of illegal White
House behavior. Ed Magnuson of *Time* portrayed Carter's news conference
as a solid performance satisfying the doubts of most critics about any legal
or ethical improprieties.[68] The *Wall Street Journal* replied that the president
handled the Billy Carter affair "in a reasonable way" and that "the real
transgressions were not Jimmy's but Billy's."[69] Yet Carter's news conference
did not dissipate the competency issue. John Lang observed in *U.S. News
and World Report*:

Carter's TV appearance deflated suspicions of gross wrongdoing. But it did
little to repair the White House's tattered image of competence.

An impressive performance on prime-time television has triggered a revival
of faith in Jimmy Carter's integrity—but belief in his judgment seems far from
being born again.[70]

A *New York Times* August 6 editorial "Billy Carter's Brother's Mess," explained that the president's news conference was a "convincing refutation" of charges of wrongdoing. Yet the *Times* criticized the president for "mismanagement" and furthering the impression that Billy Carter spoke for the U.S. government.[71]

On October 4 a Senate special subcommittee investigating the Billy Carter incident reported that the president's brother had no influence over United States foreign policy. The committee's report revealed no improper or illegal action by anyone in the Carter White House. The report inspired *New York Times* columnist David E. Rosenbaum to report that the Billy Carter affair was not worth the excitement and that the congressional report will probably sit in the Library of Congress stacks "gathering dust."[72]

The Senate report that exonerated the Carter White House of any wrongdoing criticized President Carter's judgment in handling the incident. The *New York Times* reflected on this finding in its October 5 editorial:

> The Senate's special Billy Carter subcommittee put the blame where it belongs: on Billy's brother. Yes, it was wrong for Billy to peddle his White House connection and no, not even a President can be his brother's keeper. But if Presidents are not responsible for problem relatives, they are responsible for the Government. The subcommittee does not accuse the President of doing anything illegal, but it leaves no doubt that the Chief Executive himself botched the case, with help from middle management.[73]

The Economy

Journalists subjected Carter's handling of the economy to continual criticism. By late February the prime lending rate reached 16.5 percent, and in mid-March the inflation rate reached 18 percent. After a week of emergency meetings on the state of the economy the president on March 14 called for a balanced federal budget, $13 billion in budget cuts, harsh credit restrictions and a ten-cent per gallon gasoline tax.

Time magazine's March 24 report on the economy implied that Carter attempted to blame his administration's alleged failures on citizen consumption patterns.[74] Judith B. Gardner's report in *U.S. News and World Report* began with the following statement in bold type: "Dangerous days lie ahead. The President's attack on high prices may not cool inflation fast, but signs are piling up fast that his plan will soon tip the economy into a slump."[75] Harry Anderson's *Newsweek* column focused on the irony of a Democratic president in an election year trying to stage an economic recovery through unpopular budget cuts and by proposing a balanced budget.[76]

The *Wall Street Journal*'s reaction to Carter's anti-inflation and budget cutting plan was revealed in the title of an editorial—"Have Another Arsenic." The *Journal* claimed that Carter's cure for all economic ills was "to increase taxes."[77] In response to the claim of "one senior official" that Carter wanted to balance the federal budget without harming too many people, the *Journal* exclaimed that this showed "the administration is not serious" about curing the economy's ills.[78] After more critical scrutiny the *Journal*'s editors described

Carter's proposed budget cuts "an even bigger fraud than we expected."[79] In response to Carter's proposal to put restrictions on personal credit the *Journal* asserted that Carter was not "doing his part with real budget restraint."[80] The *Journal* also criticized Carter's efforts to impose a ten-cent tax on each gallon of gasoline as "a gross abuse of power."[81]

Hugh Sidey portrayed Carter as "out of touch" with economic realities. In becoming too "isolated" the president lost his ability to intuitively understand the source of economic dislocations incomprehensible to experts:

> When Presidents get isolated, they miss firsthand observations that sharpen their judgment. They begin to lose the inner instincts that warn when statistics may be deceptive, that suggest human responses data do not reveal. In no field is it more important to have that internal receptivity than in economics.
> . . . feeling from his statistics the frustration of farmers who must plant crops while anticipating that they will lose money, or hearing in the charts the grumblings of businessmen as customers melt away, that is what being President is all about.[82]

The Carter administration's handling of economic dislocations contributed to more broadly-based assessments of the president's leadership ability. I turn now to the most revealing commentaries in 1980 concerning Carter's performance in general as president. These assessments were all prior to the 1980 elections and should be separated from retrospective analyses of Carter's presidency in the post-election stages.

Carter's "Failing" Presidency

In mid-March, Richard Levine and Karen Elliot House assessed "Mr. Carter's Inconsistent Leadership." They catalogued Carter's "flip-flops" in both domestic and foreign policy and argued that "inconsistency and a lack of follow-through are the hallmarks of the Carter brand of leadership."[83] *Time* magazine's March 17 issue also outlined Carter's "most notable flip flops" and added: "In addition to the shifts in policy, there is often an improvised quality to Carter's actions." This review recalled a number of common press evaluations of Carter:

> He too often seems as uncertain as when he first took office: an immensely dedicated, well-meaning, decent man who is not comfortable with the power of the presidency.
> An idealist, Carter tends to think that if a policy is right, it will somehow prevail. A proper moral stance, he seems to believe, is at least half the battle. He thus remains relatively indifferent to strategy. . . . He tends to react rather than anticipate, to race from one crisis to the next, always hoping for the best. He often fails to see how one event is related to another in a binding chain of circumstances that a President must always keep in mind.
> . . . Carter compounds the confusion by dividing authority among too many people. . . . His economic advisers have never been logically organized. . . . Carter has split foreign policy between Secretary of State Cyrus Vance and [National Security Adviser Zbigniew] Brzezinski.[84]

A large number of early retrospective evaluations of Carter's presidency occurred during the Democratic Party convention and just prior to the November elections. The convention week assessments found Carter to have grown into his job but still lacking many qualities necessary for effective leadership. Timothy D. Schellhardt's August 11 article outlined a number of common press criticisms of Carter: blind loyalty to the "Georgian" insiders; failure to communicate a vision for the nation's future; failure to push hard enough for his administration's programs. Schellhardt acknowledged that Carter developed better relations with Congress over time and that the administration eventually expanded its inner circle to include some leaders with experience in political Washington:

> After 3½ years in the Oval Office, he is in some ways a changed man—more knowledgeable, more savvy, more realistic. He has thus managed to correct some of the shortcomings that led to the early public perception of a likable but naive leader beyond his depth.[85]

Steven R. Weisman also discussed the assessments of Carter's critics. While acknowledging that many such criticisms were in part true, Weisman responded that Carter was "getting a measure of blame he doesn't deserve." The *Times* columnist identified a number of Carter's characteristics that confused political observers:

> Fundamentally, Mr. Carter remains as much an enigma and a contradiction as he was in 1976.
> He can be both meticulous and grandiose, cocky and defensive, extremely political and extremely self-righteous, compassionate and vindictive, a man who boasts of his many close friends and a man more alone politically than any President in modern history.[86]

In *U.S. News and World Report's* pre-Democratic convention issue columnist Ted Gest asked about Carter: "Is he big enough for the job?" Gest replied that "misgivings, fed most recently by the Billy Carter affair, have grown rather than receded over the last 3½ years." Gest continued:

> In any review of the Carter record, what stands out most sharply are the frequent dramatic policy shifts.
> . . . he is generally rated a lackluster speaker, having neither Franklin Roosevelt's fatherliness nor John Kennedy's flair for witty ad libs. . . . Carter and his aides, most of whom were fellow Georgians as untutored in Washington's ways as their boss, soon found their agenda to be unrealistically ambitious.
> . . . Confusion over priorities has been exacerbated by public disagreements among administration officials. . . . The cacophony of conflicting voices has been especially pronounced in foreign policy.[87]

In a series of editorials during the Democratic party convention the *Wall Street Journal* reflected on Carter's leadership ability. The *Journal* provided credence to the argument that factors beyond the president's control (e.g., effects of congressional reforms of the 1970s and the reforms of the political party system) were responsible to some degree for the administration's governing problems.[88] Yet the *Journal* focused on the president's leadership qualities in explaining his problems governing:

> [Carter] does suffer leadership failures, especially an apparent inability to see the connections between any two things. But his vacillations have a deeper cause. It has been his fate to be trapped between a country moving in one direction and a party pushing in the other.[89]

On the day of Carter's nomination, a *Journal* editorial offered an unflattering picture of his leadership. Rejecting Carter's "eclectic, non-ideological style," the *Journal* complained:

> The most striking thing about the record he has compiled in his first term is that it is so confusing and contradictory. One continues to look in vain for anything beyond his own reelection he wants to accomplish with the powers of his office, for any consistent purpose or vision.[90]

Hugh Sidey's column "Assessing a Presidency" appeared in *Time* magazine's August 18 issue. This early retrospective covered a number of themes frequently stressed in press assessments of Carter's administration.[91] First there was the allegation of *political inexperience:*

> When Jimmy Carter stood before the 1976 Democratic National Convention and pledged new "leadership," he had never met a Democratic President or slept in the White House. The presidency was a legend from books, the Federal Government a classroom exercise, and Washington was a distinct citadel of power that somehow had been corrupted by its residents.
> . . . In his own inexperience, the President could not define a mission for his Government, a purpose for the country and the means of getting there.

In addition to inexperience and the *failure to define a vision* for the nation's future, Sidey added that Carter's White House was *isolated*. In Sidey's view Carter's White House was run exclusively by six people—Hamilton Jordan, Jimmy Carter, Rosalynn Carter, Charles Kirbo, Jody Powell, and Stuart Eizenstadt: "There has been no room for anyone else in this select fraternity. The crusade of the Georgians had been against Washington, bigness, sin in public places and institutions as viewed and defined from Plains."

Jimmy Carter the *outsider* could not accept the rituals of legislative leadership, Sidey argued. Carter, therefore, was *consumed by problems*. Sidey added that Carter "never could come to believe in Congress or its odd rituals. . . . Carter is today a political cripple both at home and abroad because the larger issues have swamped him." Sidey assessed that Carter's attributes of *moralism* and *a belief in human goodness* blinded the president to the realities of leadership:

Carter's matrix is that found in the Scriptures, where the rules of a just and loving life are laid out. He wants to prevail by purity. Applying those patterns of human concern and behavior to the world's masses is far more difficult.

. . . In almost every political arena that Carter has entered, his conviction that fervid goodwill would carry the day has proved false, and in many instances has worsened the problems.

Within one week of the national elections there were a number of retrospectives on Carter's presidency. Martin Schram of the *Washington Post*, Christopher Ogden of *Time* and Joseph Kraft published commentaries on Carter's leadership near the elections (October 26–27).[92] These articles repeated familiar themes. In the views of these writers Carter "managed" or "engineered" but did not lead:

Ogden: He likes getting ideas across directly, without having them filtered by television and the press, which he believes is bitterly antagonistic to him.

. . . Summoning a team and then synthesizing its advice is a favorite Carter assault on a problem, and it exemplifies an inclination to manage rather than to govern.

Schram: [Carter] set about the business of engineering a presidency. His was the clockwork presidency. He was chief engineer and operating officer of the United States of America. His role, as he seemed to see it, was to study it all and then engineer the very best program a country could want, send it up to Capitol Hill for enactment, and then wait to sign the measure after congressional enactment.

Carter's alleged attention to detail, at the expense of seeing the broader picture, was another personal attribute which seemed to harm his leadership ability:

Kraft: Carter ought to raise himself above mere business with infinite detail. He owes himself and the country a large outline of the big things he expects to accomplish over the next few years.

Schram: Carter's attention to detail came at an exorbitant public price: a loss of presidential leadership that doomed his ability to accomplish the things he had once felt sure he could do.

[Carter lacked a] conceptual framework of how the great issues of the time fell into place. . . . He lacked the conceptual frame of reference that comes with a decade or two of sitting in Congress and having to take positions on the major issues, or that comes with, even, a decade or two of speaking out on the issues as a national figure.

These journalists also said Carter had so many good intentions that he tried to accomplish too many things too quickly and moved from one issue to another without a sense of direction:

Ogden: His on-the-job training has been a very painful process for Carter. He hurt himself from the start by both expecting and promising too much. He arrived in Washington with an almost limitless list of priorities that was too much, too soon.

Schram: [Carter] produced . . . a presidency of good intentions and diligent work habits, of some dramatic successes and some all-too-apparent failures; but more than that, a presidency in which he seemed to be constantly "grasping for something" and forever having to "prove my leadership."

Carter's congressional relations contributed to the generally negative view of his leadership. Ogden assessed that Carter's relations with the legislative branch had not changed much over three and a half years:

Having announced a necessary program, he seemed to believe it would move along automatically. He failed to recognize the importance of pushing and negotiating with Congress and selling the idea to the public. Governing, in other words.

. . . Carter, who never liked or respected Congress and came to office running against it, still has poor relations with the Hill in general.

In September, Albert Hunt reviewed Carter's congressional relations. Hunt argued that "on the major issues, the Carter legislative record lies in shambles." Hunt asserted that Carter had few notable legislative successes in the foreign policy realm and that civil service reform was the administration's one major domestic policy achievement. "When the quality or significance of the legislative record is considered, the Carter administration has an almost endless list of failures."

Hunt attributed such "failures" to Carter's inability to garner public support and sort out legislative priorities. Hunt added that "the White House lobbying team is second rate, and other top Carter aides are contemptuous of Congress."[93]

In the fall 1980 issue of *Foreign Affairs* Carter's White House Counsel Lloyd Cutler published a controversial article, "To Form a Government." In that article Cutler wrote, "The separation of powers between the legislative and executive branches, whatever its merits in 1793, has become a structure that almost guarantees stalemate today." Voicing his frustration with the failure of Congress to pass many of President Carter's programs, Cutler criticized a system in which a president can be elected to carry out certain policies but is then denied by Congress the means to enact those policies.[94]

A number of journalists portrayed the article not as a serious attempt to debate a constitutional issue, but rather, as a "sour grapes" explanation for the administration's failures. The *Wall Street Journal* retorted: "A lot of us suspect Mr. Carter's problems in obtaining legislation reflect less on the Congress than on the President's proposals."[95] George F. Will responded as though Cutler's views were the president's views:

If, instead of regretting the separation of powers, Carter had paid attention to its functioning early in 1977, he might have been spared his SALT failure. The Senate fired a warning shot across Carter's bow when he nominated an extreme McGovernite, Paul Warnke, as chief SALT negotiator. . . . Had Carter told the country he planned to put people like Warnke in power, Carter would never have got into a position to put anyone in power.[96]

Carter's problems with Congress on energy policy were a continual source of press criticism. The *Washington Post* admiringly described Carter's energy proposals on numerous occasions. In October the *Post* wrote: "Mr. Carter's most important—and most courageous contribution has been to begin decontrolling oil prices." Despite this praise the *Post* lamented Carter's efforts to gain congressional support for such meritorious proposals. On energy policy, the *Post* asserted:

> [Carter's] judgment has been pretty good—but there is no subject in which that judgment has been more often nullified by his inability to show Congress and the country what he wants to do, why it's right and why they ought to support him actively. His inability to persuade has had serious consequences in this area.[97]

One of Carter's worst legislative defeats concerned his proposed oil import fee. Congress repealed the president's oil–import fee leading him to veto the legislature's action. Congress responded by overriding the veto, providing Carter with only 30 House and 16 Senate votes. Peter Goldman noted that Congress's successful override of Carter's veto was "a humiliation no Congress has visited on a President of its own party since Harry Truman's Blue Period in the 1950's."[98]

The *Wall Street Journal* remarked that it was "interesting" that a president whose own party controlled Congress received only 46 votes of support from both legislative chambers. "The lawmakers are not the only ones who are not impressed by the President's energy tactics."[99] In the *Journal's* view "the trouble here is not the state of the American presidency; it is the policies Mr. Carter has tried to use the office for."[100]

The 1980 Campaign

What is most evident from the journalistic treatments of Carter during the campaign is that journalists judged his actions as both candidate and president with great suspicion. The general press impressions of Carter as honest and above politics eroded as the campaign progressed. Even the belief that Carter was a decent, fair-minded person seriously changed. The press reviews of Carter's 1980 campaign are presented chronologically to convey the journalistic assessments of Carter at different stages of the campaign.

January Through March

During the early months of the 1980 race for the Democratic party's presidential nomination Carter defeated Senator Edward M. Kennedy in a series of caucuses and primaries. These victories included the January 21 Iowa caucus, the February 20 Maine caucus, and the February 26 New

Hampshire primary. Senator Kennedy won the primary in his home state of Massachusetts on March 4. Between March 11 and March 22 Carter defeated Kennedy in five primaries and seven caucus votes assuring the president's renomination. On March 25 Kennedy won the New York and Connecticut primaries.

During the initial stages of the campaign commentators sought explanations for the political strength of a president whom Peter Goldman called "deeply mired in economic and diplomatic troubles and sliding badly in the popularity polls." Goldman noted the disparity between Carter's electoral support and political strength:

> [Carter's] Presidency is burdened with what ordinarily would be insupportable political baggage—boiling inflation, soaring interest rates, an oncoming recession, the stalemated hostage crisis in Teheran, the snafued vote against Israel in the United Nations, a Gallup poll rating that has plummeted 14 points in a month to a so-so 41 percent. But he has successfully sheltered himself in the Oval Office and . . . has escaped retribution for his pyramiding problems.[101]

Journalists identified factors contributing to this disparity between Carter's electoral strength and political strength in Washington. These included Senator Kennedy's weaknesses as a presidential candidate, and public support for the incumbent president during a crisis. More important to this study are the factors attributed to Carter himself—how he conducted his campaign and used the powers of incumbency.

The most prevalent explanation for Carter's success in the Democratic primaries was that he was a skilled politician who used the powers of the presidency for electoral gain. Joseph Kraft noted that while the administration's "policies meet defeat after defeat" the president continually won major primaries. Kraft attributed this phenomenon to Carter's "political skill." In economic policy, Kraft argued, Carter offered stimuli to "short-circuit criticism." Carter also "has wrapped himself in the flag and caused critics to look unpatriotic."[102]

Journalists criticized Carter's refusal to campaign during the hostage crisis as a "Rose Garden strategy." Hugh Sidey chastised Carter for "campaigning" from within the White House. In Sidey's view: "He still spends too much time stroking political figures in the White House, thus casting doubt on his story of total absorption in crisis."[103] William Raspberry challenged Carter's use of White House pressure on local and state officials to gain political endorsements. In Raspberry's view, this practice "seems out of character with the image Carter has sought to project."[104] Timothy D. Schellhardt added:

> Incumbency provides *big* advantages. And President Carter is no exception in using his office to win friends and influence voters in the critical Illinois primary on March 18. His message is clear: If you support me, you'll be rewarded, if you don't, you may be sorry.[105]

Schellhardt listed the many alleged instances in which the president used federal aid to influence the endorsements of local and state officials and of members of Congress.[106] Schellhardt alleged that the president borrowed the 1976 Gerald Ford strategy—staying in the White House looking "presidential"—despite Carter's strong criticism in 1976 of the incumbent president for refusing to campaign.[107]

Peter Goldman's column "See Jimmy Run—in Place" refuted Carter's claim of tending to the job of president, not politics:

> President Carter has in fact been politicking furiously, raining Federal funds and jobs on key primary states, flooding the field with surrogates and telephone calls, coaxing and flogging nonaligned Democrats aboard a once-unimaginable re-elect Jimmy bandwagon. But Carter has not ventured out of the Rose Garden. . . .[108]

Goldman continued that the "vast resources of the Presidency" kept Carter from having to abandon the Rose Garden strategy. He noted that Carter took advantage of "not just the call of patriotism but the power of the Federal purse." The article listed federal grants to states and localities, government contracts, and White House interviews that seemed to coincide with forthcoming Democratic party primaries. Goldman added: "The frontline states have drunk deepest from the well."[109]

By mid-March it was apparent that Jimmy Carter would be facing Ronald Reagan in the November elections. According to Goldman the choice between a battered president and "an aging trader in conservative simplicities, with no experience whatever in Washington . . . was viewed with great alarm by Op-Ed writers, much unenthusiasm by friends and foes abroad, and growing foreboding in the political establishment."[110]

April Through May

In the aftermath of the March 25 Kennedy victories in New York and Connecticut, journalists portrayed Carter as a weakened candidate. Goldman characterized the Kennedy victories as a referendum on Carter and not a show of support for Kennedy.[111] The logic to this argument was that voters no longer had to fear a Kennedy victory if they cast protest votes against Carter.

Even with the Democratic nomination assured Carter needed primary victories to reassert his strength as the party's nominee. Carter won the April 1 Wisconsin primary by an almost 2 to 1 margin over Kennedy. Journalists found suspicious the president's 7:18 a.m. (EST) press conference on the day of the primary to announce that proposed sanctions against Iran would be delayed, as encouraging developments in the hostage situation were occurring. On April 22 Kennedy barely defeated Carter in the Pennsylvania primary. In the concluding Democratic primary (May 3) in Texas Carter defeated Kennedy.

The Wisconsin primary incident invited serious press criticism of Carter's campaign. Carter became seen as politically desperate, willing to go to incredible lengths to assure his renomination and reelection. David Broder wrote on April 6: "Jimmy Carter's 'good news' strategy in 1980 is a textbook case in the manipulation of public opinion by a White House politician." Broder blasted the "clear pattern of pre-primary 'news' created by the White House to shape a positive public perception of the president's handling of key matters of voter concern." Broder provided a tabulation of the pre-primary White House staged media events and positive news releases and implied that this strategy provided Carter an unfair advantage in the campaign.[112] Broder was also uncomfortable with Carter's "Rose Garden strategy" because it degraded the presidency by forcing Carter to answer campaign related attacks during news conferences.[113]

The day after Carter's Wisconsin primary victory Evans and Novak observed that the president's short-term political needs dictated the administration's policies. The columnists wrote: "Carter's syndrome, what he says for immediate political impact one day, he denies the next under the stress of changed political needs. The result is that U.S. policy becomes hostage to instant political requirements."[114]

Eventually journalists regarded almost every action by Carter as politically motivated. According to William Safire, Carter's campaign strategy was to equate criticism of the incumbent president with being against the United States, smear his opponents, and portray Ronald Reagan as trigger-happy.[115]

In early May, David Broder strongly rebuked Carter for exploiting public fears of political opponents. Broder noted that it was unfortunate that Carter needed to focus on the shortcomings of opponents to win elections. Broder also claimed that Carter was "using the Iran hostages as an excuse to disappear from public view." According to Broder, Carter's strategy was to avoid in any way possible discussion of the administration's record.[116]

If some commentators lamented Carter's negative campaign, others acknowledged that he had little choice in selecting a campaign strategy. Timothy D. Schellhardt noted that an emphasis by Carter on Reagan's weaknesses perhaps was necessary inasmuch as projecting a positive future under a Carter administration or appealing to the president's leadership abilities may not have been credible strategies.[117]

Joseph Kraft agreed that Carter could not run on the administration's record. Rather, Carter's "best shot" was to focus on Reagan: "That is one fight he might well win, for the issue that now shapes up before the country is which candidate for president is the least incompetent."[118]

At the end of May, Marvin Stone noted that, "the President's actions over the past six months seem to have been dictated largely by his determination to win re-election." Carter's strategy on Iran, Stone believed, was to follow fluctuating opinion polls rather than adopt a consistent policy.[119]

June Through July

During the mid-summer months dissatisfaction with the nominees of both parties spread. Some journalists searched for answers as to why "undesirable" candidates successfully emerged from the presidential selection process. Some found the selection process itself to be wanting. David Broder believed that the "new" presidential selection process, with its emphasis on primaries, made it possible for "unqualified outsiders" to emerge victorious.[120] Meg Greenfield argued similarly that the electoral system in 1980 "has produced two thoroughly unacceptable candidates" in the views of many voters. Carter and Reagan "are loners, outsiders, men who came to political power at the edges of the life of their national parties and who had to overwhelm recalcitrant and fearful party mainstream regulars to succeed." Greenfield focused on Carter's leadership shortcomings:

> . . . what has brought Jimmy Carter to his present low estate—what we are denouncing him for—is an accumulation of flubs and failures that are almost all directly attributable to his apolitical nature and instincts.
> . . . We have developed something new in our politics: the professional amateur. It is by now a trend, a habit, a cult. You succeed in this line of activity by declaring your aversion to and unfitness for it. That will bring you the cheers of the multitude. It will also bring in time—I am certain of it— the kind of troubles the Carter Presidency has sustained and seemed, almost perversely, to compound.
> . . . [Carter] has no appetite for and certainly takes no joy in that combination of management, manipulation, inspiration, deceit, psychiatry and arm-wrestling that it takes to get things to happen when you are President. . . . He is not transfixed by power. He does not seem intrigued by the challenge of using it forcefully and to good ends without abusing it. He doesn't seem to like it very much.[121]

Combined with this view of Carter as the anti-political president, as the logical outcome of a reformed presidential selection process that rewarded personality more than political acumen, was the perception of Carter as the total politician. For example, Joseph Kraft accused Carter of exploiting the hostage crisis for political gain:

> . . . at every turn of the Iranian crisis—in big things and in small, in matters of life and death, in military, diplomatic and economic affairs—Carter's actions have at all times been ruled by a single, dominant consideration. That consideration is domestic political advantage.
> . . . Carter sacrifices all the normal rules of decent behavior to follow the one principal that has been always ranked highest with him—the principle of short-term political gain.[122]

William Safire considered Carter an expert campaigner but an ineffectual leader.[123] In a column describing European perceptions of Carter, Safire wrote that Europeans saw the administration's responses to Iran and the Soviets as designed for domestic political consumption. "Europeans see Carter-Muskie protests as palaver for American voters, not a serious statement of U.S. diplomatic aims."[124]

George F. Will wrote that Carter resorted to demagoguery to advance the fortunes of the Carter-Mondale campaign. Will's examples of this alleged demagoguery included an administration policy reversal on a proposed tax cut, Carter's stated belief that the SALT II treaty was an "achievement," the offering by Carter of a national Christmas tree to symbolize hope for the hostages, and Carter's 1979 Crisis of Confidence speech in which, Will claimed, the president said to the nation "I'm unpopular, so you're sick."[125]

Joseph Kraft perceived Carter as benefiting politically from contradictory appeals to the electorate. Kraft was not clear whether Carter's apparently inconsistent positions were the result of an inability to relate issues to one another, or a conscious effort to appeal to differing public sentiments:

> . . . that inability to see a tie between the government and himself and between what happens and his leadership—goes to the heart of the Carter presidency. It explains why . . . the president is losing the substance of power—the power to make policy.
>   . . . Carter appeals to the electorate with popular, and often opposite, themes. He favors jobs and the balanced budget. He supports solar power and energy conservation and inveighs against the oil companies and their dirty profits. He wants a strong America standing up for peace and human rights, but opposes foreign adventures and wasteful military spending.[126]

It appears that a confusing journalistic portrait of the president emerged during the 1980 campaign. The *Washington Post* pointed out in a July 1 editorial:

> Here is a president daily getting a rap for being "too political" whose campaign at the moment resembles a disaster area, a man simultaneously perceived as being 1) a devilishly clever and cynical political conniver in office who minutely calibrates all his official acts to the partisan needs of getting reelected, and 2) a hopeless klunk at making anything happen or even knowing what is going on.[127]

These assessments appear more contradictory than they are. For the most part, journalists who emphasized the "devilishly clever" Carter referred to the president's campaign-related political skills. Journalists who focused on Carter the "hopeless klunk" generally referred to the president's congressional relations.

August Through September

The press assessments of Carter after the Democratic party convention turned increasingly critical. If journalists previously perceived Carter as a decent and caring person, the media by August began to see him as "mean" and "vindictive." During these two months no other issue dominated the media assessments of Carter more than the "meanness" issue.

The allegations that Carter ran a "mean" campaign were in reaction to a number of campaign statements made by Carter when criticizing Republican candidate Ronald Reagan. Carter implied that Reagan's call for states' rights represented "code words" for reviving a racially divided nation. The president also implied that a choice between Reagan and Carter would be a choice between war and peace in our nation's future. Carter asserted that Reagan's proposed defense policies would push the world to the "nuclear precipice." Journalists characterized these and other Carter statements as excessive, demagogic appeals. The *Washington Post*'s editorial "Running Mean" summarized a common journalistic view:

> Mr. Carter, as a candidate, tends to convey a mean and frantic nature.
> [Carter has a] miserable record of personally savaging political opponents (Hubert Humphrey, Edward Kennedy) when the going gets rough.
> . . . So the President calls names, and he badly recreates his record (for the better) and that of everyone else (for the worse) and he displays an alarming absence of magnanimity, generosity and size when he is campaigning. . . . Jimmy Carter, as before, seems to have few limits beyond which he will not go in the abuse of opponents and reconstruction of history.[128]

Political commentators across the philosophical spectrum echoed the *Post*'s view. James Reston condemned the "mean and cunning tactics of [Carter's] campaign" which appeared to be "negating the principles and ideals that helped bring him to the White House in the first place." Reston was disturbed by "the conflict between Mr. Carter's moral pronouncements and his Tammany Hall tactics."[129]

George F. Will lambasted Carter's attacks on Reagan and accused the president of "sleaziness," and of speaking "viciously . . . without provocation or excuse." Will defined the Carter campaign as an "attempt to smear Reagan."[130] Will added:

> Recently Carter said Reagan loathes peace, incites hatreds, injects race into the campaign and if elected would not return blacks' phone calls. Then at a press conference, Carter said his campaign is "moderate in tone." And when asked if he was saying that Reagan was running a campaign of racism and hatred, he said, in that "I invented morality" tone of his: Golly, no. And then he accused Reagan of "reviving" racism. That same day Andrew Young, who is, increasingly, Carter's Agnew, said the election of Reagan would jeopardize the "survival" of many blacks. If this week is like the last, Carter will call a press conference and wish, rather wistfully, that Reagan should quit reviving the issue of slavery.[131]

Hugh Sidey also found the president's rhetoric largely at odds with the carefully cultivated image of a decent, caring, and fair-minded leader:

> The past few days have revealed a man capable of far more petty vituperances than most Americans thought possible even in a dark political season.
> . . . The thing that has sustained Carter through his time of leadership has been his personal appeal, a good man struggling to get experience against impossible odds and sinister forces.[132]

A *Wall Street Journal* editorial called the president's campaign rhetoric "vintage Carter" and "not very presidential."[133] Referring to Carter's rhetoric on the alleged dangers of a Reagan foreign policy and a defense buildup, the *Journal* replied that there was "not much to back up the mud Mr. Carter is slinging."[134]

Robert G. Kaiser believed that the above arguments were the reactions of responsible reporters, not of biased observers hostile to the Carter administration. In his discussion of the media's treatment of Carter's "mean streak" Kaiser wrote:

> At the White House this display was probably taken as further proof of the press corps' unrelieved hostility for Carter. In fact it was probably something else. A number of White House reporters have felt for a long time that Carter has a mean streak and in the "racism" episode they saw a legitimate way to convey that side of the president to the public.[135]

George C. Church of *Time* found Carter's acceptance speech at the Democratic convention conspicuous for its harsh attacks on Reagan and failure to enumerate a positive vision for the future.[136] The *Washington Post*'s editors noted displeasure with the rhetoric of the convention and added that it appeared that the point of the Carter campaign "is to paint Mr. Reagan as the mad bomber. If this is true, it is a terrible plan."[137]

Just prior to the Democratic National Convention Peter Goldman analyzed the dissatisfaction within the party with their nominee and the "anybody-but-Carter mutineering in the back benches of Congress." Goldman added: "Carter's renomination remained very nearly a mathematical certainty. What seemed less sure than ever was how much his victory would be worth."[138] Separate committees to draft Secretary of State Edmund Muskie, Vice-President Walter F. Mondale, or Senator Henry Jackson (D-Wash.) formed spontaneously. Carter's Harris poll rating sank to 22 percent, an all-time low point in the modern presidency. Goldman concluded that the convention "has become a further trial that [Carter] and his sundered party will be happy to survive."[139] After the convention, Goldman wrote: "What was missing as the party decamped was an affirmative reason for Jimmy Carter."[140]

Journalists perceived Carter's rhetoric as part of the strategy of a desperate incumbent campaigning for reelection without an impressive record to discuss. Norman C. Miller called Carter's criticisms of Reagan the core of "A Make-Believe Campaign." Carter "shamelessly" distorted Reagan's views to make them appear dangerous and distorted the administration's record to make it appear favorable, Miller claimed.[141]

Journalists portrayed a number of other Carter campaign related activities as the moves of a desperate candidate. Timothy D. Schellhardt accused Carter of being an "isolated" candidate, trying to divert attention from criticism by not facing the media. Evidence of this view included Carter's failure to keep a 1976 campaign promise to hold bi-weekly press conferences and his refusal to participate in a three-man presidential debate with Republican Ronald Reagan and Independent John Anderson.[142] Tom Wicker asserted that Carter's refusal to debate Anderson lent credibility to charges that Carter could not defend the administration's record.[143] And Joseph Kraft criticized Carter for patronage that coincided with the state primaries. Carter sought his party's nomination, Kraft argued, by "personalizing power."[144]

October to Election Day

The print-media analyses of the presidential campaign in the month preceding the elections often focused on the "meanness" issue. Norman C. Miller blasted Carter for "ugly smears," "gutter politics," and "mean spirited, wildly exaggerated attacks" on Reagan. Carter, Miller noted, created a "gross caricature of Mr. Reagan" in the campaign thereby ruining the president's "most precious political asset," the faith that voters had in his genuine honesty and decency.[145] One day before the November 4 elections Timothy D. Schellhardt's story "Carter and Meanness" characterized the president as "mean, vindictive, humorless."[146] The *Washington Post* characterized Carter as "a politician gone haywire." The *Post* criticized Carter's "frantic, overstated, boomerang attacks" on Reagan.[147] Evans and Novak claimed that "the Carter camp relies on the tactic it knows and practices best: assault the opponent."[148] Walter Isaacson reported in *Time* that "Carter's strident personal attacks had crossed the line of propriety for a presidential campaign."[149] A *U.S. News and World Report* story claimed that Carter alienated voters with his harsh rhetoric.[150] And Meg Greenfield observed:

> Carter, in his overwrought attacks on Reagan . . . seems determined to display precisely the same kind of temperament—impetuous, reckless, bellicose—that he says is such a menace in Reagan.[151]

George F. Will stepped up his criticism of Carter as election day drew closer. On October 12 Will mocked Carter's pledge to "moderate" the tone of the campaign and asserted:

> The evident premise of Carter's campaign is that if he is relentlessly coarse, day in and day out, his coarseness will stop being news.
> . . . There is this to be said, by way of extension, about Carter's shrillness: What else can he do? Talk about his record? It is (to borrow a phrase from the phrasemaker) "too bleak to contemplate."[152]

On October 26 Will penned a column "Three Reasons to Remove Carter." Will accused Carter of "megalomania" and of "dishonest" characterizations of Reagan's positions. In Will's assessment SALT II was Carter's "most complete flop" and the promise to resubmit the treaty in a second term "is either dishonest or vacuous." Will added that the failed hostage rescue mission ordered by Carter was "one of the most feckless uses of military power in U.S. history."[153] On October 30 Will attacked Carter's campaign once again:

There is no precedent—none—for an incumbent's campaign so thoroughly woven from distortions about his challenger.

. . . Americans should tremble at the thought of Carter's claiming a mandate for more of the same, more desolate failures, more of the dangerously second-rate.[154]

Finally, two days before the national elections Will wrote a column entitled "No More Peculiar Presidents, Please." The columnist mocked Carter's performance in the nationally televised debate with Reagan and acknowledged: "As you may have detected, I am not your basic undecided voter."[155]

In mid-October, Carter appeared on ABC television in an interview with reporter Barbara Walters. In this interview Carter confessed that some of the political rhetoric in the 1980 campaign had been "ill-advised" and that he would moderate his tone throughout the remainder of the campaign. Peter Goldman reported:

Carter's own retreat to the high ground was motivated less by remorse than by frustration. His comeback in the polls had hit stall speed. . . . His private sounding suggested that the politics of insult, and the inflamed media reaction to it, had in fact begun bloodying him more than the enemy. Jimmy the Mean accordingly gave way to Jimmy the Good.[156]

One week later a *Newsweek* poll reported by Goldman revealed that Carter's "meanness" strategy succeeded. Despite claims that Carter undermined his image as a decent, compassionate man, Goldman added, the negative campaign helped the president's reelection chances:

. . . the most corrosive problem for Reagan was the war-and-peace issue—the gut who's-got-the-button question hyped by Carter at such hazard to his own reputation for common decency.

. . . Reagan's people searched their own canvasses for offsetting signs that Carter had hurt himself with his scare rhetoric—and found only the depressing evidence that it had worked. . . . Reagan's vulnerability, unlike Carter's excesses of rhetoric, could not be apologized away.[157]

The presidential debate between Reagan and Carter invited the obligatory media assessments of "who won." The *Washington Post* did not decide, but its editorial criticized Carter's attacks on Reagan in the debate as intended to frighten voters.[158] The *Wall Street Journal* called the debate a "draw" on the merits but a Reagan victory "in electoral terms." That is, Reagan was able to overcome public fears of his alleged belligerence.[159] David Broder declared that Carter failed to destroy Reagan as a viable candidate by playing on public fears of the Republican nominee.[160]

Finally, a number of commentaries close to election day are worth examining. The *Washington Post* called the 1980 elections a test of Carter's character, instead of his policies, because of the manner in which the president handled the hostage crisis: "Repeatedly in the past year Mr. Carter has handled the issue in a way that raises suspicions that he had excessive concern for its impact on his political fortunes."[161]

In its election day (November 4) editorial the *Wall Street Journal* proclaimed:

[Carter] has mismanaged the hostage crisis from the first. . . . This record of mismanagement piled on mismanagement seems to us, far more than any belligerence by Mr. Carter's opponent, to increase prospects for war.[162]

Allan J. Mayer, in the November 3 *Newsweek* issue, offered a brief retrospective on Carter's presidency and campaign. Mayer characterized Carter's campaign as "a study in the advantages of incumbency." Regarding the Carter presidency:

Jimmy Carter is as much of an outsider today as he was when Hamilton Jordan first breezed through the West Wing of the White House in his boots and green windbreaker. The Presidency . . . has not tempered his smoldering contempt for the political establishment—nor its for him. . . . He and his tightly knit circle of Georgians have followed no one's instincts but their own— and theirs would be a victory of surpassing sweetness. "If Jimmy Carter wins this election," said a campaign aide, "he can say 'screw you' to the world."[163]

On November 4 Ronald Reagan won a landslide victory over President Carter and Independent candidate John Anderson. Reagan received 489 electoral votes to Carter's tally of 49 electors. The Republican party gained a majority in the Senate (53–46), picking up twelve seats in the elections. In the House, Republicans gained 33 seats on the Democrats' substantial majority. The *Wall Street Journal* commented that, in part, Reagan's landslide "represents the voters' rejection of President Carter's management."[164] The *New York Times* did not believe that the election signaled public support for Republican party programs:

[Carter] was defeated not by a better program but by the widespread feeling that his best efforts were not good enough. . . . Mr. Carter lost this election more than Mr. Reagan won it. The American people recoiled all year from having to choose either. . . . Americans voted against Mr. Carter not because he sponsored a complicated arms treaty or ambiguous Middle East peace; they turned him out because in a time of economic stress, he gave them no firm sense of direction.[165]

Allan J. Mayer also held Carter personally responsible for the massive defeat for reelection:

. . . in large measure the President had brought his defeat on himself. His contempt for the political establishment was as thick as his Georgia accent— and just as resistant to change. The result was an us-against them mentality that isolated the White House. His relations with a Congress controlled by his own party were the worst of any President in modern history. His refusal to compromise, consult or curry favor on Capitol Hill first baffled, then outraged legislators, who retaliated by bottling up his programs.[166]

Lance Morrow's post-election assessment of Carter emphasized a number of common press themes:

> In a sense, Carter was an irrelevance to his own party. He was never a Democratic leader either in blood or inclination. . . . He never sought, like Lyndon Johnson, to preside as paterfamilias over the great brawling Democratic coalition, rewarding and remonstrating from the head of the table while all the family factions (workers, blacks, Jews, city dwellers, the poor, intellectuals) passed around the meat and potatoes. Carter won the White House in 1976 as a sweet-psalming loner circuit riding outside the party structures. As President, owing little or nothing to the party, he practiced a cool neglect of it.[167]

George F. Will believed that Carter was the logical and unfortunate outcome of the immediate post-Watergate era. Will argued that the lesson of Watergate was, for many people, that aspiring politicians should be judged by criteria focusing on private, not public, virtues. Such a "lesson" gave us Carter as president and "made a Reagan presidency necessary." Will added that Carter's campaign was "ineffective, at best, but it was his governing that doomed him."[168]

Some analysts compared President Reagan's transition to that of Carter's four years earlier. Carter's transition was held up as a model of how not to get started. For example, Peter Goldman reported on Reagan's visits to Capitol Hill during the transition:

> Carter made a similar (though shorter) visit to Washington during *his* interregnum in 1976, to similarly warm notices. But his stubborn outsiderliness thereafter shortened his honeymoon, undermined his program and provided Reagan his working model of how not to do business in an insider's city. Reagan accordingly radiated signals that he will be different—that he will happily visit Capitol Hill, whose leaders Carter dragged to the White House and then billed for breakfast; that he will mix with the lords and ladies of Washington society, toward whom Carter was standoffish; that he means to ride in his inaugural, where Carter ostentatiously walked.[169]

Timothy D. Schellhardt wrote a November 6 column speculating on what the Carter "legacy" would be. Attempting to anticipate the judgments of historians Schellhardt wrote:

> History may treat Mr. Carter most harshly in the area of presidential leadership. There was a kind of hollowness about Jimmy Carter's administration, from beginning to end. He seldom seemed to articulate a clear idea of just what he wanted to do and how he planned to do it. While he often communicated goodness and compassion, he didn't communicate purpose. And while he remained levelheaded in times of crisis, Mr. Carter frequently appeared naively surprised when international cross-currents produced shocks like the Soviet invasion of Afghanistan.[170]

Carter's Legacy

During January 1981, as Ronald Reagan prepared to assume the presidency, the press presented many retrospectives on the Carter presidency. The early retrospectives sought to understand the so-called "failures" of Carter's administration and to predict Carter's legacy. Surprisingly, many analysts who for four years strongly rebuked the president for his leadership tactics either praised Carter's efforts or found other reasons for the voters' rejection of a second Carter administration. David Broder's evaluation is indicative:

> That the nation was uneasy with his leadership and rejected his bid for a second term may be less a reflection on his shortcomings as a president than an evidence of the fitful spirit of the age.
> . . . That he was unable to rise above the circumstances that made his election possible and shape a consensus for governing effectively is hardly a condemnation. It would have taken a leader of extraordinary skills to do that, and Jimmy Carter was not that man.
> . . . he was hobbled by his almost complete lack of eloquence and was embarrassed by his too-easy tolerance of mediocre performance by some of his all too familiar aides. He was victimized by one of the characteristic failings of the age—the belief in expertise. Some of the "expert" energy and economic advice he received was way off the mark.
> His personality was such that he could not easily gain the trust and affection of other politicians. He was unable to persuade them to take risks on behalf of his policies, even when Carter and the policies were right.[171]

Meg Greenfield characterized Carter as the victim of unreasonably high, contradictory expectations of public leaders. She noted that what brought down Carter, in part, was public relations—"the tireless and doomed pursuit of an effective image, a winning voice, the right set of symbols to project." Greenfield added:

> . . . we not only expect a projection of the right symbols—and thus values— from our presidents, but also walk around with mutually contradictory ideas of what these values are—grandeur plus cottage-hearth simplicity, for example.
> . . . Jimmy Carter was being set up by the whole 200 million of us and he didn't seem to know it. We wanted a president who *didn't* make his own bed, in addition to one who did. And, besides, the staginess of the whole thing really got to us.
> . . . Maybe the hardest thing for a President to do in this day and age is to find his authentic voice and to—forgive me—*communicate* it to all his various publics, clients and antagonists. We stack the odds against him. We tempt him to do other things. But basically this is what people are after, and it is also the crucial instrument of Presidential policy success.[172]

The *Washington Post* editors, while critical of Carter's political leadership, also believed that the public had an unclear notion of what should be expected of our presidents. In response to the question "what went wrong?" the *Post* replied:

The flaw in the Carter style was the pervasive habit of indecision. Many forces always struggle for the soul of an American president. In the past four years, the struggle was fierce and the outcome was never entirely resolved. It had a lot to do with the nature of Mr. Carter himself, but this was also a time in which American ideas about politics and the presidency were changing. Americans didn't seem to have made up their minds exactly what kind of president they wanted.[173]

Peter Goldman agreed that modern presidents are held to unreasonably high expectations. In Goldman's view, contemporary presidents adopt Franklin D. Roosevelt's leadership approach as a role model, generating policy pressures that the government is no longer equipped to handle:

> . . . the FDR of legend has become part of the problem for its inheritors— an enticement to try getting it all at once and an impossible standard of measurement when they fail. A new President typically comes to office pledged to right every wrong within reach, and some far beyond. . . .[174]

The lack of any national "consensus" on how to deal with the many problems faced by Carter also contributed to the president's difficulties, Goldman added. Yet, according to Goldman, Carter did not help his administration's fortunes:

> What presidents do command is a matchless opportunity for persuasion, if they are gifted enough at speech and timing and can get the nation to listen. . . . For a Jimmy Carter, with his singsong speech and his unmajestic bearing, it was hardly a resource at all.
> It was Jimmy Carter's misfortune to come to town with his small flair of leadership at a time when no [national] consensus existed—and when the pendulum of power was at the far end of one of its periodic swings between the White House and the Hill.
> . . . Carter, to be sure, made his own way harder on the Hill. . . . Carter proved unadept at most [political] arts—at massaging Congressional egos, at trading pork-barrel politics for votes, at mobilizing public opinion behind his programs.
> His more serious failure with Congress was that he asked it for too much.
> . . . Carter surrendered to the program-of-the-month impulse that has governed Washington for much of the past half–century, blurring his priorities and fragmenting his energies in the rush.[175]

Tom Wicker praised Carter's achievements in human rights policy and arms control. Wicker added that Carter's arms control policies were thwarted by the ill-timed Soviet invasion of Afghanistan and short-sighted domestic critics. Wicker wondered what led the American people to so thoroughly repudiate this president:

> Mr. Carter's impending return to Plains impels the question why such a disciplined and intelligent man, taking office with so much good will and

representing a majority party that controlled both houses of Congress, achieved what the American people obviously judged to be so little.[176]

Wicker offered a series of observations intended to help answer this riddle. His assessments can be summed up as follows:

1. *Economic Policy.* Carter lacked "a definite economic attitude." His economic policy was one of "vacillation and reversal," focusing on inflation one week and unemployment the next.

2. *Communication:* Carter had "an inability to persuade the American people." He persisted in the engineer's approach of devising "comprehensive programs on this subject or that, but repeatedly failed to mobilize public opinion in their support."

3. *Political Skill:* Carter was "unable to stimulate and sustain genuine commitment to his causes—perhaps because the public did not sense in him the political skills and understanding that could have built its confidence and engaged its loyalties."

Carter "never established a politically coherent Administration. No doubt that was partly owing to Mr. Carter's inexperience in Washington, and partly to his unwillingness to move outside a tight reassuring Southern circle— but more, I believe, to his apparent lack of a clear and orderly sense of possibilities and priorities."

4. *The Agenda:* Jimmy Carter took on what "one well placed Democrat" suggested to Wicker was "an agenda for a second term."

> Such divisive, even back-breaking issues were challenged—not always necessarily—before effective working relations with Congress, smaller but more popular successes and a record of practical accomplishment had given Mr. Carter sufficient public confidence and political capital. Instead of building momentum toward his major goals, he attacked them head-on and headlong.
>
> That may have been bold but it was not *political*, a word that in its best sense describes more than the art of winning elections and defines what a President must be, over all.[177] (emphasis original)

In predicting history's eventual judgment of Carter journalists frequently turned to academicians and political observers for insights. Terrence Smith claimed that the opinion of most "Presidency watchers" was that Carter's greatest achievement was winning the presidency in the first place. After the 1976 election Carter's other major achievements, in order, were the Camp David treaties, Panama Canal treaties, the opening of diplomatic relations with China, and the national energy policy. Smith consulted a number of political analysts including Harry McPherson, Austin Ranney, Clark Clifford, James David Barber, Theodore H. White, and Theodore Sorensen.[178]

Steven V. Roberts consulted other "experts" and observed: "The most common view is that while he can point to a few notable accomplishments, Mr. Carter will not bequeath a particularly distinguished legacy to the nation." For this analysis Roberts consulted Thomas Cronin, R. Gordon

Hoxie, and James Fallows. In the views of the experts, according to Roberts, historians would regard Carter's foreign policy more highly than his domestic record.[179]

The *Wall Street Journal*, despite its criticisms of Carter's foreign policy as "weak" and "vacillating," concluded its assessments of the Carter legacy in the international realm on a positive note:

> The United States under Mr. Carter has indeed espoused humanitarian values, and that should not be forgotten as we try to get a firmer grip on the world's harsher realities. The worth and dignity of the individual are deeply held American beliefs and form the core of our democratic institutions and our concepts of private property and free economic choice. Mr. Carter's failings in foreign policy had more to do with the way his subordinates translated this principle into policy than with the principle itself. They often conceived policies totally at odds with the principle, in fact.[180]

Anthony Lewis offered some flattering perceptions of Carter's potential legacy. Lewis observed that history has favorably treated many presidents condemned by their contemporaries. Lewis added: "We pile exaggerated hopes on our Presidents and then, when inevitably he disappoints us, we destroy him. . . . I think there will be rewards in history for the man now leaving office under the burden of rejection. . . . In Jimmy Carter's four years as President, no American soldier died in combat. That is a great achievement—a singular one in the last 50 years." Lewis listed the major accomplishments of the outgoing administration. These included: the courage to resist political pressure to use military force against Iran; full diplomatic relations with China; the Panama Canal treaties; the Camp David accords; support for British policy in Southern Africa which "made it possible to settle the savage war in Zimbabwe"; the human rights campaign where "American idealism was represented in the world"; an impressive environmental record at home; judicial appointments which included a significant number of women and minorities; an energy policy which "broke away from the distorting practice of holding American prices way below world levels"; and a break "with outmoded liberal ideas to begin deregulation of airlines, trucks, banking."[181]

Finally, the *New York Times's* editors on January 16, 1981, issued "The President's Report Card." This editorial, in the wake of Carter's farewell speech as president, was a sentimental farewell to President Carter:

> Jimmy Carter stood, sometimes uncertainly, for progress on [nuclear arms control, the environment and human rights]. He worked to limit nuclear weapons and the spread of plutonium for nuclear energy. If his devotion to human rights seemed piestic at times in Asia or Eastern Europe, it was inspirational in Africa and Latin America. On the environment, his administration demonstrated repeatedly that protection can be squared with development.
>   Mr. Carter brought powerful personal values to office. If his human rights pronouncements sometimes sounded moralistic, they were grounded in genuine

morality and in a sense of duty to act against poverty and intolerance. He promised an Administration that would not lie, and by and large, even at the risk of looking clumsy, it did not.

Was this a weak President or only a time of a weak Presidency? Was Jimmy Carter an outstanding President . . . or a poor one. . . . Whatever the polls say, there's no outguessing history. What is clear is that Jimmy Carter was a decent President.[182]

Conclusion

This concludes our review of the journalistic assessments of the Carter presidency from November 1976 through January 1981. In this review can be found a pattern to the assessments of the Carter presidency. In the early stages of the administration journalists identified certain expectations that they had of Jimmy Carter as president. Less explicit at this time were their more general expectations of presidential leadership and performance. These more general sets of expectations were revealed over time as reactions to particular events during the Carter presidency.

Gradually a negative perception of the Carter administration dominated journalists' commentaries. This unflattering view became increasingly evident over time as Carter appeared to many journalists to disappoint the expectations that they had of him. To review briefly, the elements of this negative press perception of the Carter administration were:

1. *Timing.* Journalists did not credit the Carter administration with a good sense of timing. They criticized the administration in the first year of the term for trying to do too much too quickly. Many journalists clearly believed that a president should begin his term with clearly focused, limited, and politically feasible agenda items. Journalists portrayed Carter's controversial first year items, especially the energy program, as ill-timed policy interventions.

The administration from early on, therefore, developed a reputation for poor political timing. This portrait became most negative in 1980 when journalists regarded the timing of White House events and policy interventions as calculated to enhance Carter's reelection campaign.

2. *Rhetoric/Symbolism.* In the early months of the administration's first year journalists portrayed Carter as the master of the symbolic act. Journalists often described his rhetorical tone as modest and conservative, leading many journalists to believe that Carter did not aspire to be a "bugle-call" president. The favorable image of Carter as an effective communicator did not last. By the end of 1977 journalists considered Carter ineffective at arousing public support for administration proposals. The prevailing image of Carter that developed was that of a lackluster speaker and ineffectual persuader. Journalists often attributed Carter's leadership problems to his failure to use the "bully pulpit" effectively and his apparent inability to articulate a vision of the nation's future.

3. *Agenda.* The major journalistic critique of Carter's agenda was that it was not politically feasible. The president, according to this view, correctly

identified the major issues of the day and proceeded to push these agenda items because they were "right." The comprehensive energy program, according to journalists, was the most controversial item on which to stake Carter's first year leadership.

The Carter agenda (energy, civil service reform, human rights, arms control) did not in itself contribute widely to the negative press assessments of the administration. Journalists tended to accept Carter's agenda items as the correct areas for government action during his term and thus frequently praised administration policy proposals. For the most part, they indicated that they would have emphasized different agenda items for reasons of political feasibility. This criticism reflects the very common view of Carter as inattentive to political necessities.

4. *Policy Development.* The negative press assessments of the Carter administration focused a great deal on the president's efforts at policy development. The most frequently reported criticisms of Carter concerned his public and congressional relations. Journalists asserted that Carter disregarded conventional political norms, sought support for proposals by appealing to the merits, and did not consider his proposals negotiable. They portrayed the Carter administration as lacking a clearly identifiable set of policy priorities and as moving haphazardly from one issue area to another.

Journalists also viewed Carter's foreign policy as inconsistent and lacking a sense of direction. Considerable press criticism focused on Carter's foreign policy-making process which was influenced by a group of philosophically diverse individuals (Cyrus Vance, Andrew Young, Harold Brown, Zbigniew Brzezinski). A major source of press criticism was the apparent lack of a single voice directing United States foreign policy in the Carter administration.

5. *Staff.* A negative view of Carter's White House staff developed early in the administration and never changed. In general, journalists perceived Carter's staff as inexperienced and out of place in political Washington. The so-called "Georgian insiders," according to most journalists, were too insular, hostile to political Washington, and lacking in a sense of political decorum. Journalists criticized Carter for placing so much trust in these "outsiders" while allegedly ignoring the sentiments of many important Washington "insiders."

This negative press assessment contributed importantly to an image of the administration in the public and in Washington as incapable of effective leadership. Many White House officials believed that the press did not present an accurate portrait of the president and his subordinates. In the following chapter I turn to Carter White House communications advisers' perceptions of the press assessments of this presidency. These White House insiders corroborate many of the press themes identified in this study.

Notes

1. Quoted in Hamilton Jordan's *Crisis: The Last Year of the Carter Presidency* (New York: Berkeley Books, 1982), p. 1.
2. "Squeezing the Soviets," *Time*, January 28, 1980, p. 13.

3. "Carter Takes Charge," *Time*, February 4, 1980, pp. 12–15.

4. Hedrick Smith, "Carter's New Momentum," *New York Times*, January 25, 1980, p. D14.

5. "Jimmy Carter's Catch Up," *Washington Post*, January 25, 1980, p. A14; see "State of the Union," *Washington Post*, January 22, 1980, p. A18.

6. "Clear and Present Danger," *Washington Post*, January 17, 1980, p. B6.

7. "Carter's Turn to Cope with Russia," *U.S. News and World Report*, February 4, 1980, p. 16.

8. "Weakness Is Strength," *Wall Street Journal*, January 21, 1980, p. 18.

9. "A Corner Turned?" *Wall Street Journal*, January 25, 1980, p. 16.

10. Joseph Kraft, "Carter's Menu, Without a Bill," *Washington Post*, January 27, 1980, p. B7.

11. Martin Schram, "Carter Speech: Outflanking, Undercutting Rivals," *Washington Post*, January 25, 1980, p. A22.

12. James Reston, "The State of the Union," *New York Times*, January 20, 1980, p. E19.

13. James Reston, "Register for What?" *New York Times*, February 13, 1980, p. A27.

14. George F. Will, "Right Out of the 1930's," *Washington Post*, January 17, 1980, p. A27.

15. George F. Will, "Open Market on Ineptitude," *Washington Post*, May 19, 1980, p. A19.

16. Joseph Kraft, "A Superpower's Job," *Washington Post*, February 3, 1980, p. C7.

17. Rowland Evans and Robert Novak, "Carter's Defense Game," *Washington Post*, February 13, 1980, p. A15.

18. "New Mood on Capitol Hill," *Time*, February 4, 1980, p. 17.

19. Tom Mathews, "Carter's Widening Crisis," *Newsweek*, January 7, 1980, p. 17.

20. Norman C. Miller, "A Real Debate," *Wall Street Journal*, January 31, 1980, p. 14.

21. Joseph Kraft, "New Men for New Measures," *Washington Post*, January 15, 1980, p. A15.

22. "Born Yesterday," *Wall Street Journal*, February 27, 1980, p. 22.

23. Joseph Kraft, "Who's Conning Whom?" *Washington Post*, March 13, 1980, p. A19.

24. "Hanging Tough," *U.S. News and World Report*, April 28, 1980, p. 19.

25. "Iran: Enough," *Washington Post*, April 6, 1980, p. E6.

26. "Enlisting in Humiliation," *Wall Street Journal*, April 1, 1980, p. 22; see also, "Minimal Response," *Wall Street Journal*, April 18, 1980, p. 20.

27. "Storm Over the Alliance," *Time*, April 28, 1980, p. 15.

28. "In the Aftermath," *Washington Post*, May 2, 1980, p. A16; and "Let's Avoid Scapegoats," *Newsweek*, May 5, 1980, p. 104.

29. "Debacle in the Desert," *Time*, May 5, 1980, p. 12.

30. Allan J. Mayer, "A Mission Comes to Grief in Iran," *Newsweek*, May 5, 1980, pp. 24, 27; see also, "Rescue That Failed: Big Setback for U.S.," *U.S. News and World Report*, May 5, 1980, p. 23.

31. Joseph Kraft, "Faulty from the Start," *Washington Post*, April 29, 1980, p. A17.

32. George F. Will, "Just What You'd Expect From this Administration," *Washington Post*, May 1, 1980, p. A19.

33. Tom Wicker, "Mr. Carter's Loss," *New York Times*, April 29, 1980, p. A23.

34. "A Surprise at State," *Time*, May 12, 1980, p. 12.

35. Peter Goldman, "Another Rescue Mission," *Newsweek,* May 12, 1980, pp. 26–28.

36. Tom Wicker, "Mr. Carter's Loss," *New York Times,* April 29, 1980, p. A23.

37. Hedrick Smith, "A Political Jolt for Carter," *New York Times,* April 29, 1980, pp. A1, 15.

38. "Cleaning Up a Mess," *U.S. News and World Report,* May 12, 1980, pp. 19–20.

39. Anthony Lewis, "What the Captain Means," *New York Times,* May 15, 1980, p. A27.

40. "Leaving Well," *Wall Street Journal,* April 29, 1980, p. 22.

41. "Muskie at State," *Wall Street Journal,* May 1, 1980, p. 24.

42. "Carter's Mission: Stop the Rot," *U.S. News and World Report,* June 23, 1980, pp. 18–19.

43. "Seven Allies In One Gondola," *Time,* July 7, 1980, pp. 10–12; see also "Carter's Impact on Europe," *U.S. News and World Report,* July 7, 1980, pp. 16–18.

44. Hugh Sidey, "Determination and Adroit Maneuvers," *Time,* July 7, 1980, p. 13.

45. David Alpern, "Carter and the Cuban Influx," *Newsweek,* May 26, 1980, p. 22.

46. "Devil's Island," *Wall Street Journal,* October 2, 1980, p. 30.

47. "Nuclear Riposte," *Wall Street Journal,* May 21, 1980, p. 22.

48. "Nuclear Cave," *Wall Street Journal,* May 9, 1980, p. 18.

49. Ibid.

50. "Proliferating Confusion," *Wall Street Journal,* October 30, 1980, p. 30.

51. "Bungle Fever," *Wall Street Journal,* March 7, 1980, p. 16.

52. Tom Wicker, "Two for the Skeptics," *New York Times,* March 23, 1980, p. E21.

53. Joseph Kraft, "Carter Plus Vance Equals Trouble," *Washington Post,* March 18, 1980, p. A19.

54. Allan J. Mayer, "Newly Vulnerable Carter," *Newsweek,* March 17, 1980, p. 27.

55. "Flip-Flops and Zig-Zags: Isolated in the White House, Carter Seems All Too Prone to Error," *Time,* March 17, 1980, p. 14.

56. George F. Will, "Transparent Blunder at the UN," *Washington Post,* March 9, 1980, p. C7; on the political ramifications of the UN vote incident see Karen Elliot House, "Carter's Turnaround On Vote at U.N. May Bring Him Varied Political Results," *Wall Street Journal,* March 5, 1980, p. 4.

57. "Billy Carter Affair: New Headache for the President," *U.S. News and World Report,* August 4, 1980, p. 17.

58. Ed Magnunson, "The Burden of Billy," *Time,* August 4, 1980, pp. 14–15; see also *Time's* July 28 cover story on Billy Carter, "To The Shoals of Tripoli," and "What Have You Done, Billy Boy?" *Time,* August 11, 1980, pp. 20–21.

59. Allan J. Mayer, "A Storm Over Billy Carter," *Newsweek,* August 4, 1980, pp. 15, 21.

60. "His Brother's Retainer, " *New York Times,* July 16, 1980, p. A22; and "Caeser's Brother," *New York Times,* July 24, 1980, p. A18.

61. "Loose Justice, Loose Canon," *New York Times,* July 30, 1980, p. A20.

62. "Billy: Fire or Smoke," *New York Times,* August 1, 1980, p. A22.

63. "Not that Heavy," *Wall Street Journal,* July 24, 1980, p. 16.

64. Of the more than one dozen commentaries by Safire on the Billy Carter controversy, the following articles are most significant: "Billy, I'm Proud of You," *New York Times,* February 4, 1980, p. A19; "The Honesty Test," *New York Times,* February 7, 1980, p. A23; "Igor and Billy," *New York Times,* June 26, 1980, p. A19;

"None Dare Call It Billygate," New York Times, July 21, 1980, p. A17; "The Hostage Profiteer," New York Times, July 24, 1980, p. A19; "Informal Brief Exchange," New York Times, July 28, 1980, p. A21; "Moral Blindness," New York Times, August 7, 1980, p. A19; "Somebody Is Lying," New York Times, September 4, 1980, p. A27.

65. Joseph Kraft, "More Problems than Billy," Washington Post, August 3, 1980, p. C7.

66. Tom Wicker, "A Watergate Parallel?" New York Times, August 1, 1980, p. A23.

67. Anthony Lewis, "Wishing Will Not Make it So," New York Times, August 4, 1980, p. A21.

68. Ed Magnunson, "First Billy, Then Teddy," Time, August 18, 1980, p. 22.

69. "Ending the Affair," Wall Street Journal, August 6, 1980, p. 16.

70. John Lang, "Has President Laid Billy Case to Rest?" U.S. News and World Report, August 18, 1980, p. 20.

71. "Billy Carter's Brother's Mess," New York Times, August 6, 1980, p. A20.

72. David E. Rosenbaum, "The Billy Carter Case: A Fizzled Bombshell," New York Times, October 4, 1980, p. A10.

73. "What Billy's Brother Did Badly," New York Times, October 5, 1980, p. E18.

74. "Jimmy Carter vs. Inflation: He Promises Budget Cuts and Credit Curbs, But More Is Needed," Time, March 24, 1980, pp. 8–9.

75. Judith B. Gardner, "A Carter Recession—How Soon, How Deep," U.S. News and World Report, May 31, 1980, p. 23.

76. Harry Anderson, "Carter's Attack on Inflation," Newsweek, March 24, 1980, pp. 25, 30; see also, Harry Anderson, "Fighting the Inflation 'Crisis,'" Newsweek, March 10, 1980, pp. 24–26.

77. "Have Another Arsenic," Wall Street Journal, March 17, 1980, p. 20.

78. "Test of Seriousness," Wall Street Journal, March 14, 1980, p. 22.

79. "One-Day Budget Cuts," Wall Street Journal, March 18, 1980, p. 24.

80. "Credit Cop Capers," Wall Street Journal, March 21, 1980, p. 24.

81. "Tiger in the Tank," Wall Street Journal, May 16, 1980, p. 22.

82. Hugh Sidey, "Losing the Inner Instincts," Time, June 16, 1980, p. 17.

83. Richard Levine and Karen Elliot House, "Mr. Carter's Inconsistent Leadership," Wall Street Journal, March 14, 1980, p. 22.

84. "Flip-Flops and Zigzags," Time, March 17, 1980, pp. 14–15.

85. Timothy D. Schellhardt, "The Inner Circle," Wall Street Journal, August 11, 1980, pp. 1, 9.

86. Steven R. Weisman, "Carter's People Face Challenge of Finding the Grand Design," New York Times, August 10, 1980, p. E1.

87. Ted Gest, "Carter as President—What Record Shows," U.S. News and World Report, August 18, 1980, pp. 30–32.

88. "Diminished Honor," Wall Street Journal, August 13, 1980, p. 26.

89. "Panic and Ingratitude," Wall Street Journal, August 11, 1980, p. 12.

90. "Unanswered Question," Wall Street Journal, August 14, 1980, p. 18.

91. Hugh Sidey, "Assessing a Presidency," Time, August 18, 1980, pp. 10–15.

92. Christopher Ogden, "Coming to Grips With the Job," Time, October 27, 1980, pp. 14–18; Martin Schram, "Carter: Toll of a Clockwork Presidency," Washington Post, October 27, 1980, pp. A1, 4; Joseph Kraft, "How Would Each Man Govern?" Washington Post, October 26, 1980, p. C7.

93. Albert Hunt, "Carter's Congressional Record," Wall Street Journal, September 2, 1980, p. 26.

94. Lloyd Cutler, "To Form a Government," Foreign Affairs (Fall 1980), pp. 470–486.

95. "Tinker Time," *Wall Street Journal*, September 25, 1980, p. 32.

96. George F. Will, "The Administration's Alibi," *Newsweek*, October 13, 1980, p. 136.

97. "In Energy, Clear Contrasts," *Washington Post*, October 8, 1980, p. A18.

98. Peter Goldman, "Fighting After the Final Bell," *Newsweek*, June 16, 1980, p. 22.

99. "A Congressional Crusher," *Wall Street Journal*, June 6, 1980, p. 16.

100. "Power and Policy," *Wall Street Journal*, June 9, 1980, p. 24.

101. Peter Goldman, "This Ball Game is About Over," *Newsweek*, March 31, 1980, p. 22.

102. Joseph Kraft, "On the Wings of Failure," *Washington Post*, March 16, 1980, p. C7.

103. Hugh Sidey, "Refuse in the Rose Garden," *Time*, February 18, 1980, p. 24.

104. William Raspberry, "Carter's Long Strong Arm," *Washington Post*, January 25, 1980, p. A15.

105. Timothy D. Schellhardt, "Carter, Who Railed Against Pork-Barrel Politics in 1976, Now Exploits Them For Illinois Primary," *Wall Street Journal*, March 6, 1980, p. 48.

106. Ibid.

107. Timothy D. Schellhardt, "Rose Garden Tactic Keeps Carter Home, Leaves Kennedy Railing Out in the Cold," *Wall Street Journal*, February 7, 1980, p. 6.

108. Peter Goldman, "See Jimmy Run—in Place," *Newsweek*, February 18, 1980, p. 45.

109. Ibid.

110. Peter Goldman, "This Ball Game Is About Over," *Newsweek*, March 31, 1980, p. 22.

111. Peter Goldman, "Carter Is In Trouble Again," *Newsweek*, April 7, 1980, pp. 21–25.

112. David Broder, "Jimmy Carter's 'Good News' Strategy," *Washington Post*, April 6, 1980, p. E7.

113. David Broder, "Self-Defeat in Self-Exile," *Washington Post*, February 17, 1980, p. D7.

114. Rowland Evans and Robert Novak, "Policy or Passing Fancy?" *Washington Post*, April 2, 1980, p. A19.

115. William Safire, "Stumbling Into War," *New York Times*, April 17, 1980, p. A27; see also, William Safire, "My Fellow Americans," *New York Times*, April 24, 1980, p. A27.

116. David Broder, "The Only Way Carter Can Win," *Washington Post*, May 7, 1980, p. A19.

117. Timothy D. Schellhardt, "Carter's Post-Rose Garden Strategy," *Wall Street Journal*, May 8, 1980, p. 26.

118. Joseph Kraft, "End of the Rose Garden Strategy," *Washington Post*, May 4, 1980, p. C7.

119. Marvin Stone, "Carter's Big Test," *U.S. News and World Report*, May 19, 1980, p. 92.

120. David Broder, "Would You Prefer a Mondale-Baker Race?" *Washington Post*, June 4, 1980, p. A19.

121. Meg Greenfield, "The Cult of the Amateur," *Newsweek*, June 16, 1980, p. 100.

122. Joseph Kraft, "Whose Political Gain . . . ," *Washington Post*, June 15, 1980, p. D7; see also Kraft's "Hostage Politics," *Washington Post*, July 15, 1980, p. A15.

123. William Safire, "Turning Whose Tide," *New York Times*, June 2, 1980, p. A17.

124. William Safire, "Won't Be No December," *New York Times*, June 12, 1980, p. A31.

125. George F. Will, "And Who's the Demagogue?" *Washington Post*, June 15, 1980, p. D7.

126. Joseph Kraft, "Losing the Power to Make Policy," *Washington Post*, June 3, 1980, p. A17.

127. "Jimmy Carter in General . . . ," *Washington Post*, July 1, 1980, p. A16.

128. "Running Mean," *Washington Post*, September 18, 1980, p. A18.

129. James Reston, "What Ails Carter?" *New York Times*, September 21, 1980, p. E19.

130. George F. Will, "The Smear," *Washington Post*, September 21, 1980, p. D7.

131. George F. Will, "Moderation, Carter Style," *Newsweek*, September 29, 1980, p. 21.

132. Hugh Sidey, "More than a Candidate," *Time*, September 29, 1980, p. 21.

133. "The Shoebox War," *Wall Street Journal*, September 4, 1980, p. 26.

134. "Threat to Peace?" *Wall Street Journal*, September 25, 1980, p. 32.

135. Robert G. Kaiser, "President Carter's 'Low Road': Heavy Media Traffic," *Washington Post*, September 26, 1980, p. A3; see also, "Back to the Real World," *U.S. News and World Report*, September 15, 1980, pp. 21–22; and Allan J. Mayer's "Oh, I'll Take the Low Road," *Newsweek*, September 29, 1980, pp. 22–23.

136. George C. Church, "Carter: Running Tough," *Time*, August 25, 1980, pp. 8–12.

137. "New York: The Finale," *Washington Post*, August 17, 1980, p. 21.

138. Peter Goldman, "The Mutinous Democrats," *Newsweek*, August 4, 1980, p. 21.

139. Peter Goldman, "The Drive to Dump Carter," *Newsweek*, August 11, 1980, pp. 18–25.

140. Peter Goldman, "Now for the Hard Part," *Newsweek*, August 26, 1980, pp. 18–23.

141. Norman C. Miller, "A Make-Believe Campaign," *Wall Street Journal*, September 5, 1980, p. 14.

142. Timothy D. Schellhardt, "This Year's Political Watershed: Containment," *Wall Street Journal*, September 16, 1980, p. 38.

143. Tom Wicker, "The Debate Absence," *New York Times*, September 12, 1980, p. A23.

144. Joseph Kraft, "The Carter Machine," *Washington Post*, August 12, 1980, p. A17.

145. Norman C. Miller, "The Price of Victory," *Wall Street Journal*, October 9, 1980, p. 28.

146. Timothy D. Schellhardt, "Carter and 'Meanness,'" *Wall Street Journal*, November 3, 1980, p. 30.

147. "Haywire," *Washington Post*, October 8, 1980, p. A18. See also "The States' Rights Issue," *Wall Street Journal*, October 10, 1980, p. 24.

148. Rowland Evans and Robert Novak, "The Campaign Style that Backfired," *Washington Post*, October 6, 1980, p. A15.

149. Walter Isaacson, "A Vow to Zip His Lip," *Time*, October 20, 1980, pp. 16–17; see also Isaacson's "War, Peace and Politics," *Time*, October 6, 1980, pp. 22–25.

150. "A Biting, Gouging Race for President," *U.S. News and World Report*, October 20, 1980, p. 11.

151. Meg Greenfield, "The Real Military Issue," *Newsweek*, October 6, 1980, p. 112.

152. George F. Will, ". . . And Boredom," *Washington Post*, October 12, 1980, p. C7.

153. George F. Will, "Three Reasons to Remove Carter, " *Washington Post*, October 26, 1980, p. C7.

154. George F. Will, "Wringing Out Mandate," *Washington Post*, October 30, 1980, p. A23.

155. George F. Will, "No More Peculiar Presidents, Please," *Washington Post*, November 2, 1980, p. C7.

156. Peter Goldman, "Two Candidates For Reform," *Newsweek*, October 20, 1980, p. 26.

157. Peter Goldman, "A Showdown, One-on-One," *Newsweek*, October 27, 1980, p. 34.

158. "90-Minute Wonder," *Washington Post*, October 30, 1980, p. A22.

159. "Good Show," *Wall Street Journal*, October 30, 1980, p. 30.

160. David Broder, "Carter On Points, But No KO," *Washington Post*, October 29, 1980, p. A1.

161. "A Test of Character," *Washington Post*, October 24, 1980, p. A22.

162. "Carter II?" *Wall Street Journal*, November 4, 1980, p. 28.

163. Allan J. Mayer, "Playing Catch-Up Ball," *Newsweek*, November 3, 1980, p. 34.

164. "Mandate for a Change," *Wall Street Journal*, November 6, 1980, p. 32.

165. "President Reagan, and Other Messages," *New York Times*, November 5, 1980, p. A30.

166. Allan J. Mayer, "Carter: A Long Day's Night," *Newsweek*, November 17, 1980, p. 29.

167. Lance Morrow, "Is There Life After Disaster?" *Time*, November 17, 1980, p. 44.

168. George F. Will, "Lesson Unlearned," *Washington Post*, November 6, 1980, p. A19.

169. Peter Goldman, "Hail the Conquering Hero," *Newsweek*, December 1, 1980, pp. 30, 32. See also, "How to Charm a City: Reagan Gives a Boffo Performance in His First Appearance in the Capital," *Time*, December 1, 1980, pp. 10–15.

170. Timothy D. Schellhardt, "The Jimmy Carter Legacy," *Wall Street Journal*, November 6, 1980, p. 32.

171. David Broder, ". . . Of An Uneasy Era," *Washington Post*, January 18, 1981, p. C7.

172. Meg Greenfield, "Carter and the PR Trap," *Newsweek*, January 26, 1981, p. 84.

173. "The Carter Years," *Washington Post*, January 19, 1981, p. A18.

174. Peter Goldman, "The Presidency: Can Anyone Do the Job?" *Newsweek*, February 26, 1981, pp. 37–38.

175. Ibid., pp. 37–41.

176. Tom Wicker, "A Failure of Politics," *New York Times*, January 16, 1981, p. A23.

177. Ibid.

178. Terrence Smith, "Experts See '76 Victory as Carter's Big Achievement," *New York Times*, January 8, 1981, p. B14.

179. Steven V. Roberts, "Analysts Give Carter Higher Marks in Foreign Affairs than in Domestic Policy," *New York Times*, January 19, 1981, p. A22.

180. "The Hostages," *Wall Street Journal*, January 20, 1981, p. 30.

181. Anthony Lewis, "The King Must Die," *New York Times*, January 11, 1981, p. E23.

182. "The President's Report Card," *New York Times*, January 16, 1981, p. A22.

7

White House Communications Advisers' Perceptions of Presidential Leadership

This chapter ascertains the convergences and divergences in definitions and evaluations of presidential leadership between Carter's White House communications advisers and presidential journalists. In retrospective assessments of their governing experiences White House staff members revealed how they viewed their own efforts to deal with the Carter presidency's press image problem. The extent to which these staff members recognized and accepted the bases of journalistic evaluations provides important corroborative evidence of the themes identified in this study, and of the similar values of leadership held by journalists and White House "insiders." The Carter White House staff members selected for investigation here include individuals concerned with the president's speechmaking and media image: speechwriters, members of the press secretary's office, and some members of the White House inner circle.

In identifying the perspectives and perceptions of these White House staff members I rely on two research sources: (1) The selected transcripts of the Carter Oral History project. These transcripts are based upon a number of interviews with Carter White House staff by panels of scholars; (2) the memoirs of White House staff.

To anticipate, there are widely shared notions of leadership among political communications elites—journalists and the White House press people and speechwriters. This finding tends to confirm other studies on shared values between specialized White House staffs and the clientele with whom these staff members deal.[1] This finding is not surprising since many of the White House staff discussed here were drawn from journalistic backgrounds. The existence of shared notions of leadership clarifies the bases of evaluations of a president who did not place great emphasis on image making and mass persuasion. Let's turn now to a review of the White House staff members' perspectives and perceptions of Carter's press image problem.

Timing

A major theme in the retrospective assessments of Carter White House staff was that of the "bridge presidency" or "transitional presidency." That is, a number of staff members perceived their four years in government as an important transitional stage in American public life. The Carter years immediately followed the conclusions of national traumas associated with Vietnam and Watergate. These four years also came at a time when a conservative tide seemed to be sweeping the country.

This unusual period in our recent history, according to some staff members, provided both unique opportunities and disadvantages for Jimmy Carter. The major benefit derived, they noted, was that this was the only time that a candidate with Carter's background and aspirations could have been elected to the presidency. Some staff members added that while many opinion leaders were uncomfortable with Carter's "outsider" image, the general public in 1976 was receptive to Carter's anti-establishment message.

In terms of press portrayals of the president, the historic context of this administration was perceived as a great disadvantage by some Carter staff members. A number of references to journalists' perceptions of public officials generally in the immediate post-Watergate years reveal the sentiment that this presidency was subjected to unusually high standards of public conduct. According to members of the press secretary's office:

> Succeeding Gerald Ford, Richard Nixon's Vice-President, [Watergate] hadn't been that long, and there was still that real residual distrust which was obviously at one point very intensely felt throughout the country, but always . . . much more intensely felt in Washington. I can remember very much references to Watergate or Watergate-like actions in the transition period and that's part of the mix that we were competing with. . . .[2]

> I found a real sensitivity among the press to being manipulated and questions were raised when we set up the radio operation and the media liaison office and [journalists] said, "You know this is just like something out of the Nixon press office. You know, going around the Washington press corps and manipulating the people."[3]

> I came to the conclusion . . .that of all the institutions in our society, the press was probably the most traumatized by Watergate—and it probably took it longer to scab over than it did anything else. If you had to refine it more, I think that the White House press corps . . . were even more bloody and bruised from it than the press corps at large. . . .[4]

> They always went away giving you the impression of believing "I just know the SOB dodged or lied to me and later I'm going to be able to say that if they'd just answered my tough questions I would have caught it." There's always that sense that they're out to catch you. Very tiring at the end of the day. I'll tell you.[5]

Press Secretary Jody Powell expressed the same sentiment in his book, *The Other Side of the Story:* "The events of Watergate, Vietnam, and that whole turbulent decade of souring relations between press and government have created a residue of cynicism that is a serious and corrosive force."[6]

White House Chief of Staff Hamilton Jordan in his *Crisis: The Final Year of the Carter Presidency* asserted that White House staff were ill-prepared for the kind of journalistic reaction they received in the late 1970s:

> We did not . . . understand or appreciate the extent to which the Washington press corps had changed in the past decade.
>
> I believe that Watergate and Vietnam pushed the American media from wholesome skepticism and doubt into out-and-out cynicism about the American political process generally and the Presidency specifically. Both Vietnam and Watergate had assumed the coloration of a struggle between the press and the President.
>
> It was against this backdrop of subtle but profound change in the media that the Carter Presidency was reported and judged. . . .[7]

White House staff commented on the administration's early difficulties brought on by an ambitious policy agenda and the crucial Bert Lance controversy. Regarding Carter's first year agenda a member of the press secretary's office assessed:

> The President started his first year with too many issues, too many priorities, too many initiatives. He started to focus a little more on the important things after that first year. . . .[8]

> Well yeah. That goes back to the question of did we fill up our tray too much. And I think we probably did. There was no lack of appreciation, on our part, that we were asking Congress to do some very painful things.[9]

A number of communications advisers noted that the Lance controversy marked a turning point for the Carter presidency. This event was particularly crucial to the development of the White House's press relations. Jody Powell wrote:

> I believe that our relations with the press began to fray in the late summer of 1977, when the prolonged and painful dispute over allegations against Bert Lance . . . led to hard feelings on both sides.[10]

The basis for the eventual press reaction to the Lance affair and other Carter administration controversies, Powell assessed, was the expectation the president himself fostered of an administration of unusually high ethical standards. Journalists accepted the "challenge" to prove that Jimmy Carter was really not very different from other public figures:

> Most journalists are convinced that no one makes it very far in politics without selling a sizable chunk of his soul. But here was a guy who not only claimed to have done it differently, but who was clearly of the opinion that politics as usual was wrong. To make things even worse, this guy was setting himself up to be not only better than most politicians, but also better than most

journalists. There was an implicit challenge involved, or at least many journalists thought there was, to prove that Carter was at least as rotten as all the rest.[11]

The Lance controversy therefore appeared to provide for many journalists the evidence needed to "prove" that Jimmy Carter's administration would not be different from its Republican predecessors. While many White House staff members admit "tactical" errors handling the Lance controversy, legislative relations and press relations, they believe that the press criticisms of the administration developed such a mindless momentum that Carter received less credit than he deserved for some important achievements. For example, Jody Powell attributed the less than enthusiastic press reception of the March 1979 Middle East peace treaty to that event's coincidence with a general negative journalistic view of the president's leadership ability:

> When the treaty was signed in March of 1979, the President received little credit for his accomplishments. . . . Unfortunately for the President I served, the culmination of what was perhaps his greatest diplomatic accomplishment came at a time when the press corp was largely unwilling to give him credit for much of anything. It was a time when I used to say that if the First Lady had conceived, the White House press corps would have declared that it had happened despite the President's best efforts.[12]

In assessing the impact of the timing of press criticisms of Carter, Powell discussed the journalistic portrayals of the administration during the 1980 elections. For example, Powell argued that the strong press reaction to Carter's statement about the hostage crisis on the morning of the Wisconsin primary could be attributed partially to the White House's failure to take into consideration the political ramifications of the timing of the announcement:

> The idea that we were devious and not above playing politics with the lives of the hostages, became part of the conventional wisdom of many who were covering us. Nothing we could do or say would change their minds. . . .
>   The primary in Wisconsin was far from our minds as we waited for the first wire service reports to come in. . . .As things turned out, we would have been better off to have given at least some thought to the political events of the day, and to the bitter cynicism with which the press viewed the President's every action.[13]

Powell was particularly sensitive to the issue of the timing of the press criticisms of Carter during the election year. Powell correctly observed that press criticism of Carter in 1980 was especially harsh, even in comparison to earlier years in the term. The Press Secretary attributed this harsh criticism to journalists overcompensating for their philosophical disagreements with candidate Reagan by criticizing the incumbent president harshly.[14] What Powell appeared to find unacceptable was the extent to which the White House's process of applying political considerations to decision making became such a major issue in the press in 1980:

For at least a year, Carter's every statement and action had been analyzed in a political context. If he did something popular, he was pandering to the public opinion. If he defied the popular mood, he was trying to combat his wishy-washy image by looking tough. If he defied Congress with a veto, he was preparing to run against a Congress controlled by his party, and blame it for his problems. If he compromised, it was a play for political backing in some key state.

Of course there were political considerations involved in almost every decision, as there have been for every president since George Washington. Whether the implication that this president almost never thought of anything else came through as strongly in print reporting as it seemed to me, others will have to judge.[15]

To conclude, Carter White House officials recognized the importance of timing as a determinant of journalistic portrayals of the presidency. The particular era in which Carter served, immediately following the national traumas of Watergate and Vietnam, was especially difficult for establishing favorable press relations, staff members asserted. Several Carter staff members acknowledged the importance of the first year in office for establishing a tone to the press evaluations. A few Carter officials conceded that early "tactical" errors contributed to perceptions that became hard to break. Finally, a number of Carter officials argued that journalists failed to give the president proper credit for his achievements. By 1980, the press portrait of Carter, some staff members asserted, became inaccurate and unfair.

Rhetoric/Symbolism

A significant amount of self-criticism by White House staff concerned the various White House efforts directed at the portrayal of Jimmy Carter. The communications advisers offered the following explanations for their own difficulties: (a) the president was inattentive to the press's portrayal of his presidency and did not make enough effort to create a favorable image; (b) the president resisted slogans and simplifying characterizations, making the job of explaining a Carter program or philosophy to the press and public difficult; and (c) the president was inattentive to, if not suspicious of, the presidential speechmaking process. Let's examine each of these explanations:

1. A number of Carter's communications advisers expressed frustration with the president for not working hard enough at fostering a favorable press image. According to a member of the press secretary's office, Carter ignored the potential effects of the day-to-day press portrayal of his presidency:

President Carter didn't spend a lot of time thinking about the press, compared to most presidents which is good and bad. I think a president can certainly be too caught up in reading every story and watching the wires and fretting over the networks every night. . . . From my standpoint, I wished at times that he was more interested in it and delighted in the game-playing aspects of it . . . that he took an interest in how you go about working this thing out from a press strategy more than he actually did.[16]

For a number of speechwriters the most important "game-playing aspect" of creating a press portrait of the president was getting favorable reactions to presidential speeches from newspaper editors and columnists. Carter's speechwriters perceived these members of the press as an important constituency that needed to be cultivated. The speechwriting office maintained files on major columnists to gain insight into what the nation's opinion leaders reacted to both favorably and unfavorably. The speechwriters were therefore frustrated to find the president unwilling to cultivate this important constituency.

Former Carter speechwriter James Fallows explained that there is an important filtering-down effect of editorial and columnist-inspired opinion. These opinion elites, according to Fallows, play a significant role in the development of public perspectives on the presidency. The president and his senior staff, Fallows contended, did not understand this process:

> One point which we [the speechwriters] tried again and again to make to Carter's old guard of warriors was that a lot of time you do not care in giving a speech whether you're boring the audience or not, because what you really care about is having a written documentation which when inspected by the editors of the *New York Times* and the columnists and by people outside the two thousand who are going to actually hear it, it will strike them as an impressive piece of reasoning and will for the next six months have a sort of ripple effect. That was never company line under Carter. But I think for any president, if he can do that well, that becomes a tremendous power.[17]

Fallows argued that President Carter did not worry about journalistic opinion of presidential speeches:

> I think to a larger degree in this administration than most, it would not occur to Carter very often to ask "Well what's the [newspaper] lead going to be about this?" That's not the way his mind works.
> I think Carter did not believe enough in, or feel accustomed to the idea of, different groups leading the opinion of people. He just didn't want to have these speeches that would bore the listeners but which would bring editorialists to an enthusiastic frenzy. So that didn't happen much.[18]

Carter's speechwriters generally agreed with Fallows' observations. One speechwriter asserted that senior White House staff members believed that cultivating opinion elites would be a fruitless endeavor. "Some staff felt a lot of that group was against them in the campaign. There was a lot of glee at times at having toppled this establishment."[19]

An exchange between several Carter speechwriters in their discussions on the function of opinion development reveals their agreement with Fallows that the White House failed to cultivate opinion leaders:

Why didn't we ever give a *New York Times* ed board kind of speech. Why didn't we ever think that we were looking at Meg Greenfield and . . . George Will and what would we say to them, and how would Carter explain himself? . . .[20]

By having contempt for those establishment media people, we set a time bomb each time we ignored them. I would even hear it said, "I don't care what so and so thinks."[21]

They are a special constituency that need to be taken care of. When they have a complaint or their squeaky wheel starts up you've got to do something about it or otherwise they'll come back at you.[22]

2. Carter's speechwriters, therefore, were frustrated by the low priority the president gave to cultivating public opinion leaders in the press. This frustration was related to the difficulty the speechwriters had portraying the Carter administration to the public in a way that was clear and unambiguous. The speechwriters observed that President Carter resisted attempts to summarize his administration's programs in a slogan that would explain the focus of his presidency. The speechwriters asserted that the president's resistance to characterization made the Carter administration appear to lack focus. One speechwriter explained:

Carter never sent out directives, "let's stick to these themes the next two weeks. . . . " [We] never got any communication from Carter in terms of philosophy.[23]

The major explanation for this problem was that the president's eclectic, non-ideological philosophy was not conducive to being simplified through the use of a slogan, a theme, or some other explanatory device. A speechwriter explained that Carter "simply resisted the idea of labelling himself in any way, shape, or form. . . . There was something in his view of reality, of life, that led him to think that he could reconcile opposites."[24] Another Carter speechwriter added:

He could give a speech about civil service reform point by point. But what he could not do was . . . show where civil service reform fit into his conception of government reform . . . and that was hard because there wasn't a Carter philosophy that you could always say this fits in here and this is part of my whole approach to government. And I think that was the problem that he had, that he could not think deductively.
   If you said, "How does your civil service reform relate to government reform?" . . . he could tell you all the tradeoffs . . . but he wouldn't do it if you said "give me a speech or tell me what Jimmy Carter's all about" . . . I think it was resistance on his part.[25]

James Fallows declared of Carter: "Things which seemed contradictory to other people all fit within the comfortable embrace of his ideas."[26] An example of Carter's apparent tendency to view opposites as reconcilable was a foreign policy speech at the United States Naval Academy at Annapolis,

Maryland. According to Fallows this speech was comprised of two policy memos, one from Cyrus Vance and the other from Zbigniew Brzezinski, that Carter stapled together and read verbatim:

> And to Carter there was no contradiction. He supported both their points of view because he could see the merit to each of them and was not drawn towards their points of contradiction. He agreed that it was important to pursue arms agreements with [the Soviets]. He agreed they should be rebuffed where they were making trouble.
> . . . In most other [policy] areas, he will decide each issue by itself and not go out of his way to have the grand scheme.[27]

3. White House speechwriters attributed Carter's inability to communicate clearly to the public to the president's lack of attention to the speechwriting process. Carter's speechwriters emphasized the frustrations they experienced having had little or no contact with the president. In their view, the president attached little importance to speechmaking. One speechwriter explained that Carter "was a man who had virtually reached the Presidency without somebody writing his words for him and he regarded the whole process of a cooked up impression prepared ahead of time with suspicion."[28] A second speechwriter was puzzled by Carter's refusal to place greater priority than he did on public speaking:

> I think that never in his life did he decide that speaking was important in itself. . . . I've seen a lot of speeches in the East Room of the White House where he gave horrendous speeches to people that came to see him. They were audiences he should have turned on, supporters. . . . He didn't try. I don't know why he didn't think it was important to turn those people on. . . . I think it's a question of priorities and his priorities were not to give a great statement most of the time.[29]

A member of the press secretary's staff explained that the president's inattention to speechmaking could be attributed to the set of skills which Carter brought to the office. The ability to sway large audiences with flamboyant rhetoric apparently was not one of Carter's attributes:

> . . . when a person becomes President, they travel on what they bring to the office. And you don't take someone who's basically good at, say, answering questions and that sort of discussion and explaining and synthesizing and so forth, and turn them into a rhetorician while they're trying to run the country at the same time.[30]

Yet a senior White House adviser admitted that this lack of rhetorical flair seriously limited Carter's ability to lead public opinion and develop support for administration programs. Carter, in this adviser's view, would have succeeded even more than he did if he had the ability to speak with force and conviction to large public audiences:

One of the greatest challenges of presidential leadership is the need for a president to be an effective communicator—the President as teacher. Carter was not an effective showman. . . . I think we were long on content and substance—and short on dramatic flair and inspiration; long on policy and position—and short on passion.[31]

If he had been a more artful, more dramatic articulator of what he was doing we would have been more successful. He *does* lack a tendency to speak with fervor, force, inspiration, and rhetorical impact, which we all needed.[32]

Carter speechwriters were particularly frustrated with the president's attitude towards speechmaking. Carter speechwriters complained of the lack of status they held in the Carter White House, and how this lack reflected the president's priorities. One speechwriter recalled:

The general experience that Carter had was not such as to make him trust [speechwriters]. The Carter White House speechwriting department was one of the smallest in recent administrations. . . . We had no researchers and just a couple of secretaries. . . . The President never worked in any consistent way or directly with the people who wrote his speeches. He always worked through somebody else. So there was this constant and futile search for an intermediary between Carter and his speechwriters who would magically produce the desired results. Of course, it was a doomed search. . . . There was surprisingly little personal contact between us and the man we were writing for. . . . Our work was often guesswork. We would have to imagine what the President would want to say in a given situation.[33]

Three other presidential speechwriters added the following observations about the president placing relatively little emphasis on speechmaking:

The "official speechwriter meets President to do work on this speech" kind of meetings could be counted on the fingers of your hand during the whole administration for us.

. . . there was no formal regular way that any of the speechwriters ever talked to the President about speeches except in unusual circumstances . . . Neither was there an informal kind of arrangement where we all talked with the President about speeches as a group on any regular basis or even on any individual basis.[34]

One of the overall problems is that the writing of a speech is such an important nexus in any administration. That's where so many fights and policy fights come together, and the role of being in charge of that was a very enviable position because of the sort of policy power it provided and also the access it provided. None of us were ever in a position to seize that access. There was always somebody who had access to Carter about speeches. But it was never the person who actually wrote the speech, or almost never.[35]

He never came back to us and said, "why don't you do another like that. I like that speech. . . . " There was no feedback on that stuff.

If you have to explain why you have to see the President then there's no way you can. Al McDonald would say, "Well what exactly did you have in mind for an agenda?" If you have to go through that crap to ask to talk to the guy you're writing for, you're in trouble. . . . We had to justify meeting with the President, which we really never justified.[36]

James Fallows' observations are consistent with those of the other speech-writers. Fallows recalled that: "For the first month or two I think all of us had a grander idea of what we had been employed to do than finally turned out to be the case."[37] He adds that Carter's first major message to Congress on the economic recovery plan was the clear exception to the rule for speechmaking in this administration. In that speech, Fallows explained, Carter delegated responsibility to the speechwriters to create a speech with clear prose and simple connecting themes. While this speech succeeded in achieving those objectives, Fallows argued, that process of speechwriter–speechmaker interaction "was virtually never repeated in [my] whole time there."[38]

Carter's speechwriters also portrayed the president as inattentive to the necessity of working on political rhetoric simply because he disliked the presidential role of mass audience persuasion. The speechwriters made clear distinctions between the president's speeches to large public audiences and his speeches to small, familiar groups. Regarding formal speeches to large public audiences Fallows asserted:

> . . . he basically does not like to give these formal speeches. He knows he's not very good at it. He knows he rarely covers himself with glory when he does so there are few things he looks forward to less than a speechwriter coming in a month ahead of time and talking the thing over. And he just sort of resigns himself to waiting 'til the last minute.[39]

The speechwriters favorably assessed Carter's speeches to small, familiar groups. The important difference between the two kinds of speeches was that large public addresses required preparation and some stage-acting ability on the part of the speechmaker; addresses to small, familiar groups required little preparation and a genuine sense of empathy with the audience. To the speechwriters this distinction was crucial to understanding Carter as a speechmaker. Unlike President Reagan, they noted, Carter could not stand before a large public audience with whom he shared no personal experiences and simply create, as actors do, a believable sense of empathy with members of the audience. Once in front of small groups with whom he shared genuine emotions, there was no need for the speechwriters to create a formal text for the president. Carter's finest speeches, they explained, were ones in which he could relate on a personal level to individual members of his audience. A speechwriter provided the following example:

> Sometimes, most often in front of a black audience, in a highly emotional situation, he could really step right up, just be himself and hit it out. There was nothing of the actor in that man. . . . The times he could plug a speech into his own personality, it worked.[40]

When he was talking to those black audiences he had real, genuine emotion. Their condition was something he knew, he experienced. An actor will learn how to either re-create that emotion in new situations if he's a good actor, or if he's a bad actor he will learn to fake it. If he's great, he'll probably combine both. Carter could neither re-create nor fake those emotions. When they were not a real part of his experience he would not try to make emotions up or learn how to make them up.[41]

A conspicuous exception to the distinction between Carter's abilities to speak to large and smaller audiences with varying degrees of success was the July 1979 Crisis of Confidence speech. In this public-televised speech Carter delivered his message to the nation with force and conviction. Carter acknowledged criticisms that he had lost touch with public sentiments and was not doing an adequate job of leading the country. The president identified for the nation his own conception of the problems we faced and of how to reestablish trust in government and our country. A speechwriter noted that initially the nation "responded overwhelmingly positively to that speech. . . ."[42]

While the immediate response to the "Crisis of Confidence" address was highly favorable, the speech became a political liability for Carter. Some White House staff members cited the speech as additional evidence of Carter's inattention to the political function of the public speech, because the president hurt himself politically by using a public forum to bring negative news to the voters. Identifying the national crisis, a speechwriter commented, "was risky because it's risky when the President diagnoses the country's illness and he can't come up with an immediate cure."[43]

Three White House officials commented on the president's propensity to bring bad news to the public and the effects that negative speeches had on Carter's standing:

Every time we would make a speech on inflation or energy, and the more we talked about it without being able ever to bring the little carrot of good news, people would more and more find Carter responsible for those things. We were more closely identified with the bad news the more we made speeches.[44]

Part of the problem was that he took responsibility once he became President so that people associated what was wrong and what was bothering them about him.[45]

[Reagan] does make people feel wonderful about the fact that he was there [giving a speech]. Our symbols got to be a bit of a problem there. "You're going to be cold, you're going to have to drive less, you're going to pay more for gasoline"—rough ways to go.[46]

To conclude, many of Carter's communications advisers believed the president contributed significantly to the administration's negative press portrait. Communications advisers portrayed the president as inattentive to the "game playing" aspects of stroking the egos of editorial writers and columnists. He also appeared to refuse to orient his speeches to the opinion leaders in the press whose reporting and commentaries greatly influenced public perceptions of the administration. Carter's speechwriters also portrayed the president as inattentive to the formal speechmaking process. Carter's speechwriters explained that the president placed little emphasis on mass audience persuasion, did not work closely with the speechwriting staff, and did not pay heed to how his frequent negative messages undermined public support for the administration. The speechwriters were particularly frustrated with Carter's refusal to cooperate with their efforts to resolve the negative press image. Carter, instead, had ways of responding to criticism other than adopting measures that would suit the expectations of others. To overcome criticisms for not being a "great communicator" would have required the president to focus on the speechmaking and public opinion leadership roles when in fact Carter downplayed these tasks and emphasized policy problem solving. As the above quotations reveal, Carter opted to stick to the skills and roles he felt most comfortable with rather than adopt suggestions that he spend time improving his communications skills.

Agenda

Some Carter staff members believed the administration's policy agenda explains much of the negative press portrait of the president's leadership abilities. Three explanations for the difficulties the president experienced enacting his policies and for the subsequent negative press reviews are provided by Carter staff members. First, the agenda was comprised of issues that were "political losers"—from civil service reform, the Panama Canal treaties, to the controversial energy program. Second, Carter's agenda was not a traditional Democratic party agenda thereby causing a great deal of in-party criticism of the administration's efforts. Third, the first year agenda was too ambitious and perhaps created an impression of poor legislative acumen in the White House. Let's first take up the issue of the politically difficult Carter agenda.

Carter White House officials asserted that the president defined his policy agenda according to his perception of the country's needs. Questions of whether or not particular agenda items were politically possible were cast aside by the president, these officials reported. Some staff members commented that Carter pushed "second term issues": that is, issues which a president can afford to focus on when he does not have to be concerned about the electoral implications of unpopular programs. White House staff members commented:

> If you back down the list of things, whether it's energy or civil service reform or nuclear proliferation or SALT or even the Mideast, the Camp David business, the Panama Canal, all of them were political liabilities for him in more than just the sense of, well, you have a certain amount of capital and you ration it, you expend it.[47]

> I asked [another senior staff member] last night if he could recall a specific bill, program or policy that we had advocated that was popular and helped

us politically. We couldn't think of a single thing. Everything was politically
a loser. Try to reconcile that with the image of President Carter in October
or November of 1980 as the ultimate politician who would do anything to get
reelected. There was no way to square what we tried to do with the way we
were perceived.[48]

. . . so many of the things that he tried to do and did both were really things
that were behind the times. I mean they were things that should have been
done twenty years ago, or ten years ago, or five years ago and the reasons
they weren't done . . . were exactly the reasons we had such a hard time
doing them. Good reasons. It was the political difficulty.[49]

Some advisers attributed the difficulties Carter experienced with his party
and the press to Carter's "new kind of Democratic program." That is, the
president's domestic policy agenda departed in significant respects from the
traditional Democratic party agenda. A member of the press secretary's
office offered the following observations:

The programs the Carter Presidency was putting forward were certainly a new
kind of Democratic program. It was more business management techniques—
taking the available funds and targeting the citizen, not taking all the dollars
there are in the world and throwing them at the problem. It caused the
President, of course, to be disowned by his own party. You know, there's a
Democrat sitting in the White House but he's not putting out Democratic bills
and the coalition was falling apart.
    . . . he looked at any problem presented to him and tried to figure out
what was the right solution. Well the right solution is not always the liberal
one and it is not always the conservative one. But the average, everyday
politician behaves in that way because he has a constituency that he must
respond to. So Ronald Reagan could no more take Teddy Kennedy's health
care bill and support it if he thought it was the best idea in the world. But
Jimmy Carter might.[50]

One senior staff member cited an administration study that linked, in
part, Carter's new Democratic programs to the negative references to the
administration in the press by Democratic members of Congress:

Carter came to Washington not particularly as the favorite of the Democratic
establishment or the people in Congress. . . . We took a survey of news in
the second year of the administration . . . and found that 85 % of the negative
statements in the *Washington Post* about Carter were from members of his own
party. It was really kind of ironic that Howard Baker was our best public
supporter in the Congress from the day we came to Washington.[51]

Finally, several staff members asserted that Carter's agenda was overly
ambitious and filled with controversial proposals. A senior White House
adviser pointed out:

We clearly did have a problem in that the President wanted to do so much
so fast. There were so many things he wanted to confront—and did—[civil]

service reform, the Panama Canal treaties, the 1977 economic stimulus program. . . . We had too many things on our agenda for our own good. We needed to be a little more "laid back." We would have been more effective in the long run had we done so.[52]

And a senior White House staff member concluded:

We were dealing with a collection of issues. The best example is the foreign policy area. We were dealing with a generation of issues that no one had dealt with because they were so politically controversial. Every one of them were [politically] losers.[53]

A member of the press secretary's office added, though, that a limited policy agenda may only have resulted in limited achievements. In this individual's assessment, a president cannot ignore problems to focus on a few priority agenda items:

. . . there is a limit to the extent that I think a conscientious chief executive can say, "well, we're just going or I as President am just going to worry about these two or three things." The other things bubble on, they get gangrene, they start to smell, and by and by maybe they kill you if you don't pay some attention to them.[54]

A senior White House adviser asserted that the president's legislative achievements were significant yet not recognized sufficiently by the press. This adviser believed that the press, which so often criticized Carter for overloading the agenda, focused too heavily on the policy process and not enough on results. Carter, therefore, received poor journalistic reviews for the same reasons that his administration achieved so many of its major legislative programs—because he refused to ignore controversial issues:

Then we can see things happening such as having legislative successes that looked like failures. We had as good a legislative record as anybody. As far as in the percentages. But what you would see happening was that the process in getting something passed was so bloody that the press would focus so much on the process and not enough on what actually happened. Every president from Eisenhower or from Truman would sweep the Panama Canal problem under the rug. Carter got the damned thing passed. . . . Civil service reform. For better or worse we had the first energy program.[55]

A number of Carter staff, therefore, recognized the importance of the policy agenda as a source of journalistic criticism of the administration. Several staff members asserted that the president set himself up for press criticism by focusing his agenda on controversial items. Most of these staff members agreed with Carter's agenda and praised the president for taking on controversial issues ignored by previous administrations. Several Carter staff members also argued that the administration's legislative achievements were underrated by the press because the process of enacting some programs appeared unorthodox and chaotic. Finally, many Carter staff members agreed that the administration's ambitious agenda was a legislative liability.

In response to criticism for proposing too many policies too fast, Carter eventually scaled down the number of administration priority items. What Carter could not change was the nature of the agenda itself. Journalists criticized Carter for forcing controversial items on the agenda. Yet Carter did not always have discretion in setting the agenda. Carter staff members noted that many pressing issues pertaining to energy, natural resources and the economy had to be dealt with. On issues such as the Panama Canal treaties where public support of administration policy was lacking Carter believed that as president he had the responsibility to do what was "right." To the more politically-minded White House staff members Carter's propensity nearly to ignore the electoral implications of his policy actions was a frequent source of frustration.

Policy Development

A great deal of press criticism of the Carter administration focused on the process of policy development. Journalists criticized the administration for speaking with too many conflicting voices, especially in the foreign policy realm, and for lacking a sense of policy priorities. Journalists criticized Carter for failing to engage in the kinds of wheeling, dealing, and horsetrading with members of Congress expected of all presidents. Finally, some journalists noted that institutional reforms of the 1970s made presidential leadership difficult.

Carter White House officials made similar observations. The difference is one of degree. Journalists placed great emphasis on the conflicting voices and lack of policy priorities; Carter officials acknowledged these criticisms as legitimate for the early stages of the administration but added that major and unrecognized improvements were made. Both journalists and White House staff made a great deal of Carter's apparent refusal to participate in the coalition building rituals of political Washington; yet a number of Carter officials emphasized the importance of political changes brought about by institutional reforms in the immediate post-Watergate years.

James Fallows asserted that too many administration officials had a role in influencing the development of Carter's speeches. This speechwriter believed that Carter should have vested responsibility in one individual to make sure that his speeches were clear and coherent. Fallows claimed that the administration appeared to speak with many conflicting voices:

> I think it's inevitable in the absence of one condition which is the President giving his clear support to a coherent result. I mean if he is not weighing that way then all of this squabbling below will produce a confused and badly drafted document. And so that can be changed if you have somebody like Sorensen, or Safire, or whomever, who has the backing of the President to knock all the other people out at the end and just write a coherent document.

. . . I did not have the standing with Carter to do that so these things inevitably became incoherent.[56]

Fallows added, though, that the addition of Gerald Rafshoon to the White House staff brought about much needed coordination of speechmaking and the public statements of administration members. The White House, therefore, greatly improved in communicating a consistent message to the public:

One of the first things that occurred after Rafshoon arrived was that Carter decided to veto the defense bill and Rafshoon saw to it that all of us wrote up little talking points about why this was a good thing and that those were distributed to the people who had to make speeches. Now this seems like a fairly basic thing but it just was not done before; having somebody responsible for coordinating the communications.

. . . Much more of our time was spent after he came writing up sample speeches for cabinet officers just so they would be spouting the same line as the President was. And doing proposals for speeches you should give over the next two months to set a common theme.[57]

A senior White House adviser recalled that he often complained to Carter that "the cabinet people are just talking too much and with so many different voices."[58] And a member of the press secretary's office acknowledged that the independence provided Cabinet members by Carter and the publicized Vance-Brzezinski debates fostered the impression of an administration speaking with conflicting voices:

That you can have in the White House a fellow who has a very strong view on balancing the budget which is not the same view as that of the Secretary of the Treasury. And if you have them both, one guy on *Meet the Press* and another on the *Today Show* the next morning, you are going to have stories about policy incoherence. Quite the same situation applies when the views are different about . . . blockading Ethiopia. . . . When the views are different particularly between the National Security Adviser and the State Department . . . then you get these incoherence stories.[59]

This apparent policy "incoherence" also fostered the perception that the administration lacked clear policy priorities. Carter officials acknowledged that this perception created serious problems for the administration. According to a senior White House adviser:

In some areas the President was overexposed, jumping out and making a statement on every issue, which I thought was just awful. It showed he had no priorities. The importance was to focus our efforts on the economy. . . . To always have a semblance of disarray by always having the President out front on every issue was unhelpful.[60]

Yet the president allegedly responded defensively to this adviser's pleas to focus on pre-defined priority agenda items. The president argued that such an approach was unrealistic:

> We'd say, "Mr. President, you're spending too much time on foreign policy when the country's priorities are inflation and energy." He'd look at you and say, "OK, well tell me, do you want me to forget about the Middle East?" Sometimes he'd get defensive about it. "You want to say that the Middle East has nothing to do with energy? If you knew what you were talking about maybe you'd know these things are interrelated." But what we meant was that there was just too much.[61]

Some staff members discussed the press portrait of Carter as apolitical and opposed to compromise. A senior staff member commented: "The perception that Carter did not enjoy politics, and found it anathema, was exaggerated."[62] This staff member recognized that Carter was assessed according to the Johnsonian model of legislative activism:

> [Carter] understood that part of the problem was maintaining some political support, especially in Congress, for the things he believed in. But people expected him to be Lyndon Johnson. He was not that kind of person. But even Lyndon Johnson would have had a difficult time in 1976, because Lyndon Johnson wouldn't have had to cajole and twist [only] fifteen or twenty arms.[63]

A White House communications adviser reflected a common press criticism of Carter's legislative leadership tactics:

> You'd always want to see him kind of reach out and grab [members of Congress] and say, "OK George" and throw his arm around him and slap them on the back and say, "come on, let's go up and have some pop" or something. That was not Carter's style. It's the style which Washington is used to and Carter suffered from it. . . . How do you change the personality of the man? You really can't. I think there should have been a structure built around the personality of the man that took into account the potential problems of somebody who was not a back-slapper and who was not that kind of communicator. That didn't happen.[64]

A number of quotes by White House communications advisers were equally reflective of journalists' conceptions of how a president succeeds as a legislative leader.[65] Yet a number of White House staff asserted that congressional reforms in the 1970s created a new environment for presidential leadership. This perspective was reflected by the senior White House adviser who asserted that "even Lyndon Johnson would have had a difficult time in 1976, because Lyndon Johnson wouldn't have had to cajole and twist [only] fifteen or twenty arms." This staff member lamented:

> Twenty years ago if a President wanted to pass a bill to the Congress he'd get Speaker Sam Rayburn and Majority leader Lyndon Johnson and George

Meany and maybe somebody from the business community. They could sit down in the Oval Office and write a tax bill and leave with a high degree of confidence that it would pass pretty much in the form they'd agreed on. Our experience was that you could have the President and the Speaker and the committee chairs putting on a full court press on a piece of legislation on the Hill, and you could get defeated in subcommittee by a group of people whose names were barely recognizable to you.[66]

A member of the press secretary's office offered a similar assessment:

It is no longer possible to assemble a small group of congressional leaders in the family dining room at the White House or wherever and have a couple of drinks with them and reach some meeting of the minds and then be certain that the wheels will turn and that the thing will be produced at the other end of the legislative process.[67]

The perspectives of White House staff members on Carter's approach to developing support for public policies share a good deal in common with the press portrayals of the Carter presidency. These staff offered a fair degree of self-criticism of their efforts at building congressional and public support for their agenda. Some White House staff members pointed out that any assessment of the president's agenda leadership must take into account two factors: (1) that the president's leadership style was not traditional by political Washington's standards and should be understood on its own terms; and (2) that institutional reforms of the 1970s have made presidential leadership of Congress more precarious than in the Lyndon B. Johnson years.

Carter's communications advisers accepted journalistic criticisms of the White House for "speaking with too many voices" and for an apparent lack of policy priorities. Yet White House officials added that important and often unrecognized improvements were made in White House operations (e.g., scaling down the agenda, instituting procedures for coordinating White House statements). Such improvements, staff members noted, often went unrecognized and the negative press image of Carter's leadership stood uncorrected.

Staff

Journalists subjected members of the White House staff to harsh criticism. In his memoirs Jody Powell discussed at length and refuted specific journalistic criticisms of White House staff members. Regarding a more general press portrait of the White House Powell observed:

. . . we failed to appreciate until too late the repercussions of our failure to socialize in the traditional Washington manner. We missed an opportunity to get to know Washington better. . . . We failed to establish personal relationships with individuals who could have been helpful to us professionally.[68]

A White House adviser also acknowledged and corroborated a major press criticism of the administration:

I think it was loose the first year. I think we became more businesslike after that first year. We really did not anticipate how much press scrutiny would be given and how much attention would be given to the ways the rest of us acted. Hamilton [Jordan] and myself were stunned. It just never entered our mind[s] that we would be issues, that a lot of attention would be paid to us. We came to the White House in sports shirts and windbreaker[s]. We didn't realize that you don't do that. As much as we said we were going to be different than the way things had been done, there was no need to uselessly and unnecessarily look for trouble.[69]

Some staff members asserted that the president was not served well by his White House staff. A common theme in journalists' criticisms of Carter was the lack of Washington "insiders" in the president's inner circle of advisers. A few communications advisers reflected this assessment of Carter:

. . . he was ill-served. I don't think that was particularly the fault of his staff or any one person but rather his spokes of the wheel system. The White House was as incoherent and inductive as one of his speech outlines.[70]

I think we made a mistake in not bringing more of those people in. Yes. I really do. Yet you don't realize how much more we did than we've been given credit for. I can name you people that were called a lot. Probably not in the first year.[71]

In their reflections on the Carter presidency, therefore, a number of staff members recognized and acknowledged press criticisms of the White House staff. The administration, they observed, could have done a better job of deflecting press criticism with a more experienced and well-organized White House staff.

Conclusion

This examination of Carter's communications advisers' recollections reveals shared notions of presidential leadership between journalists and White House communications aides. It appears that journalists and White House communications aides share specific conceptions of leadership and of the criteria for evaluating presidential leadership and performance. Before discussing the implications of this finding, let's review the major themes of this chapter:

White House communications specialists understood the importance of *timing* to the press assessments of Carter. First, the post-Watergate context was perceived as an important determinant of press evaluations of Carter. Second, these aides understood that the timing of the administration's activities influenced press assessments. Regarding the first year in particular, these aides noted that Carter needed to limit the agenda and make enduring political friendships in Washington. That Carter apparently did not do so opened him up to criticism for trying to do too much too fast, and for ignoring political elites.

Regarding *symbolism and rhetoric*, a number of White House communications specialists offered criticisms of Carter that reflected the press's assessments. The speechwriters explained that the president did not take the speechmaking task seriously enough and that he failed to orient his statements to what journalists and editorialists would favorably report. White House staff explained that Carter's *agenda* contributed to press criticisms. These aides observed that Carter knowingly took on many "second term issues" rather than focus on "achievable" agenda items. As a speechwriter explained: "he was unusual in that there were things to him that were much more important than getting reelected." Staff members added that Carter should have opened his term with a less ambitious agenda. They acknowledged the press's criticism of Carter for not beginning his term with achievable objectives as a means of establishing a reputation for strong leadership.

White House staff members were most critical of the administration's approaches to *policy development*. Communications specialists in the White House criticized Carter for not emphasizing the importance of such rituals of political Washington as compromising and "horsetrading." These staff aides added that the White House's tactical political errors harmed a number of Carter's legislative proposals.

Finally, a number of White House communications aides criticized Carter's *staff* system and the relative lack of "Washington insiders" in the White House inner circle. Their views also reflected very common press criticisms of Carter. These aides noted that the White House's somewhat informal style in the early months of the term and ignoring of the Washington social scene contributed to the press portrait of the Carter White House as contemptuous of the political establishment.

These themes show a great deal of convergence with the journalistic assessments of the Carter presidency. This finding is important because it reveals that among communications elites there are notions of presidential leadership that are prevalent in political Washington beyond presidential journalists. This finding also appears to confirm other studies on White House staffs. Studies show that there are shared values between specialized White House staff and the clientele with which they deal. As James Sterling Young notes, authors of what he calls the "captive presidency" school of thought have shown that

> . . . the organization originally created in the 1930s to help the president had over time developed distinctive interests of its own, and that the people on the staff who served as the president's surrogates for extending his influence downward into the bureaucracy and outward into Congress had come to act also as surrogates for those institutions in influencing the president.[72]

An example of such a perspective is Thomas Cronin's "Everybody Believes in Democracy Until He Gets to the White House." Cronin's findings pertaining to White House congressional liaison aides are revealing. According to Cronin these aides often act as surrogates of Congress within the White House:

> . . . the congressional relations aides have frequently mirrored the . . . views of congressional chairmen in White House staff deliberations. . . . [They] argue the case as viewed on Capitol Hill to their White House colleagues.
> . . . They define their task as helping the President get his program passed by Congress. . . . [They] necessarily seek to minimize conflict and maximize cohesion. . . . Because they, more than any other staff at the White House, are conscious of the ingredients that go into the making of the box scores of wins and losses that characterize presidential-congressional relations, the legislative liaison aides favor "practical" proposals.[73]

Additional evidence for this point is William F. Mullen's study of Capitol Hill and congressional liaison perceptions of Carter's legislative achievements. Mullen's study often stresses divergences in interpretations of Carter's "successes" and "failures." Yet on basic notions of presidential leadership, Mullen's study reveals important convergences:

> There was general agreement among both liaison aides and those who serve on the Hill that the skills and talents of individual presidents (and perceptions about them) are the most crucial variables in presidential influence on Congress.[74]

Liaison aides acknowledged that Carter's legislative record was not as impressive as Lyndon B. Johnson's because of the nature of Carter's agenda.[75] Mullen adds that congressmen and liaison staff both believed that Carter needed to have cultivated personal relationships on Capitol Hill more than he actually did.[76] Mullen concludes that "both liaison aides and House members share the perception that individual presidential skills and interpersonal relationships are crucial in structuring the nexus between executive and legislative branches."[77]

This chapter, therefore, is compatible with other studies exhibiting shared perceptions between specialized White House staff and staff members' clientele. The study of Carter's communications elites shows that these staff members lobbied the president to do those things they believed would make him succeed in the arena they knew best—public relations and the press. Carter's speechwriters expressed frustration with Carter for not focusing on presidential roles such as speechmaking and image cultivating. They were frustrated that Carter did not accept their advice to orient public speeches to the opinion leaders, cultivate personal relations with columnists and editorialists, spend more time improving public speeches, and adopt a grand theme for administration goals. The advice of Carter's communications staff appeared to try to make the president over to suit journalistic expectations. That Carter did not do so opened him up to criticism from communications elites both outside and within the White House.

Notes

1. See Thomas Cronin, "'Everybody Believes in Democracy Until He Gets to the White House . . . ': An Examination of White House-Departmental Relations," in Aaron Wildavsky, ed., *Perspectives on the Presidency* (Boston: Little, Brown and Co.), 1975, pp. 362–392; William F. Mullen, "Perceptions of Carter's Legislative Successes and Failures: Views From the Hill and the Liaison Staff," *Presidential Studies Quarterly* 12 (Fall 1982): 522–531; Joseph Pika, "White House Boundary Role," American Political Science Association paper, Washington, D.C., 1979; and James Sterling Young, *The Puzzle of the Presidency: An Inquiry on Political Leadership in America* (Baton Rouge: Louisiana State University Press, forthcoming), especially the discussion of the "President as Captive" in chapter 2.

2. White Burkett Miller Center of Public Affairs, University of Virginia: Project on the Carter Presidency. (Hereafter cited as CPP), Vol. 10, p. 15.

3. CPP, Vol. 10, p. 16.

4. CPP, Vol. 10, p. 17.

5. CPP, Vol. 10, p. 18.

6. Jody Powell, *The Other Side of the Story* (New York: William Morrow and Company, Inc., 1984), p. 173.

7. Hamilton Jordan, *Crisis: The Last Year of the Carter Presidency* (New York: Berkeley Books, 1982), pp. 359–360.

8. CPP, Vol. 10, p. 102.

9. CPP, Vol. 10, p. 102.

10. Jody Powell, p. 50.

11. Ibid., p. 206.

12. Ibid., p. 55.

13. Jody Powell, pp. 209, 215–216.

14. Ibid., p. 42.

15. Ibid., p. 195.

16. CPP, Vol. 10, p. 78.

17. James Fallows, "Rhetoric and Presidential Leadership," Miller Center Research Project, University of Virginia, March 1, 1979, p. 6.

18. Ibid., pp. 34–35.

19. CPP, Vol. 8, p. 37.

20. CPP, Vol. 8, p. 37.

21. CPP, Vol. 8, p. 38.

22. CPP, Vol. 8, p. 39.

23. CPP, Vol. 8, p. 130.

24. CPP, Vol. 8, pp. 84–85.

25. CPP, Vol. 8, p. 112.

26. James Fallows, p. 24.

27. Ibid., p. 25.

28. CPP, Vol. 8, p. 11.

29. CPP, Vol. 8, pp. 18–19.

30. CPP, Vol. 10, p. 81.

31. CPP, Vol. 3, pp. 95.

32. CPP, Vol. 3, p. 97.

33. CPP, Vol. 8, pp. 1–2.

34. CPP, Vol. 8, p. 8.

35. CPP, Vol. 8, p. 11.

36. CPP, Vol. 8, p. 26.

37. James Fallows, p. 2.
38. Ibid., p. 3.
39. Ibid., p. 54.
40. CPP, Vol. 8, p. 14.
41. CPP, Vol. 8, p. 24.
42. CPP, Vol. 8, p. 64.
43. CPP, Vol. 8, p. 64.
44. CPP, Vol. 21, p. 32.
45. CPP, Vol. 8, p. 138.
46. CPP, Vol. 8, p. 32.
47. CPP, Vol. 10, p. 111.
48. CPP, Vol. 7, p. 7.
49. CPP, Vol. 10, p. 114.
50. CPP, Vol. 10, p. 113.
51. CPP, Vol. 21, p. 12–13.
52. CPP, Vol. 3, p. 100.
53. CPP, Vol. 7, p. 15.
54. CPP, Vol. 10, p. 23.
55. CPP, Vol. 21, p. 12.
56. James Fallows, p. 40.
57. James Fallows, pp. 18–19.
58. CPP, Vol. 21, p. 8.
59. CPP, Vol. 10, p. 55.
60. CPP, Vol. 21, p. 14.
61. CPP, Vol. 21, pp. 10–11.
62. CPP, Vol. 7, p. 67.
63. CPP, Vol. 7, p. 67.
64. CPP, Vol, 5, p. 60.
65. See CPP, Vol. 7, p. 67; Vol, 5, p. 60; and Vol. 10, p. 28.
66. CPP, Vol. 7, p. 10.
67. CPP, Vol. 10, p. 90.
68. Jody Powell, p. 111.
69. CPP, Vol. 21, p. 48.
70. CPP, Vol. 8, p. 125.
71. CPP, Vol. 21, p. 47.
72. James Sterling Young, *The Puzzle of the Presidency* (Baton Rouge: Louisiana State University Press, forthcoming), Chapter 2.
73. Thomas Cronin, "'Everybody Believes in Democracy Until He Gets to the White House . . . ': An Examination of White House-Departmental Relations," in Aaron Wildavsky, ed., *Perspectives on the Presidency* (Boston: Little, Brown and Co., 1975), p. 380.
74. William F. Mullen, "Perceptions of Carter's Legislative Successes and Failures: Views from the Hill and Liaison Staff," *Presidential Studies Quarterly* 12 (Fall, 1982), p. 523.
75. Ibid., p. 525.
76. Ibid., p. 531.
77. Ibid., p. 532.

8

Conclusion:
Evaluating the Evaluators

This study reveals the generally negative tone of print reporting and analysis of the Carter presidency. The negative journalistic interpretations of the Carter presidency are evidenced by both judgmental press commentary and the discussions of Carter White House communications advisers. What were the bases of journalists' negative evaluations of the Carter presidency? How did these journalists define the leadership task? In this concluding chapter I turn to these important questions. I begin by identifying and discussing intellectual and contextual influences on journalists' assessments of the Carter presidency. I then analyze the differing values and criteria journalists relied upon in their judgments of the Carter presidency. I close by discussing the implications of my findings for the modern presidency.

Intellectual and Contextual Influences on
Journalistic Assessments of Carter

Journalists interpreted the Carter presidency on the basis of their understanding of historic lessons and the particular context in which Carter served. These influences on journalistic conceptions of leadership help explain the negative press perception of Carter's leadership. The major intellectual influence on journalists' assessments of Carter was derived from a nostalgic recollection of past Democratic presidents. I call this press ideal the "Activist-Democrat Model of Leadership." The major contextual influences on journalists' assessments of Carter I call the "Post-Watergate" and "Post-Reform" era influences.

1. *The "Activist-Democrat" Model of Leadership.* An important journalistic theory of presidential leadership applied to Carter was based upon a nostalgic recollection of previous Democratic presidents. Many journalists expected Carter's leadership to emulate their conceptions (real or imagined) of Franklin D. Roosevelt's and Lyndon B. Johnson's leadership approaches. These journalists based their perceptions that Carter needed to adopt the leadership approaches of his Democratic predecessors upon the belief that Democratic presidents with large party majorities in Congress naturally aspire to achieve

large-scale reforms (especially in the spheres of the domestic economy and public spending programs).

This theory of "successful" leadership by a modern Democratic president as entailing policy activism prevailed throughout much of Carter's term. Journalists frequently drew unflattering comparisons of Carter with FDR and LBJ. Early in the term a number of journalists expressed hope that the Carter administration would propose domestic policy reforms compatible with majority sentiments in Congress. When Carter chose to focus the agenda on controversial energy and budget cutting proposals, journalists criticized him for lacking LBJ's political savvy. When Carter's early legislative output did not match the pace of FDR's "kinetic 100 days," journalists concluded that Carter lacked Roosevelt's lust for power. When Carter appeared to emphasize presidential roles such as problem solving and managing the government, instead of congressional negotiation and public speaking, journalists assessed that Carter did not learn from FDR's and LBJ's experiences how to use the power of the presidency. According to almost all journalists studied here, Carter lacked specific attributes of effective leadership such as the abilities to persuade, coerce, cajole, manipulate, and convince.

It is interesting to note that the notion of presidential leadership as entailing Rooseveltian activism probably conflicted with Carter's own conception of governance. From the previous chapter we learned that Carter's communications advisers did accept journalistic bases for evaluation. Understanding the importance of a favorable press portrait to any modern administration, these White House aides tried to convince Carter to take more seriously the communications tasks they considered essential. Yet some of these White House insiders added that journalists should have tried to understand Carter on his own terms, not evaluated him against the backdrop of earlier "activist-Democrat" presidents. The activist-Democrat standard apparently created expectations that Carter never presumed to meet. Journalists therefore measured Carter against LBJ's welfare-state program accomplishments even though Carter often sought to reduce benefits distributed under these same programs. The lack of any Roosevelt-era political, economic or foreign policy crisis in the 1970s did not deter journalists from criticizing Carter for "failing" to emulate FDR's leadership style.

Journalists relished the image of the activist-Democrat president who loves the game-playing aspects of politics. Yet Carter never appeared enamored with the political presidency. On a number of occasions since leaving office President Carter has endorsed the one-term, six-year presidency. Presumably this constitutional reform would enable the president to act in the national interest without factoring in political considerations. In a *Family Weekly* magazine interview Carter revealed an important aspect of his own conception of leadership:

> I would hope that I have not let any sort of political threats interfere in my doing what was best for the country. When I served as Governor of Georgia, at that time the [state] Constitution only permitted one four-year term. And

I felt complete freedom in putting forward controversial programs, but no
more so than I try to maintain now.[1]

Undoubtedly, Carter's conception of leadership differed from his predecessors' and could not withstand criticism for failing to be something that
Carter never intended it to be. In the inaugural address and the 1978 and
1979 State of the Union addresses, to cite relevant examples, Carter appealed
to traditional Democrats to understand the "limits" on government's ability
to solve public problems. Yet even as late as the 1979 State of the Union
address many journalists interpreted the use of the word "limits" as though
it signaled an entirely new theme for the Carter presidency. This example
suggests in part that those journalists who adopted the "let Carter be
Roosevelt" standard did not take seriously Carter's own rhetoric or goals.

2. *The Post-Watergate Era Influence.* Journalists evaluated the Carter presidency in the wake of events surrounding Watergate. This context must be
acknowledged and assessed in order to understand journalistic assessments
of Carter's leadership. Two major factors influenced journalists' reporting
and commentary on the presidency at this time: (a) the public's desire for
honesty and frankness in government; and (b) the recapturing of the White
House by the political party holding a sizable majority in Congress.

Clearly the Nixon and Ford presidencies made possible the Carter presidency and helped define the context in which journalists assessed Jimmy
Carter. President Carter also contributed to press expectations of his presidency. Carter's many public statements declaring his administration to be
completely honest and open to public scrutiny created severe standards by
which to be judged. If in the immediate post-Watergate context journalists
expected highly ethical conduct by public officials, Jimmy Carter's rhetoric
heightened these expectations. The Bert Lance controversy is a perfect
example. The memory of the events surrounding Watergate influenced how
journalists portrayed the Lance controversy. Jimmy Carter's declared intent
to maintain an administration of rigid ethical standards also fueled press
criticism of the administration's handling of Lance's case.

Many journalists believed that the capturing of the White House by the
party holding a strong majority in Congress created an opportunity for
aggressive presidential leadership of Congress. After the end of eight years
of divided rule (Republican-controlled executive branch and Democratic-
controlled Congress), a number of journalists expected a "new era" of
presidential-congressional cooperation. This new era presumably would be
characterized by a chief executive asserting leadership on a number of
domestic and economic issues, with most congressional Democrats following
the president's lead.

It is interesting to note the kinds of conditions journalists focused on
when defining Carter's leadership context. Journalists placed considerable
emphasis on the conclusion of Republican-control of the executive branch,
the end of the Nixon-Ford era, and the emergence of one-party controlled
government. They gave comparatively less emphasis to the nature of Carter's
agenda. Journalists who did discuss the nature of Carter's agenda often

criticized the president for focusing on controversial issues and thereby making executive–congressional cooperation difficult.

Undoubtedly much of the president's policy agenda lacked any significant following in Congress. Much of Carter's agenda required cut-backs in federal support for domestic spending programs that were popular with Democratic members of Congress. His energy program demanded sacrifices in individual lifestyles and behavior. The civil service reform package, though widely viewed as meritorious, lacked an impassioned following. In foreign policy the administration's pursuit of a Middle East arms package, the Middle East peace process, Panama Canal treaties, and the Turkish arms embargo invited a great deal of hostility from various interest groups. In her memoirs First Lady Rosalynn Carter exclaimed: "Often during his term, we used to sit around and try to think of something he was doing that was popular."[2]

Carter's "unpopular" agenda generated occasionally tense legislative-executive relations. If Stephen Hess is correct in asserting that the national press is "the medium of Congress," then the negative press portrayals of Carter's legislative leadership are not surprising. Carter's agenda also did not easily lend itself to the interventionist-legislative leadership approach that journalists idealized. Despite poor congressional relations the Carter administration eventually passed many of its major agenda items. It is conceivable that Carter's proposals would not have passed had he adopted a different leadership approach. Journalists focused in their evaluations on the process by which the administration sought congressional and public support. Much less press attention centered on whether the administration's legislative strategy had anything to do with policy victories such as civil service reform and the Panama Canal treaties. Frequently journalists assessed that Carter attained such victories despite the administration's efforts.

3. *The Post-Reform Era Influence.* Another contextual influence on press perceptions of the Carter presidency was the nature of governance in the immediate post-reform era. Reformists in Congress, reacting to the abuses of power during the Nixon years, enacted significant changes in the legislative process. Reforms of Congress intended to make the institution more "democratic" and responsive to constituents became particularly important to the president's leadership position. During the Carter years journalists emphasized how these reforms created increased demands on the president to play a vigorous leadership role in the political system. Journalists placed great importance on the ability of the president to act as a unifying force in American national politics. To provide such integrative leadership, journalists assessed, Carter needed to define a common purpose or vision for the nation and to persuade congressmen of the wisdom of that vision.

Journalists frequently criticized Carter for failing to define a coherent policy direction for the nation. When Carter did appear to clearly define some broad national goal (e.g., energy policy, human rights abroad), journalists criticized (1) his choice of unifying issues, and (2) his methods in seeking to unify political leaders and the public behind his proposals. For example, some journalists criticized Carter for choosing an issue as controversial as the nation's energy policy to focus on in the early stages of the administration. In the views of these journalists Carter would have benefited from focusing on a less controversial issue so as to attain an early legislative success and establish a reputation for "effective" leadership.

Journalists most severely criticized Carter's legislative leadership tactics. In the post-reform era journalists may have expected presidents to be especially sensitive to the sentiments of the congressional membership. The ability of members of Congress to frustrate the political plans of the executive was greater than at any point in recent history. Journalists perceived Carter's alleged failures to negotiate and compromise with members of Congress as important reasons for what these journalists described as the president's inability to bring coherence to an increasingly chaotic policy environment. Significantly, while the Carter administration achieved many of its legislative priorities (e.g., much of the requested energy package, civil service reform, Panama Canal treaties, lifting of the Turkish arms embargo), journalists tended to focus on the antagonisms created on Capitol Hill in trying to enact controversial items rather than on the legislative victories themselves.

Carter staff members often concurred with the press assessment that Carter needed to place additional emphasis on the rituals of political compromise and "horse trading" with congressmen. Staff members also criticized Carter for overloading the legislative agenda. In *Keeping Faith* Carter acknowledged that with "hindsight" he realized that he should have proceeded with a little less haste in introducing legislation. Interestingly, Carter also revealed that he could have done more to enhance good relations with Congress, even though more cordial relations with Congress may have resulted in fewer legislative accomplishments.[3]

Ingredients for "Effective" Leadership

Based on this summary of influences on journalistic assessments we can outline some journalistic ingredients for effective leadership. These ingredients do not comprise a single theory of presidential leadership. The following, instead, summarizes journalistic bases for evaluating presidential leadership and performance. These bases for evaluation pertain to the president's *personal* characteristics, the leadership *context*, and the president's success at *integrating* disparate policy centers.

Personal Factors

An important journalistic ingredient for effective leadership is the president's ability to project an aura of being in command of the government and current events. The president is expected to exude a degree of personal "stature" that enhances respect for his leadership. This personal projection of leadership presumably strengthens the president's public position, his standing abroad, and his influence over the legislative branch. In assessing Carter's leadership abilities journalists often inquired: Is he "big enough" for the job? Has the presidency elevated the man or has it diminished him?

Is he in command of the office and current events or is he imprisoned by them? Does he love to exert his power and influence? Does he project the aura of a leader and thereby command the respect of others?

By these criteria, journalists developed a generally negative view of Carter's abilities. They criticized Carter for failing to project the kind of leadership image that compelled members of Congress, the public and foreign governments to follow his dictates. Journalists portrayed Carter, rather, as opening himself to public and congressional criticism for his actions. As a result, he allegedly lacked the "stature" needed to convey the impression of being in command. Journalists perceived this lack of personal "stature" as a major leadership liability. From the journalistic standpoint, Carter failed the test of the power-seeking president.

Contextual Factors

When evaluating presidential leadership and performance, journalists are also cognizant of the importance of the political context. The situation under which one leads influences the possibility of exhibiting strong personal leadership. As noted earlier, the post-Watergate, post-reform years shaped journalistic perceptions of Carter's leadership. It appears that after eight years of legislative-executive feuding journalists held high expectations for a kind of party government under Jimmy Carter's leadership. The political context presumably called for an end to the legislative "stalemate" of the Nixon-Ford years and the inauguration of a "new era" of cooperation between the political branches.

The journalistic scenario for effective leadership under these conditions began with arguments pertaining to how the president should open his term. In their assessments of Carter's leadership journalists complained that the president opened his term with an overly ambitious, controversial legislative agenda. Many asserted that the president needed to open his term with a limited, achievable set of agenda items, thereby creating the conditions for early legislative successes and a reputation for effective leadership. According to this scenario, after establishing a reputation for legislative leadership, Carter could have proceeded by proposing more controversial agenda items. Carter's failure to follow this advice subjected him to criticism for not taking advantage of his allegedly unique leadership situation.

Political Integration

In addition to assessing leadership behavior journalists also evaluate leadership results. In the post-Watergate, post-reform years when Congress's ability to frustrate presidential plans was increasing, journalists still perceived the president as the major political actor for bringing the political branches together to enact public policies. The president, therefore, was perceived as responsible for overcoming the effects of pluralism, or the stalemate engendered by the separation of powers system. According to political journalists, presidents overcome the separation of powers and foster policy integration in the following ways:

First, a president must define a common purpose for the nation. As the one elected leader of all the people, the president establishes a vision for the future and a clear set of goals to achieve that vision. Journalists criticized Carter for failing to adopt some overriding theme or objective for his presidency. They perceived the lack of a unifying theme like the "Great Society" or "New Deal" as a symptom of a much deeper problem: Carter's inability to convey a coherent governing philosophy to the press and the public. Many journalists believed that Carter gave too much emphasis to the "nuts and bolts" aspects of the presidency (e.g., managing the government, understanding the details of legislative proposals) while he paid little attention to molding his policy proposals into some overriding framework.

Second, journalists expect the president to focus on policy issues that enhance collective action. When Carter did define some broad purpose or national goal such as energy policy, journalists criticized the president's choice of a unifying issue. Journalists lamented the choice of controversial issues like energy policy as the bases for collective action. They portrayed a number of Carter's policy proposals as overly divisive and as making too many demands on the public and political elites.

Third, while exuding an aura of decisive leadership, the president is also expected to be flexible in his dealings with members of the legislative branch. The effective leader, therefore, is perceived as one who is capable of striking deals with members of Congress and making political compromises to garner support for administration proposals. Of the ingredients for effective leadership the ability of a president to bargain and "horsetrade" with members of Congress may have been the most prominent journalistic standard of presidential leadership applied to the Carter administration.

Assessing Presidential Evaluation by Journalists

How accurately or completely did journalists portray the Carter presidency? From this study we find a consistently negative press portrait of Carter's presidency. While certain themes dominated these negative assessments, journalists did not always provide a consistent portrait of Carter. For example, they portrayed Carter as too cautious in his legislative agenda, not exuding the image of an activist-Democrat, and destroying his leadership position through an overly ambitious agenda. They perceived Carter early on as too concerned with symbolism and later in the term as too mired in legislative details. Journalists, finally, portrayed Carter as incapable of defining a purpose for his presidency while criticizing him for trying to define a political purpose by focusing on controversial issues. The findings of this study therefore confirm James Sterling Young's assertion:

> In the first round of study, during incumbency, much was learned from Washington observers about the way the 39th presidency did *not* go about getting things done in Washington, what it did *not* do to push its policies

through, what it did *not* do to project its power. Far less was learned about the kind of presidency it was, the way it did go about getting things done, what it did do to push its policies through, the way in which it did use a President's power to persuade.[4]

Focusing on what this presidency did *not* do, therefore, tells us little about how the Carter presidency did seek to lead. The implication of Young's statement is that contemporary observers of the Carter administration did not present an accurate picture of this presidency. Given the nature of presidential journalism we cannot, of course, expect a complete or accurate portrait during any presidency. As Young adds, we have to wait years until White House documents are opened to the public before we can develop a more complete or accurate portrait of a presidency. Recent scholarly accounts of the Truman and Eisenhower presidencies are illustrative of this point. Nonetheless, the implications of journalistic analysis of the presidency are immediately relevant to the president's ability to govern.

These implications will be discussed from two vantage points: (1) that of a White House attempting to deal with press expectations; and (2) that of the presidency as an institution.

(1) As reviewed earlier, members of Carter's White House staff perceived and reacted to press criticisms of the president. Despite a great many efforts to deal with press criticism, the White House could not fundamentally change the journalistic portrait of the president. This finding reveals the great difficulty associated with attempts to alter a basic press image of a president. In the journalistic reviews of Carter we found that a negative press image began to develop in the first year of the term. Once this image became established it appeared that journalists assessed almost all of Carter's actions in light of this perspective.

Carter White House staff members recognized how this negative image hurt the president's standing, yet they could do little to overcome the problem. For example, Carter's speechwriters tried to get the president to adopt a unifying slogan for the administration and to work harder at improving public relations skills. Yet Carter would not accept proposed solutions to the negative image problem that required he conform to journalists' expectations.

(2) It is also necessary to inquire into what difference these findings make to the institution of the presidency. The first point is that presidents operate in an environment of continual press scrutiny. This press scrutiny has important implications for the development of a presidential image. Journalists, in a sense, teach the public about what presidents should and should not be doing, how presidents should lead, and whether presidents are succeeding or failing the task of leadership. As James Sterling Young notes, journalistic roles in evaluating presidential leadership and performance changed significantly in the post-Watergate years, and we are beginning to understand this phenomenon. Journalists' teachings about the presidency, he adds,

. . . now regularly offer what used to be called "inside dope" on the president and his staff. This includes information about the president's *modus operandi*, about the political methods and strategies, about his possible motives and his probable next moves, about the soft spots and the political intrigues within his administration, and about his personal probity and that of his key aides— together with periodic assessments of his successes, failures, present and future political vulnerabilities.[5]

This regular public airing of the president's political secrets and craft, this turning of spotlights on the seamier side of political leadership, and this continuing watchfulness for impeachable behavior were hardly part of the citizenry's political education about Franklin Roosevelt and his White House. That it has become so now—the legacy of Vietnam and Watergate—suggests how far the Washington academy has moved away from the orbit of presidential power, into the gravitational field of other institutions that have been challenging, curbing, and policing the presidency.[6]

The judgmental standards of journalists influence not only public perceptions, but presidential performance as well. Cognizant of the effects of the press image on the president's agenda, White House officials often orient their own behavior and actions to deal with press portrayals. Yet as this study reveals, it is questionable how much success a White House can have in managing its own press image after a basic journalistic perception of a presidency develops.

In the case of Jimmy Carter it appears that the negative press image was a major element of the president's leadership difficulties. The almost daily press discussions of the president's leadership skills, competence, character and political acumen placed continual demands upon the White House to explain its activities, goals and priorities. The negative press portrait of the president significantly influenced the ability of the White House to carry out its daily activities.

The findings of this study raise questions about the extent to which presidents can influence their general press images. It appears that presidents have three options: (1) try to manage the overall press image of the White House; (2) try to influence press portrayals at the margins, but not the basic image; and (3) treat press portrayals like natural disasters—acts of God over which men have no control.

From this study it appears that the second option is the most that a White House today can hope to achieve. As Young notes, presidential journalism changed significantly in the post-Watergate years. Journalists today will not allow themselves to be managed or controlled by the White House.

If FDR and JFK showed them the benefits of being co-opted by the White House, the Johnson and Nixon years revealed some of the costs. . . . [Journalists discovered] the risks of complicity in a leadership system that not only misled them but got many of them into trouble with their constituents, clients, or principals outside the capital.[7]

Earlier in this study I identified the two sets of press expectations of presidential leadership applied to Jimmy Carter: (1) A general set of press expectations drawn from history. These expectations concerned the proper "ingredients" for successful leadership. These ingredients included personal characteristics exhibited by Franklin D. Roosevelt such as energy, persuasiveness and forcefulness. The leadership context comprised another basic ingredient for effective leadership. (2) The more specific press expectations of Jimmy Carter as leader. These expectations pertained to what journalists thought Jimmy Carter would and should do as president based on their understanding of Carter's own intentions and attributes.

It is more likely that Carter could have influenced the second set of press expectations than the first set. The general set of expectations is relatively stable and difficult to alter. These expectations carry over from one presidency to the next. Little can be done to change the basic notions of leadership held by journalists. It appears that Carter could have influenced the more specific expectations that journalists had of him. Yet White House aides revealed that Carter downplayed presidential roles such as public persuasion and cultivating press relationships in favor of other important roles such as problem solving and decision-making. Carter, it appears, resisted advice from staff members who sought to change him in ways that would suit the press image of presidential leadership.

Therefore, while presidents can no longer manage press expectations and reporting to the degree that Franklin D. Roosevelt was able to, it is possible for presidents to influence their press images to some degree. Whether presidents do so reflects the emphasis they put on this aspect of the mixture of presidential roles and demands of the office.

Carter perhaps should have done more than he did to manage press expectations. As this study reveals, a president plays a significant role in establishing journalistic expectations of his administration. If the president can gain the upper-hand in managing press expectations, encouraging journalists to see the world through White House lenses, he has potential leverage in his efforts to lead public and elite opinion. Jimmy Carter did encourage journalists to adopt certain expectations of his presidency. Unfortunately, these expectations were difficult, if not impossible, to meet, thereby encouraging severe press criticism of the administration for failing to meet its own standards of success.

The press assessments of the Lance controversy provide a good example. As a presidential candidate in 1976 Carter promised that his administration would maintain the highest standards of ethical conduct. Carter made clear his belief that the private virtues of individuals were important criteria for suitability to serve in a public capacity. Undoubtedly the severe press reaction to the Lance controversy is attributable to the standards of evaluation Carter established for his presidency. Journalists, not surprisingly, held Carter and his staff to what Carter called in his memoirs "the very stringent standards I established for serving with me."[8]

A number of other incidents illustrate the same point. Carter announced that his first year leadership could be judged a success or failure on the basis of whether Congress enacted his energy program. A number of journalists adopted Carter's standard and proclaimed the president's first year leadership a "failure." The Carter White House even published a list of over 200 campaign promises made by Carter. Journalists therefore had a useful tool to tally Carter's record. The unfavorable press reactions to the Marston firing and Cabinet shake-up were influenced by Carter promises to avoid politicizing the Justice Department, to avoid appointing a Chief of Staff, and to maintain an "independent Cabinet." This is not to suggest, as many journalists have, that Carter failed to remain true to his principles. Rather, the findings of this study raise questions about the importance of managing press expectations of the presidency. It is unlikely that Carter could have fundamentally altered the negative press portrait of his presidency. It appears that Carter could have avoided the severity of the press reaction to particular incidents had he thought more carefully about the need to manage press expectations.

Carter's apparent inattention to press portrayals became an important leadership liability. As media analysts Grossman and Kumar argue, "Carter's reputation, as shaped and hardened by the media, contributed to his difficulty in getting control of his office."[9] They add that negative news stories tend to "accelerate the decline of a man who is perceived to be not up to the job."[10] For Carter, "[u]nfavorable stories produced a momentum for continuing unfavorable stories."[11]

President Carter focused on presidential roles other than managing press expectations. Yet the negative press portrait of Carter made difficult the accomplishment of those goals that Carter valued most. Carter's difficulties reveal that presidents need to be attentive to the management of press expectations. A president who can convince the press to accept his political definitions and priorities without creating unreasonably high expectations has important leverage in the quest to enhance his public standing and power.

Notes

1. Jimmy Carter interview with *Family Weekly*, September 30, 1979, p. 8.
2. Rosalynn Carter, *First Lady From Plains* (New York: Ballantine Books, 1984), pp. 155–156.
3. Jimmy Carter, *Keeping Faith* (New York: Bantam Books, 1982), p. 87.
4. James Sterling Young, from the forward to Charles O. Jones, *The Trusteeship Presidency* (Baton Rouge: Louisiana State University Press, 1988), p. xxi.
5. James Sterling Young, from an early draft of *The Puzzle of the Presidency* (Baton Rouge: Louisiana State University Press, forthcoming). Quoted by permission of the author.
6. Ibid.
7. Ibid.
8. Jimmy Carter, *Keeping Faith* (New York: Bantam Books, 1982), p. 129.

9. Michael Baruch Grossman and Martha Joynt Kumar, "The Refracting Lens," in Doris A. Graber, ed., *Media Power in Politics* (Washington, D.C.: Congressional Quarterly Press, 1984), p. 198.

10. Ibid.

11. Ibid.